# NEW!

||||||||||||||||||||||

D0167458

BACK GUARANTEE

# Toddler

# BARGAINS

## S E C R E T S

to saving 20% to 50%
on toddler furniture,
clothing, shoes, travel
gear, toys and more!

DENISE & ALAN FIELDS
Authors of the
Best-seller, Baby Bargains

## Copyright Page, Credits and Zesty Lo-Cal BBQ Recipes

Congas, cuica, stand-up bass and mothering by Denise Fields
Flugelhorn, bassoon, steel guitar and dad stuff by Alan Fields
Congas on "Grandparents" by
Max & Helen Coopwood, Howard & Patti Fields
Cover/interior design and keyboard solo by Epicenter Creative
Saxophone on "(Don't Touch My) Potty Seat" by
Charles & Arthur Troy
Backing harmony vocals on "Jogging Stroller Blues"
by Ed Robertson and Steven Paige
Guitar and vocals on "Ants in My Training Pants" by Lyle Lovett
Band photography by Moses Street

This book was written to the music of the Barenaked Ladies,
which probably explains a lot.

Distribution to the book trade by Publisher's Group West, Berkeley,
CA 1-800-788-3123. Thanks to the entire staff of PGW for their support. Extra thanks to Heather and Mark. And Kevan.

To order this book, call 1-800-888-0385. Or send $14.95 plus $3
shipping (or, in Canada, $25 plus $4 shipping) to Windsor Peak
Press, 436 Pine Street, Boulder, CO 80302. Questions or comments?
Please call the authors at (303) 442-8792. Or fax them a note at (303)
442-3744. Or write to them at the above address in Boulder,
Colorado. E-mail the authors at authors@toddlerbargains.com.

Updates to this book are on the web at www.ToddlerBargains.com

Library Cataloging in Publication Data

Fields, Denise C.
Fields, Alan S.
   Toddler Bargains: Secrets to saving 20% to 50% on toddler fur-
niture, clothing, shoes, travel gear, toys and more/ Denise & Alan
Fields
   *320 pages.*
   Includes index.
   ISBN 1-889392-16-2
   1. Child Care—Handbooks, manuals, etc. 2. Infants' supplies—
Purchasing—United States, Canada, Directories. 3. Children's para-
phernalia—Purchasing—Handbooks, manuals. 4. Product Safety—
Handbooks, manuals. 5. Consumer education.
   649'.122'0296—dc20. 2003.

### *Version 2.0*

# CONTENTS

## *Introduction*

## *Chapter 1*

ICE WATER IN YOUR PANTS

## *Chapter 2*

FURNITURE & DECOR

## Chapter 3

### Clothing & Shoes

## Chapter 4

### Potty Training & Bath

## Chapter 5

MEAL TIME! BOOSTER SEATS, CUPS & MORE

## Chapter 6

CAR BOOSTER SEATS

## Chapter 7

ON THE GO GEAR & FAMILY TRAVEL
STROLLERS, JOGGERS, BIKE TRAILERS & MORE

# Chapter 8

## SEASONAL & OUTDOOR

# Chapter 9

## TODDLER PROOFING: AFFORDABLE SAFETY ADVICE

## Chapter 10

### Happy Birthday!

## Chapter 11

### Toys & Media

## Chapter 12

### What does it All Mean?

# ICONS

 *Getting Started*

 *Money-Saving Secrets*

 *Sources*

 *Best Buys*

 *Parents In Cyberspace*

 *The Name Game*

 *What Are You Buying?*

 *Do it By Mail*

 *Safe & Sound*

 *Email from the Real World*

 *Smart Shopper*

 *More Money Buys You*

 *Wastes of Money*

 *Bottom Line*

# CHAPTER 1

ICE WATER IN PANTS

## Ice water in your pants
### Welcome to toddlerhood

### Inside this chapter

**W**hat's it like to raise a toddler? As parents who have raised not one but two children, we can sum it up in one simple experience.

When our first son was a certified toddler, we took him out to eat at a local restaurant one night. As we all sat at the table, happy and content with our toddler secured in a high chair, we noticed the waiter out of the corner of our eye. Before we knew it, he dropped off a full glass of ice water at everyone's place . . . including that of our toddler.

What followed next was like a scene out of those nature films slowed down to show the wing motion of a hummingbird. In slo-mo, you could see both us parents lunging for the huge glass of ice water in front of our son. Unfortunately, he was (and is) much faster than his parents. With one swift move, the entire glass of ice water was knocked over—directly into the lap of his mom.

That kind of sums up what it is like raising a toddler—you're always chasing your child around in a perpetual state of disaster prevention. And while you are proud your toddler can now grab a glass of water, it is less exciting when that glass of water ends up in your shorts.

That story also sums up the cost of raising a toddler—just when you think everything is under control, along comes another financial hit that you may or may not have seen coming.

### So how much does it cost to raise a toddler

Funny you should ask. Here's a look at the average yearly costs to raise a toddler in a middle class family.

## The Average Cost of Raising a Toddler

*(costs per year to raise a child from age two to five)*

| | |
|---|---|
| Housing | $3450 |
| Food | $1280 |
| Transportation | $1120 |
| Clothing | $410 |
| Health care | $610 |
| Child Care | $1630 |
| Misc. | $1010 |
| **TOTAL** | **$9480** |

*Source: U.S. Department of Agriculture for families earning $39,700 to $66,900. Estimates are based on a 1990-92 Consumer Expenditure Survey updated to 2004 dollars using the Consumer Price Index.*

Ouch! Yes, we are talking close to $10,000 a year. When you factor out items like housing, health care, transportation and child care, the "running costs" for raising a toddler are more than *$2600 a year*—that's the diapers, food, clothing and so on.

Does raising a toddler have to cost that much? We say no. As authors of a series of money-saving books, we firmly believe you can raise children without going bankrupt.

## Why do a book on toddler bargains?

The short answer: we ran out of room in our *Baby Bargains* book. Readers of our first book on parenting may remember that *Baby Bargains* focuses on products for babies age birth to two. But over the years, we got requests to do more—parents wanted to know about toddler topics like potty training and "next step" items like booster car seats and double strollers.

If we were to add all this to our first book, it would soon weigh 17 pounds and rival Moby Dick for page count.

So, we have decided to divide all the bargains into two books. *Baby Bargains* will continue to focus on babies up to age two. This book (*Toddler Bargains*) will focus on products for toddlers age two to five. Okay, we realize most folks don't think of a five year old as a toddler, but just bear with us.

Before we get on to the bargains, let us take a moment to go over a couple of topics for those readers who have not read our previous books. First, let's talk about our "no ads" policy. Then we'll go over how we came to write these books in this first place.

## What? There's No Advertising in This Book?

Yes, it's true. This book contains zero percent advertising. We have never taken any money to recommend a product or company and never will. We make our sole living off the sales of this and other books. (So, when your friend asks to borrow this copy, have them buy their own book!) Our publisher, Windsor Peak Press, also derives its sole income from the sale of this book and our other publications. No company recommended in this book paid any consideration or was charged any fee to be mentioned in it. (In fact, some companies probably would offer us money to leave them *out* of the book, given our comments about their products or services).

As consumer advocates, we believe this "no ads" policy helps ensure objectivity. The opinions in the book are just that—ours and those of the parents we interviewed.

We also are parents of two small children. As far as we know, we are the only authors of a consumer's guide to baby and toddler products who actually have young kids. We figure if we actually are recommending these products to you, we should have some real world experience with them. (That said, we should disclose that our sons have filed union grievances with our company over testing of certain jarred baby foods and that litigation is ongoing.)

Of course, given the sheer volume of toddler stuff, there's no way we can test everything personally. To solve that dilemma, we rely on reader feedback to help us figure out which are the best products to recommend. We receive over 100 emails a day from parents; this helps us spot overall trends on which brands/products parents love. And which ones they want to destroy with a rocket launcher.

Finally, we have a panel of moms who also test new products for us, evaluating items on how they work in the real world. One bad review from one parent doesn't necessarily mean we won't recommend a product; but we'll then combine these tests with other parent feedback to get an overall picture.

What about prices of products? Trying to stay on top of this is often like attempting to nail Jell-O to a wall. Yet, we still try. As much as we can confirm, the prices quoted in this book were accurate as of the date of publication. Of course, prices and product features can change at any time. Inflation and other factors may affect the actual prices you discover in shopping for your child. While the publisher makes every effort to ensure their accuracy, errors and omissions may exist. That's why we've established a web site where you can get the latest updates on this book for free (www.ToddlerBargains.com). You can also talk directly to us: call

(303) 442-8792 or e-mail us at authors@ToddlerBargains.com to ask a question, report a mistake, or just give us your thoughts. Finally, you can write to us at "Toddler Bargains," 436 Pine Street, Suite 700, Boulder, CO 80302.

What about the phone numbers listed in this book? We list contact numbers for manufacturers so you can find a local dealer near you that carries the product (or request a catalog, if available). Unless otherwise noted, these manufacturers do NOT sell directly to the public.

## So, Who Are You Guys Anyway?

Why do a book on saving money on toddler products? Don't new parents throw caution to the wind when buying for their child, spending whatever it takes to ensure their toddler's safety and comfort?

Ha! When our first son was born in 1993, we quickly realized how darn expensive this guy was. Sure, you expect certain expenses when having a child (crib, car seat, etc.), but the sheer volume of choices out there overwhelmed us.

And those product decisions don't get any easier when your baby morphs into a toddler—now you have to consider which booster car seat (among the 50+ on the market) is best, what toys are safe, how to plan that birthday party and so on.

Becoming a parent at the turn of the century is both a blessing and curse. The good news: parents today have many more choices for juvenile products than past generations. The *bad* news: parents today have many more choices for juvenile products than past generations.

Our mission: make sense of this stuff, with an eye on cutting costs. As consumer advocates, we've been down this road before. We researched bargains and uncovered scams in the wedding business when we wrote *Bridal Bargains*. Then we penned an expose on new homebuilders in *Your New House*. Our best-seller *Baby Bargains* has sold over 500,000 copies and was featured on Oprah.

One of the biggest frustrations as a parent: separating out the good stuff for your toddler from questionable products that don't live up to their hype—and making sure to avoid products that are outright dangerous. We were surprised to learn how most juvenile items face little (or no) government scrutiny, leaving parents to sort out conflicting safety claims.

So, we've gone on a quest to find the best toddler products, at prices that won't send you to the poor house. Sure, we've sampled many of these items first hand. But this book is much more than our experiences—we interviewed over 1000 parents to learn their experiences with products. We also attend juvenile product trade shows to quiz manufacturers and retailers on what's hot and what's not. The insights from retailers are especially helpful, since these folks are on the front lines and often see which items unhappy parents return.

Our focus is on safety and durability: which items stand up to real world conditions and which don't. Interestingly, we found many products for toddlers are sold strictly on price . . . and sometimes a great "bargain" broke, fell apart or shrunk after a few uses. Hence, you'll note some of our top recommendations aren't always the lowest in price. To be sensitive to those on really tight budgets, we try to identify good alternatives in different price ranges.

## Let's Go Shopping: 3 Tips To Keep in Mind

Before we get rolling, let's go over three things about shopping for a toddler that no one tells you:

**1** **YOU'RE NOT IN CHARGE ANY MORE.** Toddlers want to assert their independence and that means more than just stuffing that piece of toast into your DVD player. Parents who used to call all the shots when it came to what their little one wore, ate and played with suddenly find themselves negotiating with a little pint-size Colin Powell. To recognize this fact, use this book to narrow down the choices for certain products for your toddler—but involve your toddler in making the final choice. Your toddler and your sanity will thank you.

**2** **SAFETY IS AN ONGOING PROCESS.** Just because you baby proofed your house even before your baby was born doesn't mean you're done. Nope, keeping a toddler safe is a never-ending experience that requires vigilance. In each chapter of this book, we'll include "Safe & Sound" tips to keep this topic front and center.

**3** **POTTY TRAINING.** It's not a job. It's an adventure. Yes, we're sure you are tired of changing diapers. But remember that potty training is more than just picking out a shiny new potty at Babies R Us. We'll discuss the in's and out's of making this important transition in Chapter 4.

But now, let's talk about that first big transition from baby to toddler—moving from the crib to the big boy or big girl bed. That's the focus of the next chapter, as well as how to save when decorating a toddler room. Let's dive in.

# CHAPTER 2

## Furniture & Decor
### Toddler rooms on a budget

### Inside this chapter

How can you buy a twin bed for your toddler at half off retail? Or hardwood bunk beds at wholesale prices shipped direct to your house from Canada? We'll discuss those bargain secrets, plus share the best outlets, deals and web sites for toddler decor. Our readers will share their creative yet simple ways to decorate a toddler's room on a budget. Finally, check out name brand reviews of the best toddler furniture and bedding makers.

Your baby's crib and nursery furniture was probably picked out after weeks or months of shopping, web surfing and careful consideration. You might have visited several stores, scoured books like ours for safety ratings and talked with other moms-to-be. In the end, you selected a crib and other nursery furniture that had the right combination of looks, safety and features.

Contrast this to the selection of a twin or toddler bed.

Most parents who buy a "big boy/girl" bed are in a state of panic, after discovering their baby for the first time crawled out of his or her crib in the middle of the night. That's what our oldest child did, greeting his stunned parents at 2am with a "Hi Mommy and Daddy." And once baby learns to climb out of the crib, there is no going back—they'll keep doing it until you find them alternative sleeping accommodations.

We set out for the furniture store the next day, picking out a floor sample twin bed in a process that took about 17 minutes. We relate this story to point out that despite your best intentions, your search for toddler furniture may not be the same leisurely adventure you embarked on for the crib.

## Getting Started:
## When Do You Need This Stuff?

There is no one "right" age to switch a child from crib to twin bed. Some children can stay in a crib until age 3 1/2; others are out at 18 months. In general, most kids transition out of a crib between ages two and three.

Of course, there can be other factors that come into play here. You might be expecting a second child and need the crib for the new infant. Another factor: your child might be potty training and need to get out of bed in the middle of the night to use the toilet. That's a lot easier from a toddler or twin bed than from a crib, of course.

Despite the story we wrote in the introduction, we realized (later) that just because baby climbs out of the crib, there is no need to panic and buy a new bed immediately. You can leave the crib rail down, which enables baby to climb out without falling from a great height. This might buy you some time, but your crib days are numbered as you can imagine.

We recommend planning for the transition to a "big boy" or "big girl" bed five to eight weeks BEFORE you actually make the move. If you are having another baby, that means doing this transition in your eighth month of pregnancy (about 30 weeks).

Those five to eight weeks will let you shop and (if need be) special order a new bed. This should be an exciting time for a child; involve them in the shopping and selection of a new bed. (See the section on page 10 for more tips on how to ease the transition from crib to big kid bed).

Of course, you can delay the new bed transition if a new baby sleeps in a bassinet for the first two or three months. The advantage to this strategy is the possible smoother transition, as your older child adjusts to the newborn. There is no one right way; it's your call.

You have two choices when it comes to buying kids' furniture (twin beds, bunk beds and other bedroom furniture): buying a sample off the floor or special ordering. For some reason, stores that sell kid's furniture seem to stock more items than baby stores. Hence you are more likely to be able to buy something "off the rack." If you decide to special order, however, the same standard wait times apply as when you ordered your child's nursery furniture—four to six weeks on average, with some items taking up to ten and even 12 weeks.

The trend in recent years is for furniture manufacturers and retailers to offer more "quick ship" items for youth bedrooms. So even if you have to wait for a special order item, it may be just two to four weeks (instead of the old days with waits that stretched out as long as 12 weeks).

Of course, beds are just the beginning. Other items like tables and chairs, toy storage and desks can be added as time goes by. Most of those items are in stock at most stores. If you order online, you'll need to allow 2-4 weeks for shipping.

Later in this chapter, we'll talk about money-saving tips that include making certain toddler items (like storage cubes) yourself. While these projects can be done in a weekend, it's realistic to start planning several weeks out in order to get materials, paints, etc.

## Sources

The kid's furniture and decor business is a $9.4 billion a year industry. As has been the trend in recent years, discounters lead the pack of juvenile furniture retailers. The big three—*Target, Wal-Mart* and *Kmart*—ring up $6 billion in kid's furniture sales or 63% of the entire market.

Next in line of dominance is *Babies R Us*, which accounts for about 20% of the market. At last count, Babies R Us (www.babies-rus.com) had about 183 stores nationwide. Nipping at the heals of BRU is *Burlington's Baby Depot*, with 295 locations nationwide.

*Pottery Barn* ranks eighth on the list of kids furniture retailers with its innovative "bricks and clicks" strategy. Pottery Barn (www.potterybarnkids.com) is a triple threat with retail stores (nearly 80 locations and growing rapidly), a mail order catalog and a cool web site (more on that later).

Independent juvenile retail stores round out the list of top kids furniture retailers. There are four big "associations" of baby/kid stores: *Baby News (*www.babynewsstores.com) with 40 locations; *USA Baby* (www.usababy.com) with 55 locations; Baby Furniture Plus (www.babyfurnitureplus.com) with over 130 stores and *Baby and Kids Express* (NINFRA; www.ninfra.com) with 100+ stores. Baby News, Baby Furniture Plus and Baby and Kids Express (see Figure 1 on the next page) operate like a co-op, with member stores operating in a loose confederation. USA Baby is a franchised chain.

Other furniture retailers with major kids selections include *Rooms to Go Kids* (www.RoomsToGoKids.com), which has locations in five southeastern states (Florida, Georgia, North and South Carolina and Tennessee) as well as Texas. *Ethan Allen* (www.EthanAllen.com) has also increased its kids offerings in recent years (more on this company later).

*Figure 1. Tired of chain stores? You can find over 100 independent kids furniture stores by clicking on Ninfra.com, a trade association of indie retailers since 1973.*

## Easing the transition to the big bed: Our six tips

Every child reacts differently when it comes time to graduate to a big boy or big girl bed. Our second child was excited to move out of the crib, wanting to sleep in a big boy bed just like his older brother. First-born kids, however, might resist, as they don't want to give up "their" crib to a newborn baby sister or brother. Here are our six tips to making this transition easier:

**1** **MATTRESS ON THE FLOOR TRICK.** Going to a big bed can be scary. Ease the transition by first putting the mattress on the floor next to the bed and letting Junior sleep there for the first week or so. This also allays fears that your child might fall out of the toddler or twin bed in the first few days. Eventually, transition the mattress onto the bed frame. Another advantage to this tip: you can do the mattress on the floor trick BEFORE you buy the actual twin bed frame, which will give you some more time to shop.

**2** **PUT THE NEW BED IN THE SAME POSITION AS THE CRIB.** That way the child's perspective of the room (nightlight, door) is the same and will be comforting.

**3** **LEAVE THE CRIB SET UP IN THE ROOM FOR A FEW DAYS.** This can make the transition less jarring, as they see the crib still in the room. Of course, it's no big deal if the child goes back to the crib for a few days after trying out a big bed.

**4** **USE THE SAME FAVORITE CRIB BLANKET.** It may be tempting to chuck the crib bedding for twin bedding, but using the same crib blanket can be helpful during the transition. And don't forget the all-important "lovey." Telling your child that his or her lovey is excited to sleep in the new bed can be encouraging too.

**5** **HAVE A BIG BED PARTY.** This is an exciting time; celebrate the move from crib to bed with an informal party with friends and family (we always love an excuse for cake and ice cream anyway).

**6** **INVOLVE YOUR CHILD IN SHOPPING FOR A NEW BED.** Build excitement for the transition by taking your child with you shopping. They might be more excited about this change if they can choose their new bed. Of course, you can always limit choices by having your child choose between two or three options if you think this will be too overwhelming.

### Parents in Cyberspace: What's on the Web?

### Wallies
*Web:* www.wallies.com, see Figure 3 on page 14.
*What it is:* Wallpaper cutouts you just wet and stick to the wall.
*What's Cool:* Wallies are pre-pasted, vinyl coated wallpaper cutouts that are sold at craft and fabric stores. Available in packs of 25, Wallies also offers borders and murals in a plethora of themes—263 at last count. And there is no messy pasting—you just wet the back of the Wallies and stick 'em to the wall. Or a lampshade. Or furniture. And so on. Best of all, they are designed to be removed without damaging the surface underneath. Wallies' web site includes a good FAQ, projects, locations to find the product and more. Sign up for their mailing list for info on special deals. Even at regular retail, Wallies are an affordable and easy way to give your toddler's room some pizzazz without spending a fortune.

### Pottery Barn Kids
*Web:* www.potterybarnkids.com, see Figure 4 on page 14.
*What it is:* The mother of all kid's decor sites.
*What's Cool:* What isn't? Pottery Barn Kids has just about re-written the rules for kids' decor and furniture.

*Continued on page 14*

# Do It Yourself Smarts: Kid Decor on the Cheap

HGTV's "Room by Room" is a great show that features ideas on affordable decorating. You gotta love their creative yet low-cost solutions. We spoke with hosts Shari Hiller and Matt Fox via email. Here are their ideas on how to do kids decor on the cheap:

**Q. LET'S TALK STORAGE. WHAT ARE SOME QUICK/EASY IDEAS?**
A. Wooden cubes made out of birch plywood are easy to assemble and can be painted in a variety of fun colors. They're very versatile since they can be stacked in a pyramid for one child, and then easily moved to another room and stacked into a vertical tower for that one! An important safety note here is that the cubes should be screwed together and even attached to the wall since children have a tendency to want to climb and pull on things.

**Q. WE USE BASKETS AS A CHEAP AND EASY WAY TO ORGANIZE TOYS. HOW CAN YOU UTILIZE BASKETS IN A KID'S ROOM AND STILL MAKE IT LOOK NICE?**
A. We've had luck building a long, three-shelf unit that holds square handled baskets. Baskets are easy places to stash toys for little ones and a great tool for them to learn how to clean up. Plus, once they're neatly arranged on the shelves, the room can look spic and span in minutes!

**Q. WHAT ABOUT BOOKS?**
A. Several years ago, Matt and I built some small bookracks complete with the child's initials on the ends. They had slightly slanted bottoms so the books would stay put, and I'd guess they were about 12" - 15" in length, just enough to hold a good supply of bedtime stories!

**Q. LET'S TALK ABOUT WALL DECOR. WHAT ARE YOUR IDEAS FOR HANGING ARTWORK?**
A. Many times, we have created tack surfaces for kid's to pin up their artwork, and we've simply wrapped brightly colored felt around homosote board. One time we cut the homosote board in the shapes of a city skyline, wrapped each one in a different felt color, and butted them together to fill a long wall up about 2/3 the distance to the ceiling. Aside from being a great tack surface, the homosote added sound absorption, and softness to the room. This is a great way for kids to learn their colors, as well as learn how to spot the tallest and widest buildings.

**furniture**

## Q. What other decorating tips have you used for kid's rooms?

A. There's almost nothing we like better to do than paint murals on kids' walls. They can be as creative as your imagination and as colorful too. We've painted hot air balloons, apple trees, palm trees and circus acts. It's great fun for the adults to create, and it turns the child's room into a place beyond the imagination! And, like everything we've mentioned, it's really inexpensive!

In a few rooms, we've actually hung swings. A toddler "bucket" type swing is safe and of course must always be attended by an adult. Make sure to position the mounting hardware to go into the joists, and even an adult could swing . . . but leave that to the kids!

Finally consider a children's perspective when decorating a kid's room. Imagine living in a giant's house. You can't get up onto a chair or eat at the dining table. That's the world of a child. To compensate, we try to add kid-sized furniture to children's rooms. Even if it is just one chair, or maybe a tiny table with little benches that you make yourself. The smaller scale makes them feel more in control. It's a confidence builder of sorts!

*Figure 2. Go to HGTV's web site (www.hgtv.com) to see an archive of the projects featured on "Room by Room."*

*Figure 3. Toddler decor on the cheap—check out Wallies's web site (wallies.com) for detailed projects, an FAQ and more.*

PBK's smart, contemporary looks have won fans from coast to coast. This stuff is just so darn cute. PBK's secret sauce is their coordinating looks, with all manner of adorable accessories. Among our reader's favorite items are PBK's bed linens. "I am sold on PBK bed-

*Figure 4. Pottery Barn Kids' (PBK) web site is a great placed to get ideas for your toddler's room . . . even if you don't buy it at PBK.*

ding," one mom emailed us. "They are reasonably priced for the good quality they provide." Yes, the matching accessories can be pricey, but frequent sales can make it less so. "I just purchased online their airplane bedding on sale—I got the twin quilt, pillow sham and a seat of sheets for $170 or 40% off," a reader reported.

PBK's web site has beds & trundles, kid's tables and chairs, dressers, bookshelves, desks, nightstands and armoires. Among the cool features of their web site is their "Tips and Advice" section a collection of articles and movies to help you decorate your baby's room. The "shop room" section includes entire room vignettes in various themes. The best part of PBK is the design ideas, whether you decide to buy their products or not. (In addition to their catalog and Internet site, PBK also has nearly 80 stores nationwide).

*Other sites to consider:* Readers have found theme bedding and accessories at sites like *Domestications.com* and *JCPenney.com.* (One tip: go to Google.com to look for a web discount coupon for those sites).

A reader in the Northeast gave a thumbs up to *Seaman's Kids* (www.seamanskids.com), with six locations in New York and New Jersey. "A great selection and they are easy to deal with," said this mom. Their web site includes a large catalog to browse through, with special sections for bunk beds and bedding.

*Lands End* (www.landsend.com) and *Company Store* (www.thecompanystore.com) are two other web sites we like for bedding and accessories. Both have excellent customer service and fair return policies.

*PoshTots.com* may have outrageous prices ($39,500 for a Cinderella Coach bed, anyone?), but you've got to love their web site just for its sheer creativity. Gathering over 1000 items from 100+ artisans, PoshTots is a great place for ideas (not to buy, of course).

Finally, we would be remiss if we didn't mention *eBay*. The auction site (www.ebay.com) is a great source for gently used (and sometimes new) toddler decor items. Look for items for sale in your hometown; that way you can save on shipping since you can pick it up instead.

## Safe & Sound

**I** **ANCHOR IT TO THE WALL.** All dressers, bookcases and nightstands should be anchored to the wall. A reader found out how important this was the hard way: "My kids knocked over a six drawer dresser, which I didn't think was even possible. Wrong! No one was hurt but we anchored it to the wall that day."

**2**    **BE WARY OF BUNK BEDS.** Even though new federal safety standards were enacted way back in 1999, we are still concerned that a good number of bunk beds are not conforming to the law. We will discuss this more in detail later.

**3**    **LOOK FOR DRAWER STOPS.** The best dressers for kid's rooms have drawer stops. As it sounds, these stops keep the drawers from being pulled out of the dresser. A significant number of injuries occur to children each year from drawers that have been pulled completely out of a dresser by accident.

**4**    **SKIP THE PORTABLE BED RAIL.** We've been troubled by the number the injuries (and deaths) attributed to this so-called "safety product." Designed to keep a toddler from falling out of a bed, portable bed rails have caused 12 deaths and 40 "near miss" incidents in the past decade (CPSC statistics, 1990 to 2000). During the same time, there have been several recalls for defective bed rails that caused death and injury.

Most of the cases of death and injury were caused when a child became entrapped in an area between the mattress on the bed and the attached bed rail, according to the CPSC.

But isn't it dangerous to put a two or three year old in a bed without a rail? No, it isn't. While the CPSC noted 47 deaths involving young children who fell out of beds from 1990 to 2000, the vast majority (38) were to children *under a year old* and most children died when they fell into or onto an object (a bucket, for example). Any parent who puts a child under one year of age in a twin bed (instead of a crib) should have their parenting license revoked.

Bottom line: cases of children who fall off a twin bed and die "due to blunt force trauma are rare," says the CPSC.

The CPSC has been so concerned with portable bed rail safety they voted in 2000 to begin development of mandatory safety standards for these products. "Although most manufacturers label their bed rails for children ages two through five and while the CPSC warns against placing younger children to sleep on adult beds," parents sometimes put children under two on beds when a crib is not available. If the bed rail is pushed out from the mattress, a younger child can fall into the space and suffocate or strangle," the CPSC announced in 2000.

We admire the CPSC for its effort to improve bed rails and we recommend parents NOT use these products. Consider these tips instead:

♦ *If you are worried about your child falling out of a twin bed, put the mattress on the floor until he gets used to sleeping in it.*

♦ *Never put a young child to sleep on an adult bed.*

♦ *Avoid putting your child's bed or mattress up against a wall.* Entrapment could occur between a mattress and wall.

♦ *Never put objects (buckets, toys, etc) next to a bed that a child might hit if they roll off the mattress.*

## Bunk Beds:
### Are the new safety standards being ignored?

It's the perfect solution for a space squeeze—bunk beds, that quintessential piece of juvenile furniture that is in thousands of kids' bedrooms nationwide. Yet bunk beds have a dark side: they have been responsible for 91 deaths by entrapment since 1990; in 1998 alone, over 34,000 children where sent to the emergency room for bunk bed-related injuries. In a five-year period ending in 1999, more than 600,000 bunk beds were recalled because they were unsafe—they put children at risk for falling, entrapment or strangulation.

To address these alarming problems, the federal government issued new mandatory safety rules in December 1999. Actually, the government's efforts to make bunk beds safer can be traced back to 1992, when a voluntary safety standard was enacted. Unfortunately, as you can see from the injury and death statistics from the 1990's, that effort was not successful, prompting the Consumer Products Safety Commission to enact tougher mandatory rules.

Beginning in July 2000, the CPSC required all bunk beds made or imported for sale in the U.S. to meet these requirements:

♦ Any bed in which the underside of the foundation is over 30 inches from the floor must have guardrails on both sides and the wall side rail must be continuous.
♦ Openings in the upper bunk structure must be small enough (less than 3.5 inches) to prevent passage of a child's torso.
♦ Openings in the lower bunk end structures must be small enough to prevent entry by a child's head or torso, or large enough to permit the free passage of both the child's torso and head.
♦ The bed must have a label identifying the manufacturer, distributor or seller, the model number, and the date of manufacture.

◆ Warnings must be on a label affixed to the bed and in instructions that must accompany the bed. The label warns not to place children less than six years of age on the upper bunk and specifies mattress size.

Yet, despite the new rules, we are troubled that unsafe bunk beds are still being sold nationwide. A loophole in the new federal law allows retailers to sell off old bunk bed stock that predates the new regulation with no warning to consumers. Unfortunately, stock can sit on store shelves or in warehouses for *years* as we've discovered.

Even more troubling: we still hear reports from parents who see bunk beds on the market that don't meet the new federal safety standards. Here are the key problems we've witnessed with bunk beds still for sale today:

◆ *Guard rails on the back side of the bunk bed that do not run from end to end of the bed.*

◆ *Openings on the top bunk that exceed the 3.5 inch space rule mentioned above.*

◆ *Bunk beds that do meet the new weight standard.* New rules call for the top bunk to withstand 400 pounds of pressure for five minutes. The problem? Many manufacturers don't have equipment to check this.

Some of these dangerous bunk beds are at second-hand stores or at garage sales. Others are in discount retail stores. One bed manufacturer who we spoke with at an industry conference said he is troubled by unsafe bunk beds that are still being made today, long after the new safety rules have been enacted.

While we don't have a list of specific bunk bed manufactures that are violating the federal rules, we urge parents to exercise caution. The CPSC's publication on bunk beds (http://www.cpsc.gov/cpscpub/pubs/071.html) provides good tips as well as illustrations:

## 1. Selection
Choose bunk beds that have:
◆ Guardrails on all sides which are screwed, bolted or otherwise firmly attached to the bed structure.
◆ Spacing between bed frame and bottom of guard rails that is no greater than 3 1/2 inches (89 mm).
◆ Guardrails that extend at least 5 inches (127 mm) above the mattress surface to prevent a child from rolling off.

◆ Cross ties under the mattress foundation which can be securely attached.

◆ A ladder that is secured to the bed frame and will not slip when a child climbs on it.

◆ A feature which permits the beds to be separated to form two single beds if you have children too young to sleep safely on the upper bunk.

◆ And finally, choose a mattress that correctly fits your bed, whether regular or extra long. (Be wary of extra long mattresses, as bedding can be hard to find).

## 2. Use

◆ Always use two side guardrails on the upper bunk. Keep guardrails securely in place at all times no matter what the age of the child. Children move about during sleep and may roll out of bed.

◆ Do not permit children under six years of age to sleep in the upper bunk.

◆ Be sure cross ties are under the mattress foundation of each bed and that they are secured in place even if bunks are used as twin beds.

◆ Emphasize to children to use the ladder and not chairs or other pieces of furniture to climb into or out of the top bunk.

◆ Teach children that rough play is unsafe around and on beds and other furniture.

◆ Use a night-light so that children will be able to see the ladder if they get up during the night.

## 3. Maintenance or Safety Repair

◆ If spacing between guard rails and bed frames is more than 3 1/2 inches (89 mm), nail or screw another rail to close the space to prevent head entrapment.

◆ Keep guardrails in good repair and securely in place.

◆ Replace loose or missing ladder rungs immediately.

◆ Repair or replace loose or missing hardware, including cross ties immediately.

## Smart Shopper Tips

There are two schools of thought when it comes to a toddler's room:

*School #1:* Decorate your child's room for a *toddler*, with a theme (characters, etc.) that reflects what a two-to-five-year-old would like. The pro to this is, well, your child just HAS to have the 101 Dalmatians bedroom. Or the Bob the Builder theme. The downside? What appeals to a two-year-old may be old news by the time your child hits kindergarten, prompting a re-do of the room (and the added expense of new decor).

**School #2:** Decorate your child's room to last until they are ten (after which, all bets are off and you are on your own). This involves picking a more generic theme (flowers, robots, trains, construction) that doesn't lock you into a baby-ish theme. The pro: you don't have to buy that 101 Dalmatians theme bedding. The con: *telling* your daughter you won't be buying that 101 Dalmatians theme bedding.

Of course, there is always the middle ground. You can pick that more generic theme and spice it up with a few character accents (a picture, lamp, etc). The Priss Prints and Wallies (discussed later in this chapter) enable you to affordably do a character theme—and best of all they can be easily removed when your child tires of them.

◆ *When it comes to bedding, buy three of everything.* "Sounds like a lot, until you have a potty trainee gone bad," one parent told us and we agree. "You do NOT want to run out of fitted sheets during the night. I actually have three of everything—mattress pads, blankets and sheets."

◆ *Avoid unusual bed sizes.* Some parents told us they thought it was a good idea to choose a bigger bed (full or queen size) for their child, so their room could double as a guest room. The problem? Most kid's bedding only comes in twin size, not full or queen. While you could go with solid color sheets, if you have your heart set on more of a "kid look," you might just stick with the twin bed.

◆ *Think outside the box.* Pick an unusual theme that no one else has (a Wizard of Oz room, anyone?). That way, you avoid overpriced and low-quality character or theme accessories. Yes, this requires a little more creativity on your part but you'll save in the end.

◆ *If space is tight, consider a "captain's bed."* Let's say you live in New York City and your toddler's room is about the size of well, a shoebox. Conserve space by buying a "captain's bed," basically a twin bed with integrated storage. These beds have under-mattress storage drawers as well headboards with additional storage. The downside? Captain's beds aren't cheap—most start at $700 and styles can soar over $1000 depending on the brand. On the plus side, you don't have to buy a separate dresser. A good example: Berg's captains bed (see above) from their Sierra collection with an integrated desk, drawers and bookcases.

*Figure 5: Short on space? A captain's bed, like this one from Berg, squeezes more storage into a small space—but at a price. This bed is $700.*

◆ **Master the bed lingo.** When shopping for a twin bed for your toddler, you'll come across a plethora of styles and options. Some beds have "bunky boards" (a piece of 3/4" medium-density fiber board that replaces the slats that would normally hold up the mattress). Sometimes these are referred to as posture boards. Other twin beds are designed for a box spring to hold up the mattress. Which is best? It's a toss-up. Either way provides enough support, although twin beds with box springs are probably more comfortable (which might be a consideration if your child's room also doubles as a guest room).

Of course, which style is best is purely a personal decision. A good web site that shows you a variety of twin bed options is Rooms to Go Kids (RoomsToGoKids.com). This small chain with locations in North Carolina, Texas, Georgia and Florida has great value packages that pair twin beds with matching dressers, night-stands and more.

◆ **Twin mattress shopping pointers.** First, forget about model names—the major mattress companies will sell the exact same mattress to one store with X name and then to another store with Y name. Every mattress company makes a variety of mattresses—think of them as different levels. For most kid's beds, the basic cheap-o mattress is just fine. Yes, the weight of a mattress will determine how long a mattress will last (the heavier, the better). But most kids weigh so little, there is very little chance they will wear out the mattress before college.

What about fancy mattresses with pillow tops? These are basically regular mattresses with a layer of extra padding. These tops can add $100 or more to a mattress—and they are a waste of money. You can buy a basic mattress pad for much less and get the same effect.

Should you buy a hard or soft mattress for your child? While it was important that their crib mattress was firm, this factor is less critical for toddlers and older kids. Basically, we'd reject mattresses that are too hard or soft. Something in the "medium" firmness range will work just fine.

## Money Saving Tips

**1 STICK AROUND.** Okay, your child HAS to have the latest character decoration for their room, but you don't want to spend a fortune on pricey accessories and decor? Priss Prints (847) 803-9200 has a solution—removable borders, appliqués and growth charts in a variety of character themes. "They make the room bright and colorful and are very easy to put up and take down," said a reader in Oregon. Toys R Us and Babies R Us sell Priss Prints in sets for $10 to $12 or so. We also found a Priss prints dealer, Modellbahn Ott Hobbies of Gilbertsville, PA who has a web site (www.prissprints.com) with an online catalog and special deals (30% off) on closeout patterns. Another online retailer of Priss Prints is www.StoryBookLane.com. Finally, don't forget about the Wallies (wall paper cutouts) we discussed in the Cyberspace section earlier in this chapter.

**2 SKIP THE "TODDLER BED."** Yeah, all those toddler beds (racecars, animals, etc) that use a crib mattress are cute . . . but unnecessary. All toddlers can go straight from a crib to a "big boy" or "big girl" twin bed without suffering any major psychological trauma (although parents may wish they could sleep in a crib until age 18). Skip the toddler bed and its associated $50 to $150 price tag.

**3 GO CANADIAN.** The favorable exchange rate makes Canadian furniture a bargain to US shoppers. Major Canadian furniture makers include AP Industries, Morigeau and EG.

**4 WHOLESALE CLUB DEALS.** Yes, BJ's, Costco and Sam's wholesale clubs do sell toddler furniture from time to time. The best deal: a reader snagged a solid pine bunk bed from BJ's for $199. "What I liked about this bed is you can use the two beds side by side or as a bunk bed. The quality of the wood and general con-

*Figure 6. Bunk beds for just $379.99? We found these sold birch bunks at Costco, but you can also find similar deals at Sam's and BJ's wholesale clubs.*

struction is very good." Read the following box for tips and hints about shopping at warehouse clubs. Costco also lists toddler furniture like bunk beds on their web site (www.costco.com) at good prices. Other readers have seen oak and maple bunks in warehouse clubs for $380 to $500—compare to over $1000 in specialty stores. Sometimes they have matching pieces like dressers.

**5 GO SECOND HAND.** Many parents buy second-hand twin beds, dressers and the like at garage sales, second hand stores and other discount places. Paint and refinish it yourself to give old furniture a new life. Funky new hardware (sold even at stores like Target) can freshen up an old dresser. Be sure any second-hand bunk bed meets the safety requirements discussed earlier in this chapter.

**6 LESS IS MORE.** Toddlers are rather simple—they just need a place to sleep and a place for their clothes. Yes, a place for books and toys is nice too—but this can be done affordably. Skip the computer work station and fancy armoire for now; desks and computers can be added down the road! Antique dressers and other fragile items should be banished to other rooms until the toddler is older.

**7 PICK A NON-TRENDY COLOR.** Paint your toddler's room with a good base coat of washable paint in a neutral color. Simple colors like yellow or light blue (or heck, even white) can adapt to a variety of decorating schemes down the road. Skip the "Martha Stewart's Orange Jumpsuit" paint.

**8** **DO A THEME WITH "SPOT DECORATIONS."** Instead of buying expensive linens or wallpaper, use simple decor to make a statement. A cute lamp, curtain, pillow sham can add pizzazz without major cost—and can be swapped out later if your toddler tires of them.

**9** **GO UNFINISHED.** A reader from California wrote about her unfinished furniture deal: "I stenciled a wonderful toddler table, chair seat and toy box from IKEA for my daughter—everyone thinks I paid lots of money for them at a specialty store. I figured I saved 60 percent!" You can use this tip for just one or two simple items, like a bookcase. Another reader echoed this tip as a bargain: "We have saved a lot of money by purchasing furniture at an unfinished wood store and staining it ourselves. One plus is the furniture is usually 100% real wood and not particle board or filler and stain-

## *Warehouse clubs do's and don'ts*

Okay, we admit it—we are warehouse club junkies. We love the incredible deals we get on kid's stuff, parent stuff . . . well, just about every kind of stuff. What kind of deals, you say? How about kid pj's for $10 that would retail for $28 in stores? We love the toys, swimsuits, coats, and more. Yes, we discussed warehouse club deals for diapers and formula in our BABY BARGAINS book, but there is so much more for kids and families today in most warehouse clubs. How can you get the best deals? Here are our five tips:

**1** **SCOPE OUT THE CHOICES.** The three big players in the wholesale club biz are Sam's (samsclub.com), Costco (costco.com) and BJ's Wholesale (bjswholesale.com). Go to each company's web site to see which locations are near you. Costco and Sam's are nationwide, while BJ's is east of the Mississippi.

**2** **COMPARE MEMBERSHIP FEES.** Yes, you must pay a membership fee to get access to wholesale clubs and that runs $30 to $40 a year, depending on the club. We've found the savings often pays for the membership fee several times over. Another bonus: some clubs sell gasoline. Our local wholesale club regularly undercuts local gas stations by 10¢ to 25¢ gallon.

ing it is no great chore. Trust me, we are the klutzes of the home project world so if we can do it, any one can!" One hint: some stores even offer to do the staining for you (one reader said she bought a twin bed, five drawer chest and night stand for $450—and staining was FREE with their purchase!).

**10 IS IT WASHABLE?** Boy, that cute rug from Pottery Barn is to die for—until junior spills paint on it. Or gets sick on it. If it is not washable, don't buy it.

**11 ONE WORD: TARGET.** Target has a tremendous number of fashionable and funky accessories for kids' rooms (pictures, lamps, pillows, shelves, coat hooks, decorative knobs and more). Target usually has three or four different "themes" for kids' rooms on display at one time (see Figure 7 on the next page). Best of all, you can do an entire theme for less than $100. They also sell the removable appliqué stickers discussed earlier in this section. Like that Pottery Barn look but not the price? Target usually sells a

**3 DON'T FORGET THE WEB.** All of the major warehouse clubs have companion web sites that offer great deals, sometimes on products not in their stores. Example: we saw Peg Perego Pliko strollers on Costco's web site for as little as $119 (retail $200+). The site had Baby Jogger strollers for $229 (about $70 less than comparable retail) These strollers weren't sold in their stores at the time of this writing. Costco even lets non-members purchase products online for a 5% additional fee.

**4 IF YOU SEE IT, BUY IT.** Remember the golden rule of warehouse club shopping: he who hesitates is lunch. If you see a great buy at a club, don't wait to buy it next week. Odds are, it will be gone. Merchandise turns over so quickly at most clubs that you have to move immediately to scoop up deals.

**5 COSTCO IS A BIT MORE FAMILY FRIENDLY.** While we love all the wholesale clubs, we have to admit that Costco is our favorite—their products seem to be aimed more at families (the aforementioned strollers, juvenile furniture and more).

*Figure 7. It's like Pottery Barn—for the rest of us. Target's affordable decor accessories have that PBK look . . . at half the price.*

knock-off look at bargain prices. Sample: Pottery Barn's cute little bathroom step stools were priced at $69. At Target a similar stool sells for $20.

**12** **SKIP THE THEME BEDDING.** Most readers tell us the quality of character-themed bedding (sheets, comforters, etc) is terrible—and the prices are sky high. If you want to do a Thomas the Tank Engine theme (for example), decorate with Thomas accessories and go for solid color, coordinating bedding. "Avoid licensed products, especially those for a movie," one mom emailed us. "The stuff's more expensive and a toddler's love affair with the character/movie/toy will last about as long as a Drew Barrymore marriage."

**13** **THINK TWICE ABOUT WALLPAPER.** Paint is cheaper and easier to change.

**14** **IF YOU STILL WANT TO DO WALLPAPER, CHECK OUT HOME DEPOT.** A reader of our baby book found Home Depot had the best price on wallpaper (50% or more off book prices) and cute patterns like Beatrix Potter. To save, Elizabeth and her husband put up a chair rail and wallpapered under the chair rail (hence, they needed only half the wallpaper required to do an entire room).

**15** **FRAME IT UP.** Here's a great idea a reader emailed us for decor on the cheap: buy a second copy of your child's favorite book, remove the pages and put them in inexpensive frames! Poof! Instant decor at a fraction of the price of framed children's prints.

**16** **KEEP THE THEME.** Having more than one child? Buy furniture in the same finish (maple, oak, white, etc). Why? That way you can move pieces from room to room as they are needed, but they still coordinate.

**17** **MATTRESS DEALS.** Again, the wholesale clubs like Sam's and Costco have the best deals—$100 or less. That's half the cost of other stores and most clubs sell good name brands to boot. Another tip: look for sales at mattress stores in January and February when they change over their inventory. Buy last year's model in January and you can save 30% to 50%. One mom used this tip to save $90 on her son's mattress.

**18** **WATERPROOF MATTRESS PROTECTORS ARE A STEAL AT TARGET FOR $8.** A reader noted that "rather than hassle with waterproof mattress pads, these protectors are like big vinyl bags which you put the whole mattress in (like a baggie) and zip shut!"

**19** **DON'T GO FOR SOMETHING OVERLY BABYISH.** Yes, your two-year-old may be into Dora The Explorer right now—but what happens when she hits three? Five? Locking into a character that your child will tire of quickly might mean an expensive re-do down the line. One tip: keep it relatively generic. Instead of Thomas the Tank Engine, go for a general train theme with a few Thomas items. Other good generic themes are flowers, farm animals and so on.

**20** **CLOSET ORGANIZERS CAN ELIMINATE THE EXPENSE AND SPACE OF A DRESSER.** A reader in Ohio found this was a great solution: "We installed closet organizers with drawers, shelves, etc. in our two toddler rooms. This is great because 1) it removes all the furniture from the kid's room so that they have more room to play 2) keeps everything out of site—I can simply close the door and voila! the mess is gone and 3) it's pretty cheap—got it from Home Depot and installed for under $200 per closet."

**21** **HIT WAREHOUSE SALES.** Most baby/kid stores have to unload their excess stock from time to time. An increasing trend: warehouse sales, where stores blow out stock at savings of 50% or more. A reader in Sacramento told us the local kids' store (Goores) has warehouse sales twice a year. She scored designer bunk beds for just $300 (half price). How do you find out about these deals? Just call your local kids furniture stores. Most are happy to tell you their sale schedule or put you on a mailing list for future sales. Also watch local newspapers and network with other parents to ferret out these sales.

**22** **RECYCLE AND REUSE.** Wondering what to do with your infant's Moses basket now that your baby is a toddler? Convert it to toy storage. The same goes for a changing table, if you have one. Most changing tables have drawers underneath for diaper supplies; after the diapers are gone (yes, that will happen some day), use them to store toys.

### E-MAIL FROM THE REAL WORLD
### *Trundle beds:*
### *the perfect guest solution*

*We realize space is tight out there and many parents don't have a guestroom—what can you do when company arrives? The solution: a trundle. Carolyn Kimball of Pasadena, California writes about how a space-saving trundle can do the trick:*

"I'm not sure that this qualifies as a money saver, but it's definitely a nice convenience. We have an almost 2-year-old boy and I'm expecting another, due at the end of July. Since our toddler will be ready soon to graduate from crib to a real bed, we intend to follow my sister's lead in decorating (she also has two kids) to allow for the frequent visits we anticipate from out-of-town relatives. We plan to get him a twin-size bed with a pop-up trundle. Then, when grandparents and other guests arrive, we can pop up the trundle and make a nice king-size bed for them, and move the toddler into our room or the baby's room on a rollaway or mattress during their stay. Real estate prices (especially in areas like ours, Southern California) mean it's hard to afford a house with an extra bedroom just for guests, so this will be our less-expensive solution. And when baby #2 is old enough, if we want the two boys to share a room, we've got two twin beds all set to go."

*Figure 8. Don't spend $200 on a fancy toy box—hit the Container Store for affordable toy storage solutions.*

**23** **SKIP THE PRICEY TOY BOX.** Instead, use clear plastic shoeboxes for toy storage. The Container Store (www.containerstore.com) and Target both sell these for $5 to $10 each (see Figure 8). It's much easier to find toys in plastic shoeboxes than one giant container and you save the $100 to $200 a pricey toy box can run. Hint: get a variety of sizes to accommodate various toys.

**24** **YARD SALES.** Okay, you have a son who's into sports. Instead of expensive wall hangings, why not hang some real hockey sticks and old jerseys. An old tennis racket, pucks and balls can be found at yard sales for a fraction of their retail prices.

### Outlets

◆ A reader in Georgia email us with kudos for the *American Home Showplace* in Dalton, GA (www.carpetsofdalton.com; 800-262-3132), saying "this is a great place for kids furniture. Their prices are 40% to 60% off retail and they often run specials and sales with additional money off."

◆ *Pottery Barn Kids.* Love that PBK look but can't afford the PBK price tags? Try the Pottery Barn outlets (eight locations, check outletbound.com for the latest). A reader near the Dawsonville, GA outlet said she found bedding and furniture at 50% off retail. Many of the items are returned catalog orders and are in excellent shape.

◆ **The furniture outlets of North Carolina** offer great deals on just about everything for a kid's room. Prices can be 20% to 50% off retail. There are two options for getting deals: you can visit the outlets yourself in High Point and Hickory or order over the phone. Either way, we'd recommend getting a good guidebook—the best is **The Insider's Guide to Buying Home Furnishings** by Kimberly Causey ($24.95, Home Décor Press; 800-829-1203). This 356-page book is a great resource for bargain furniture shoppers. While the book sports a 1996 copyright, much of the info is up to date (the author updates it with every printing). The same author has also published a book called the **Furniture Factory Outlet Guide** ($24.95, 2002 edition) with more updated material. You can surf the author's web page at www.smartdecorating.com.

◆ **Gothic Cabinet Craft** (nearly 50 locations in and around New York City and New Jersey, www.gothiccabinetcraft.com) boasts "all wood furniture at incredible prices" and our readers agreed. Erin Polenski emailed us her take on Gothic: "What a deal! They offer an extensive selection of reasonably priced, all-wood furniture. Perfect for infant and toddler rooms. Furniture can be ordered finished or unfinished. I finished a few pieces myself and it was fun. It

*Figure 9. NY-based Gothic Cabinet Craft has 50 stores in the tri-state area that feature great all-wood furniture deals, including unfinished items.*

### E-Mail from The Real World
**Murals on the cheap: project it!**

*Reader Michelle Roush found the price of wallpaper and designer decor too much to handle . . . so, here's her creative idea for creating a mural on the cheap:*

"I have decided to get an overhead projector from our local library and make transparencies of my son's favorite book characters, etc. These are easily projected onto the wall, traced, and then painted in. I am not an artist but this is very easy to do (I helped a friend do it at her home). It is also much cheaper than a border, easy to change with growth, and customized for my child."

*Reader Alissa Brandon of Washington, DC wrote with similar tips:*

"It's easy to have a beautifully painted room in any theme, for just a few dollars—basically the cost of the paint. If you can work a copier, an overhead machine and paint within the lines, you can easily save yourself $500 to $1000.

1. Pick out your toddlers favorite pictures from storybooks, coloring books or posters.
2. Copy them on to transparency film.
3. Borrow an overhead projector from work or your local church, preschool or synagogue.
4. Make the images as large or small as you like and trace the images on the walls with a pencil.
5. Paint inside the lines.

It's THAT easy! Even if you have no artistic talent and no creativity of your own, if you can paint inside the lines, you will look like a hero to your little one, and save yourself a bundle in the process. And you can do this in a weekend. The cost of hiring an artist to paint a mural is outrageous! Save the extra money you would have spent on hiring a painter and put it toward his college fund. Or get him a nice swing set for the back yard with the money you saved."

Bottom line: with a little effort, you can create a beautiful mural for your child's room and save a bundle.

could also be painted to go with any decor. They now have a web site that features a store coupon, www.gothiccabinetcraft.com. I have sent several friends there and everyone has been more than satisfied." We have to agree—this is one amazing option. If you don't live near NYC, you can order online from their web site.

◆ *Lands End* has both bricks and mortar outlets and an overstock section of their web site (www.landsend.com). One reader scored a kid's comforter for $35 (half price) online and others have emailed us with similar bargains. It might be worth checking out for toddler bedding and accessories.

## The Name Game: Reviews of Furniture Manufacturers

Following are reviews of some of the best-known brand names for juvenile furniture and bedding sold in the U.S. and Canada. There are well over 100 companies in North America that manufacture and/or import furniture and at least as many bedding manufacturers. Because of space limitations we can't review each one. We decided to concentrate on the best and most common brands. If you've seen a furniture or bedding line we haven't reviewed, please feel free to call or email us (see our contact info in the back of this book).

*Please note: Most of these manufacturers do NOT sell directly to the public. We've included their phone numbers and web sites so you can find a dealer near you. Those companies that DO sell direct are noted with the tag line "to order . . ." Just an FYI.*

### The Ratings

- **A** **EXCELLENT**—*our top pick!*
- **B** **GOOD**— *above average quality, prices, and creativity.*
- **C** **FAIR**—*could stand some improvement.*
- **D** **POOR**—*yuck! could stand some major improvement.*

**Ethan Allen** *To find an Ethan Allen store near you, check their web site at www.ethanallen.com.* Ethan Allen Kids (EA Kids) is not a discount store, but one mom we interviewed considered the twin bed she bought there to be a bargain. "It has a special finish that is very durable and it's a bed that our son should be able to sleep in until

*Figure 10. Expensive but great quality is how our readers describe Ethan Allen's kids' line. Bonus: their web site includes their kids' catalog, complete with prices.*

he's an adult. Ethan Allen's prices are comparable to or less than Pottery Barn Kids and the quality is much better." Best of all, Ethan Allen's web site features all of their kids' items complete with prices and other helpful info. Twin beds run $600 to $1000 and bunk beds are pricey at $1000 to $1300. But there are frequent sales. Although prices were on the high side, they do include free delivery and set-up. Of course, EA Kids has all manner of accessories, including night tables, bookcases, desks, area rugs and more. Given the quality and the breadth of offerings, we'll give Ethan Allen a thumb's up, however, we've slightly lowered their rating over the last edition because they've raised starting prices. This makes Ethan Allen less of a value for kids furniture. ***Rating: B+***

***EG Furniture*** *To find a retail dealer near you, check their web site at www.egfurniture.com.* Quebec-based EG Furniture has been in the youth furniture business since 1988 and offers 13 collections in 32 different finishes. Made of solid birch wood, EG's quality is excellent. Prices are in line with other Canadian furniture makers (an EG twin bed is about $600; an oversized armoire that can house a computer is $950). Styling is a bit more contemporary than what we typically see coming from the Great White North; the "Mission" in particular is a standout. Bunk bed selections in this line are somewhat sparse, but EG has expanded the bunk beds to three options from only one in the past. All three options are available as twin over twin, twin over double or double over double configurations. ***Rating: B+***

**Flexa** *To find a retail dealer near you call: 973-599-1300. Web: www.flexa.dk.* Flexa is the Denmark-based furniture maker that has been in business since 1970, but only recently invaded the U.S. We were most impressed with their Lego-like bedding "systems," made of solid wood (Scandinavian pine). We loved the space saving designs and the whimsical touches like bunk beds with castle turrets or those with an attached slide (for that quick escape, we suppose), even a triple bunk option. Best of all, the prices are affordable: a basic bunk bed is $549; an L-shaped configuration is $649. And Flexa sells regular twin beds plus a large number of accessories. Also cool: Flexa's web site, which has a "Flexa 3D" room design program you can download to design your toddler's room (see Figure 11 below). Quality is excellent, as are the safety features of the furniture. The only bummer: Flexa furniture comes in only two finishes (a clear or white wash) and is only sold in about 60 stores nationwide. Nonetheless, we think it is worth the effort to seek out. ***Rating: A***

**Moosehead** *To find a retail dealer near you, call: 207-997-3621. Web: www.mooseheadfurniture.com* Readers of our *Baby Bargains* book may recall our brief discussion of Moosehead, the Maine-based furniture maker that recently expanded into cribs and juvenile furniture. We saw their collection at a trade show in High Point, North Carolina and were impressed—their shaker-style twin bed retails for about $400 and a matching dresser was $500. The drawers on Moosehead's case goods are dovetailed, although the glide wasn't as smooth as we found elsewhere. Bunk beds weighed in at

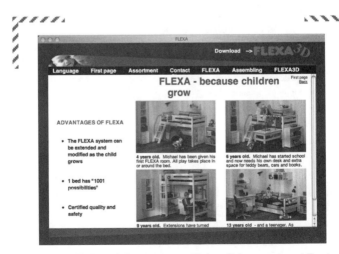

*Figure 11. Danish furniture giant Flexa offers several cool "bedding systems" that can be re-configured as your child grows.*

$1200. All models are made of solid maple and ash and manufactured in Maine. Moosehead offers two basic styles: a Shaker look in maple and a Mission-style in ash. Sold in about 200 stores nationwide, Moosehead isn't everywhere but is probably worth the effort to see if you have a dealer near by. By the way, Moosehead has a factory outlet store if you happen to be in Dover-Foxcroft, ME. Check their website for more info. **Rating: B+**

**PJ Kids** *To find a retail dealer near you, call: 609-683-5437. Web: www.pjkids.com.* PJ Kids offers a wide variety of toddler room decor, accessories and theme beds. We liked their funky headboards, which would be the way to dress up a plain twin bed without breaking the bank. One such headboard we saw at a recent trade show retails for about $175. PJ Kid's complete twin beds retail for about $500, while bunk beds are close to $1000. PJ Kids has scaled back some of their novelty beds in recent months (their web site still shows a few theme options including the Bug Off butterfly headboard), but the remaining styles retain a somewhat whimsical spin. Quality of this line is average; the furniture is made in China and Indonesia. Dressers feature dovetail joints, but we noticed the glide wasn't as smooth as other competitors. **Rating: B-**

**Rumble Tuff** *To find a dealer near you, call: 800-524-9607. Web: www.rumbletuff.com.* Readers of our baby book may recognize the name of this furniture maker; we recommended their affordable matching dressers as a good bet for nurseries. We should also mention Rumble Tuff also makes twins and bunk beds, both with above average quality. While we would not rate Rumble Tuff at the top of the heap quality-wise (they are still a step or two behind the Canadians like EG), they are a good value for the dollar. In the past few years, Rumble Tuff has expanded their line to include options with decorative molding (the Classic line) and bead board accents and bun feet (Del Mar). All in all, we recommend Rumble Tuff—good quality furniture at a decent price. **Rating: A**

**Sauder Furniture** *To find a retail dealer near you, check out their web site at www.sauder.com.* Sauder is the biggest RTA furniture maker in the country. RTA stands for "ready to assemble;" Sauder pioneered this concept back in the 1950's. By shipping furniture in flat boxes (later assembled by a consumer at home), Sauder was able to lower the prices of the furniture. Parents rave about the quality, even though most acknowledge it does take some time and effort to assemble. "We have used Sauder in his nursery and it has held up very well," one parent emailed us. "The children's line is well constructed, durable and very affordable. They also feature a drawer stop, which keeps a child from opening more than one drawer at a time for safety." One cool feature of Sauder: their new Qbits line of design-it-yourself modular furniture (www.qbits.com) lets you combine drawers, bookcases and other components at affordable prices. Sold at stores nationwide like Target and Lowe's Hardware, prices for Sauder's RTA dressers are about 50% less than traditional furniture. ***Rating: A-***

***Stanley*** *To find a retail dealer near you, call: 276-627-2000. Web: www.youngamerica.com* Stanley is probably the country's largest youth bedroom manufacturer. At last count, the company had a whopping 19 kid's collections, from the wrought iron "Garden Party" grouping to "Summerhaven," which mimics those hip color styles by Pottery Barn and Ethan Allen. Each collection contains a couple of dozen matching items, from twin beds to dressers, chairs to bunk beds. All of Stanley's beds come with three storage options: attached storage units, a trundle bed or additional under-bed storage. (See Figure 12 below for a sample configuration). Bunk beds also have three configurations: twin over twin, twin over full or a loft position bed (where there is space underneath the top bunk for a desk or dresser. It's the little touches that impress us about Stanley; their bunk beds feature a top bunk that is six inches higher than most bunk beds. Why? So parents don't hit their heads when they go to sit down on the lower bunk. The down side? Stanley uses maple veneers on some items (although the rest is solid

*Figure 12. Stanley's integrated storage and desk options make the most out of limited space.*

birch; all made in the USA). The joints on drawers are dovetailed, but the glide isn't as smooth as we've seen on other brands. And prices can be high, depending on where you shop it (most Stanley furniture is sold in those large furniture store chains). We priced a twin bed in maple from the "Simple Pleasures" line at $678. A bunk bed from the same collection is $1053; a captain's bed is $1012. On the plus side, delivery was quoted at just one week from a local furniture store, as Stanley has a quick turn around. **Rating: B**

***Vaughn*** *To find a retail dealer near you check out their web site at: www.vaughanfurniture.com* Vaughn Furniture of Virginia is an 80-year old furniture maker that recently expanded their juvenile offerings by teaming up with designer Pam Scurry. Scurry's "Cottage Garden" collection represents a departure from the more traditional look that Vaughn has done for years. The Cottage Garden is definitely aimed at girls, with its "classic yet romantic" styling (see Figure 13 below). Unfortunately, this collection isn't featured on Vaughn's web site (which is rather primitive and incomplete), so you'll have to take our word or try to see it in person. We were impressed with Vaughn's quality features, which included solid wood corners and specially molded doors on dressers. And the prices aren't bad either: twins are about $400, as are most dressers. A computer desk with hutch was $700. Vaughn is similar to Stanley in terms of distribution; you'll see it at "full-service" furniture retailers and warehouses. **Rating: B**

*Figure 13. We liked the edge detailing featured on this sleigh bed and painted dresser, part of Vaughn's Pamela Scurry's "Cottage Garden" collection.*

**Vermont Tubbs** *To find a retail dealer near you, check out their web site: www.vermonttubbs.com.* If you are looking for the top-of-the-line in bunk or twin beds, we'd recommend Vermont Tubbs. In business since 1840, Vermont Tubbs beds are made of solid ash and feature a raft of quality and safety features, exceeding the new federal guidelines. All their bunk beds can detach and become two twin beds if you need to split them. The styling (particularly the clapboard bunk bed in "blueberry") is among the best we've seen on the market. All Vermont Tubbs furniture comes in 11 finishes; the company also makes dressers, desks and chairs. Prices, as you might expect, are high—bunk beds start at about $1000 and go to $1600. Twin beds run $400 to $650. A five drawer chest, featuring dove tail joints and a very smooth glide, is $900. Realizing those prices are a bit hard for most parents to swallow, Vermont Tubbs recently launched two collection of bunk beds that are made in China.

### E-MAIL FROM THE REAL WORLD
#### Sheet Metal 101: Creative Decorating

*We are constantly amazed with the creativity of our readers. Here is a sample from parents nationwide, including an innovative use of greeting cards, sheet metal and carpet rolls:*

"For my daughter's room, I framed several greeting cards that featured really cute cats. They were super cheap (about $3 each). I had them framed with a discontinued frame, so the frames were really inexpensive as well (less than $20 each - you could also do it yourself at the Great Frame Up). I ended up with really great custom-looking wall hangings at a really great price. Plus my daughter loves them!"

*Another reader showed creativity with sheet metal:*

"A friend had this idea. Get sheet metal from a plumbing supply store (a 3 x 8-foot sheet cost $11) and cover a wall with it. Then use strips of wood to create a grid of framed sections—paint strips to suit room colors. An alternative idea is to get just one sheet, screw it to the wall, and frame it with wood strips. (I'm cutting one sheet in half and framing two 3 x 4-foot sections for each of my boys' rooms. They cut easily with tin snips.) Then get fun magnets so the kids have a place to hang their artwork without sticking pieces of tape all over your walls."

These bunks run $700 to $800 and are also made of solid ash; the styling isn't as fancy as their regular collection, but this might a good alternative to check out. We should note that Vermont Tubbs hit a rough patch in 2003—battered by competition from cheap Asian imports, the company almost closed until new investors came forward and bought the company. The new management cut Tubbs delivery time (from 12 weeks to six) and the company has subsequently seen a sales rebound. All in all, Vermont Tubbs is a great brand if you want to splurge. ***Rating: A***

## Bedding

Kid's bedding is a $443 million a year business and is ruled by one simple premise: cartoons sell. Whatever the hot licensed char-

*How about carpet rolls? Anneliese Dickman of Milwaukee, IL came up with this creative idea:*

"To keep all your kid's stuffed animals off the floor, use a cardboard carpet roll. (What the carpet was rolled on.) Carpet stores will give you one free or for very cheap. Paint it to match the room and then cut it to just fit from the floor to the ceiling (wedge it in there good so your little one can't knock it over). Tie a ribbon around each animal and hang them on the roll using drapery hooks (you'll have to drill a hole in the roll for each hook). You can hang the animals entirely around the roll, and from floor to ceiling. Put in a corner this looks great, especially in a jungle- or farm-themed room. Hang less favorite animals higher and well-loved ones lower so your child can access them more easily."

*Angela Garvie told us about how her husband used a digital camera to create unique toddler room decor:*

"We went a little crazy with paint and fake brick paneling from Home Depot to make our three-year-old's room look like a construction zone. My husband took digital pictures of road signs, printed them and mounted them on foam-core and had them laminated. Much cheaper than wallpaper or framed prints and more unique!"

acter is, you can bet a bedding pattern (and lunch box . . . and so on) are not far behind. Here's a look at the bigger players in the twin bedding market:

## The Name Game: Reviews of Bedding Makers

*Please note: A few of these bedding manufacturers do NOT sell directly to the public. We've included their phone numbers and web sites so you can find a dealer near you. Those companies that DO sell direct are noted with the tag line "to order . . ." Just an FYI.*

## The Ratings

**A** EXCELLENT—*our top pick!*
**B** GOOD— *above average quality, prices, and creativity.*
**C** FAIR—*could stand some improvement.*
**D** POOR—*yuck! could stand some major improvement.*

**Dan River** *To find a retail dealer near you, check out their web site at: www.danriver.com.* Name a popular cartoon character and odds are, Dan River has a bedding line for it. Racking up $128 million in bedding sales last year, Dan River is the biggest name in twin bedding—and that's in large part to their large stable of character licenses. You'll find everything here, from old standbys like Barbie to the latest and greatest—Spiderman, Thomas the Tank Engine and Bob the Builder. Other major licensees include Tonka, Blues Clues, Dragon Tails, Sesame Street, Franklin, Clifford, Dora the Explorer, Scooby-Doo, Looney Tunes and the Powerpuff Girls. Dan River has a large collection of sports themed bedding (including Major League Baseball, the National Hockey League and NASCAR licenses). If that wasn't enough, the company also markets bedding under the names Casual Kids and Olive Kids. The latter has its own web site where you can purchase their whimsical bedding and accessories directly (most other Dan River licensed bedding patterns are sold in discounters and chains). The Olive Kids "Happy Flowers" bedding included a twin comfort $46, pillow sham $17 and twin sheet ($30). Almost everything is a cotton/poly blend and that's our biggest gripe with Dan River—you often pay a premium price (again, that $30 twin sheet set) for only average quality. *Rating:* **C+**

**Company Kids** *To order call 800-323-8000. Web: www. compa-nykids.com.* If you want choice, consider Company Kids—this web site and catalog features over 50+ bedding patterns at last count. Separated by gender, Company Kid's web site features both basics (solid and ginghams) and prints. A solid color, all-cotton sheet runs $16 in cotton percale; $15 to $24 in jersey knit (see box on this page for discussion of these different fabrics). Some sheets (especially the more detailed patterns) can run $50, although that's the

## Ikea deals and steals

*Ikea may only have 18 locations in the US (and nine in Canada), but they have an amazing following. When we asked parents about their all time best buys for toddler furniture and decor, Ikea came up on top. Here's a sample:*

"I found the cutest kids' furniture at IKEA. The line is called Mammut—a wardrobe is $249, nightstand is $119 and a twin bed is $199. We furnished our son's entire room for $747 including tax. The colors are so vibrant! It's like something you see at FAO Schwartz. The downside? You have to put it together and the quality is only average."

"Ikea is the all time best place for sturdy inexpensive furniture. You can get unfinished furniture and paint it whatever color you want or get it finished. Plus, if it gets damaged (as toddlers are often destructive, at least mine is) it won't make the owner fret."

"Our son's room is pretty small, about 10' x 12'. We purchased a bed frame (no mattress) from IKEA that converts in several ways. It's designed to be either a bunk bed, a low loft, or a high loft. It has a six-foot-high frame. Here's the way we're planning to use it: right now, it's at a low bed height, and the bed has a railing that goes all the way around, so he won't fall out. When he's a little older, we'll move it up to the low loft position (about 4' high), and he can have a small play area underneath. When he's even older, we'll move it to the high loft position, so that we can put a desk underneath. We shopped all over for beds that would do this combination for us, and IKEA was the only place that had exactly what we wanted. The IKEA bed isn't as pretty as the $1,000 beds we found, but for $199, we're not complaining."

*Figure 14. Company Kids bedding combines the best of both worlds—snazzy designs (this shot is of their boy's collection) at affordable prices.*

exception. Bed skirts run about $55 and a comforter cover is $109. The Company Kids web site isn't as slick looking as Land of Nod, but it is easy enough to navigate (see Figure 14 above). You'll find a raft of accessories, from comforters, furniture, curtains, rugs and more. If you live in or near Wisconsin, be sure to check out Company Kids outlet stores (four at last count; check their web site for the latest locations). And watch out for the outlet stores "tent liquidation" sales, held twice a year (usually in May and September).
**Rating: A-**

**Garnet Hill** *To order call 800-870-3513. Web: www.garnethill.com.* Garnet Hill's specialty is their embroidered quilts. Pick a pattern and their web site will match a quilt or comforter cover (duvet); we liked all the detailed info on their web site, including washing instructions. While Garnet Hill doesn't have a wide selection (nine patterns on our last visit), the creativity and design elements make it worth a look. Sheets are $20 to $30; a comforter cover is about $80. A quilt with embroidery can run $168. Garnet Hill also sells matching rugs and blankets for their patterns, but no hard goods (like tables or chairs). We thought the quality of this bedding was excellent.
**Rating: A-**

**Land of Nod** *To order call: 800-933-9904. Web: www. landofn-od.com.* "Clever" and "sophisticated" are the two words most frequently used to describe Land of Nod, the mail order catalog and web site that sells whimsical kid's bedding and accessories. You gotta love a company that names a robot bedding theme "Danger Mrs. Robinson!" . . . or a plaid theme set "I'm a Lumberjack and I'm Okay." Well organized and easy to navigate, Land of Nod's web site is divided into several "rooms" for boys, girls, gifts, etc. We were impressed with the high quality and nice touches like detailed embroidery. Of course, prices are high as well—a sheet set can run $30 to $70. A comforter (duvet) cover is $100-$130. If that's a bit too much to swallow, consider just buying the duvet cover and matching it with inexpensive solid color sheets from sources like Land's End. And don't forget Land of Nod's online outlet store, "Nods and Ends" with savings of up to 80% off. On a recent visit, we saw a girl's bedding set marked down 60% with a fitted sheet for just $15. Land of Nod's biggest strength is their vast selection of matching accessories; you'll find rugs, shelves, storage, toys, lamps and more. Look for Land of Nod bedding in Crate and Barrel stores (the companies are partners); Land of Nod has three stores at last count (two near Chicago, one in Seattle). If you live near Chicago, check out their outlet store in Wheeling, IL (847-459-9900). **Rating: A-**

**Lands End** *To order call: 800-345-3696 Web: www.landsend.com.* This is the place to go for high quality basics. Lands End's bread and butter bedding offers are a selection of sheets in solids, stripes or checks. The solids are $18 to $22 per sheet; patterns are a bit more at $22-$30. A comforter is $75, while a bed skirt runs $50. While you won't find a large amount of accessories (there is a basic offering of matching shelves, lamps and a bedside table), Lands End offers some of the best quality in the biz—most sheets are 100% cotton and 220

### Jersey knit versus cotton percale?

Many web sites and catalogs offer two types of sheets: jersey knit and cotton percale. What's the difference? Jersey knit sheets feel more like a t-shirt; the fabric is thick and has a warmer feel. Cotton percale is a smooth, woven fabric that has a crisper feel. Since cotton percale sheets can feel cold to the touch, they might be more appropriate for warmer climates. By contrast, jersey knit sheets are perhaps better for locations with long, cold winters. Or consider flannel sheets, which are usually available seasonally.

thread count. Compare that to "character bedding" sets that are often cotton/poly blends with lower thread counts yet still cost more money. And don't forget about the Lands End outlet stores (mentioned earlier) and the overstock section of their web site, where you can find great deals. As you might of heard, Sears bought Land's End back in 2002. So far, little has changed with the brand . . . and now you can find some Lands End products in Sears stores. ***Rating: A***

***Springs Industries*** *To find a retail dealer near you, check out their web site at: www.springs.com.* Nipping at the heals of Dan River is Springs Industries, the second-largest player in the kid's bedding market with $105 million in sales. While Springs doesn't have the marquee name licenses that Dan River has, it still has a few formidable ones, including Disney (which it shares with WestPoint Stevens, see below). There's also "My Little Pony" bedding and "Cat the Hat" themes, as well as Nascar. What they lack in licenses, Springs sometimes makes up for in quality—Springs also markets the more upscale Wamsutta Baby, Springmaid and Natural Basics brand. Like Dan River, Springs quality is often average—most character sets are poly/cotton blends (but the upper-end brands like Wamsutta are more likely to be all-cotton). You'll see Springs sold in stores like Target, which also features their bedding on their web site. ***Rating: B-***

*Figure 15. Most of Target's kids bedding is made by Springs, which counts Harry Potter and John Deere among its licenses.*

## When boys share with girls

What happens if you only have one room that is to be shared by both a boy and girl? At first glance, it might seem like a difficult task, as many bedding themes are overly boyish or girlish. But there are solutions: First, go with a neutral color scheme like cream or taupe for the walls. Second, consider a decorating theme like farm animals or a character theme like 101 Dalmatians. Both can be accessorized without looking specifically like a boy or a girl's room. Finally, choose accessories in bright primary colors (pastels are more likely to look more gender specific).

**WestPoint Stevens/Martex** *To find a retail dealer near you, check out their web site at: www.martex.com.* WestPoint Stevens' (also known as Martex) biggest license is Disney—this is the home of Mickey, Winnie the Pooh, Tigger and Buzz Lightyear bedding. Their "Disney Home" bedding label churns out bedding based on whatever Disney's latest movie characters. We did like their web site, which offers detailed info and pictures of their Disney bedding (but alas, you can't purchase online from the site directly). Most WestPoint Stevens bedding is sold in chains like Bed, Bath & Beyond, JCPenney, Wal-Mart as well as a slew of department stores and even warehouse clubs like Costco. A bargain tip: the company also has 52 outlet stores where you can score deals on discontinued items. Check their web site or call 800-533-8229 for the latest locations. **Rating: C+**

## The Bottom Line: Our Top Picks

Don't waste money on a toddler bed—every toddler can go straight from a crib to a twin bed, even if you have to leave the mattress on the floor for a while. Fancy twin beds can run $800 at pricey boutiques, but you can find the bed for half or less on sale at furniture stores or at wholesale clubs. Speaking of clubs, Sam's and Costco have the best deals on twin mattresses as well. As for good brands, we thought Moosehead's twin beds combined the best of both worlds—good quality and decent prices. For bunk beds, we thought Canada's Forever Mine had a great deal—$600 for a solid birch bunk bed that converts to two twins.

For bedding, we thought Lands End and Company Store

offered the best quality at the lowest prices. A little creativity goes a long way in decorating a toddler room—consider Wallies (pre-pasted wallpaper cut-outs) and cheap chic at Target to give your toddler's room pizzazz on a budget.

# CHAPTER 3

## Clothing & Shoes

### Inside this chapter

W*here are the best deals for toddler clothes? And how you can get quality shoes that won't break the bank? We've got all the deals and steals here in this chapter, plus the low-down on the best brands, outlets, wastes of money and more!*

Ah, those care free baby days! Remember when you could actually pick your son or daughter's outfit without any protests or discussion about the merits of this color versus that one? When a cotton sleeper is what they'd wear all day? When shoes were just a decorative accessory?

Welcome to toddlerhood and clothes, where discussions of which outfit is appropriate approach the complexity level of nuclear disarmament talks. And where shoes are now an expense threatening to overtake your mortgage payment.

Of course dressing your toddler doesn't have to cost a fortune. When we polled readers of our *Baby Bargains* book, we were amazed at the sheer creativity of parents in stretching their toddler clothing and shoe dollars. In this chapter, we'll talk about secrets to saving on all of it from everyday clothes to designer jackets, sneakers to special occasion shoes.

Among the key lessons: think outside the box. Yep, it's easy to pop into a mall and buy toddler clothes—but you'll often be socked with retail prices. The best bargain shoppers use a variety of tactics to win the clothing battle: discounters, outlet stores, warehouse sales, end-of-season deals, second-hand stores and even the Internet. Let's break it down:

## Getting Started: When Do You Need This Stuff?

Readers of our past books may recognize one of our bargain mantras: shop early for deals. One of the classic blunders in life (right after "Never get into a land war in Asia"—apologies to the *Princess Bride*) is waiting until the last minute to shop for something, as you usually get soaked in the process.

Yet, shopping for toddler clothing and shoes often defies that rule. Trying to shop for clothing deals months before your toddler will wear them is usually difficult to near impossible. That's because it involves guessing your toddler's shirt/dress/shoe size several months out, all the while factoring in the season (perfect fitting sandals don't work in December; a winter coat deal isn't worth much in June). And it is hard to anticipate some clothing/shoe needs, like getting a month's notice that your toddler will be the flower girl at your sister's wedding.

So while we will talk somewhat about buying "ahead" one or two seasons when you see a deal, we realize most folks have to shop in season. Hopefully, you can take advantage of many of the deals in this chapter with little or no advance planning.

## Parents in Cyberspace: What's on the Web?

Most parents we interviewed still buy clothes the old fashioned way: they go to a store, see what fits and then buy it. Or they hit second-hand stores, garage sales or outlets. The Internet ranks a distant last place where folks shop. Why? Most moms and dads we spoke to said concerns about sizing, not being able to see items in person, high shipping charges and return hassles kept them from shopping online.

Of course, that doesn't mean the 'net isn't useful at all. There are quite a few sites that offer good info and great deals . . . and we'll talk more about the toddler bargain bazaar on eBay later in this chapter. Here's a look at what's out there:

◆ **Lands End's overstock area (www.landsend.com).** Looking for coats and outerwear at bargain prices? Check out the overstock area of the Lands End web site. Reader India Fraizer emailed us her kudos for the deals here: "I adore this site. Click on the overstock link and you are transported to a wonderful array of discounted kids clothes. This is a great way to buy winter coats and rain gear.

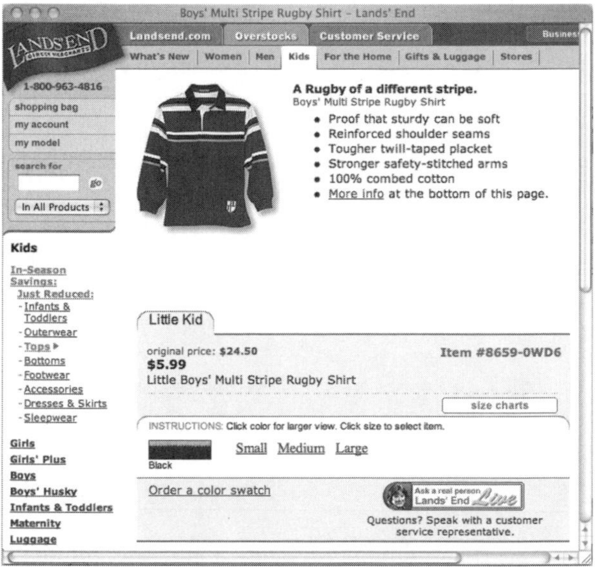

*Figure 1: Why pay $24.50 for this shirt when you can buy it for $5.99? Lands Ends' web site overstock section is a great bargain source. Be sure to look in both the Infant/Toddler and Kid's sections for deals.*

I got a very nice Gore-Tex fleece lined winter coat for $39, originally $70. I was so blown away by the prices that I bought my three year old coats for the next two years!" One tip: be sure to check the site first thing on Wednesdays and Saturdays. Those are the days new stuff goes online.

And one reader noted that Lands End carries hard-to-find toddler sized snow and rain boots. Even at the regular price, finding the right sizes make Lands End a plus for this cold weather gear.

We should also mention Lands End unconditional return policy, one of the most generous in the industry. Now that Lands End is owned by Sears, you can return mail-order purchases to your local Sears store.

◆ **Preschoolians.com.** When you visit this shoe web site, we know you're going to check the cover of this book to make sure it still says "Bargains." And we agree that kids shoes for $60 ain't no bargain. But some parents absolutely swear by Preschoolians. Why? Every shoe Preschoolians makes comes with a clear "window" in the sole so you can make sure the shoe actually fits your child. (The company claims that the old fashioned way of pushing on the shoe's toe to see if there is enough room for growth is inaccurate). The site offers three options to make sure parents size their kids' shoes properly: they'll send you a free measuring device, you can use a ruler or you can download a sizer from the site. They also offer a live chat option to help you size your child. They claim parents are best at measuring feet and that standard shoe measurement devices simply aren't good enough. If you have a hard to fit child or are frustrated with the shoes you're finding, Preschoolians may be an option. However, at $60, we're hard pressed to give them our wholehearted recommendation. Remember, toddlers may have to be fitted for new shoes as much as four times a year. So your total outlay may be as much as $240 a year. Ouch!

◆ Looking for some shoe advice? *StrideRite.com* has some good articles and advice on shoes. Check out the "Why Stride Rite" section and look at the "custom fit" area for good info on how to properly fit a child's shoes.

◆ *Payless.com* has a free "Kids Shoe Sizer" with a printable chart that not only shows your child's current size, but also whether they need regular or wide widths.

◆ *Keds.com* has a "sale" section on their site with 25% off deals. One bonus: you can usually find odd sizes (such as extra width) online. On a recent visit, we saw a girl's canvas tennis shoe for $15, regularly $25.

◆ What's the best site to buy toddler clothes online? We surveyed our readers and the winner was: *The Gap* (www.gapkids.com). Their site earns kudos for its ease of use and frequent sales.

## What Are You Buying?

How much do parents shell out for clothing for an average toddler? Here are the answers, based on government statistics and broken down by family income level:

Average annual clothing expenses per child, ages 2 to 5:

### Dual-Parent Family

| Income | Clothing expense per year |
| --- | --- |
| Less than $44,000 | $350 |
| $44,000 to $66,900 | $410 |
| $66,900 and up | $540 |

### Single-parent family

| Income | Clothing expense per year |
| --- | --- |
| Less than $40,000 | $340 |
| $40,000 and up | $480 |

*Note: Income is before-tax. Figures are based on the Consumer Expenditure Survey by the US Department of Agriculture conducted from 1990-92, updated to 2004 dollars using the Consumer Price Index.*

For our Canadian readers, the figures look very similar: about $450 to $550 spent per year on toddler clothing, according to a 2001 survey we found by the province of Manitoba. (Those figures are in Canadian dollars).

Does it cost more to clothe a girl versus a boy? Are you kidding? Of course there is a difference—in that same Canadian survey parents of girls spent 13% to 15% more on clothes than parents of boys. (The U.S. government survey we discuss above didn't break out costs by gender; we assume the figures are averages for both boys and girls).

Now that you know the average costs, what are the basic parts of a toddler's wardrobe? Most parents divide their kids' clothing purchases into the following categories:

◆ **Day care clothes.** Yep, this is the everyday wear that gets the full frontal abuse of day care. Obviously, the cheaper the better but watch out—sometimes the cheapest clothes wash poorly or shrink too much. Many readers have success with Target's house brands such as Circo; a few readers say Wal-Mart's Garanimals also does well for basics—hey it is hard to beat $2.88 for a t-shirt! In the past, Wal-Mart's kid clothes were not our pick for best quality. To Wal-Mart's credit, however, they have improved quality dramatically in the past year or so—parents we interviewed now say they wash and wear well.

We'll discuss which additional brands are the best deals later in this chapter.

◆ **Pajamas.** We've seen the gamut here: from $38 pajamas in catalogs to fancy options at nearly that price in department stores. But you don't need to spend that much—we'll go over our best discount source for PJ's later in this chapter and discuss alternatives that can also cost much less.

◆ **Dress up outfits.** Most folks have a few of these outfits for a nice occasion. But how do you find the better brands at a discount price? eBay is the answer for many readers; we'll discuss more about

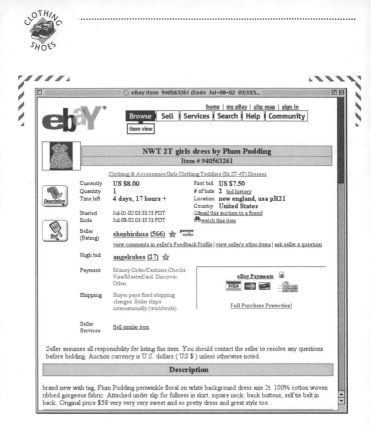

*Figure 2: Why pay top dollar for a dress-up outfit? This brand new, designer floral print dress retails for $58 but went for just $8 on eBay! Hint: look for listings with NWT, which means "New With Tags."*

eBay deals later in this chapter. (See Figure 2 above for a sample eBay deal). Other parents find fancier clothes at Gymboree to be fairly indestructible . . . "just promise yourself you won't buy anything here that isn't on sale," added one mom. Gymboree also has one advantage in sizing: their "Grow Cuffs" that give you an extra inch or two in pants. That might mean a few more months of wear.

◆ *Shoes*. This is a tough one for many parents—the choices here seem split between high cost and discount options. On one end are the full price shoe stores (like Stride Rite, although you can get these on sale at discounters and at outlet stores . . . more on this later). The advantage here is you can correctly fit your child and the shoes are often high quality. Full price shoe stores offer half sizes and other special sizes for kids with hard to fit feet (like extra-wide widths). You also get perks like free check ups every three months to make sure the shoes are still fitting correctly. Some parents believe that buying quality shoes and getting them sized right is worth the extra money.

On the other hand, discount stores offer great prices—50% or more off retail. But you have to judge your child's size yourself, as the selection is self-service. And hope your child fits into standard sizes, as you often can just find the basics (few half sizes or special widths). And here's a little secret: guess who makes Target's shoes? Yep, it's Stride Rite according to our sources inside the industry.

Some parents split the difference—they spend a bit more on shoes their children wear every day, but hit the discounters for shoes their children might wear just once or seasonally (dress up shoes, sandals for a beach vacation, etc.).

There is a widespread belief among parents we interviewed that investing in quality shoes prevents foot problems down the road. Parents seem to have the fear that if they buy cheaper, discount shoes for their kids, those kids will have deformed feet later as adults. We're not sure how much of this is truth or just effective marketing by shoe companies, but it's a "perception is reality" thing by now. Does this mean you have to shell out $40 for a decent pair of sneakers for your toddler? Of course not—we'll talk more later in this chapter about getting quality shoes at reasonable prices.

◆ *Special considerations.* Younger toddlers still in diapers need diaper-friendly clothes. Yes, overalls look cute but think about how you are planning to get them off for a diaper change. As your toddler enters the potty training phase, clothes that can be quickly removed (no fancy snaps or buttons) are critical. Dressers or skirts for girls (and pull-on pants for boys) who are potty training are a smart idea.

## More Money Buys You

When does quality matter when it comes to toddler clothes? As the parents of two boys, we can give you a one-word answer: pants. Toddlers' pants/jeans take a ton of abuse; shirts on the other hand get less abuse, but more stains.

So it makes sense to invest in quality pants and skimp a bit on the shirts. What makes a quality pair of pants or jeans? Look for pants with rivets and triple rolled hems. Go for better, thicker fabric. As for shirts, better quality options have snaps/buttons on a reinforced band.

As with baby clothes, higher priced or designer toddler duds tend to be more generously sized than bargain basement brands. This is important to remember if you plan to bid for designer items on eBay or if you hit second-hand stores.

## Safe & Sound

Watch out for clothes and jackets with drawstrings. These were eliminated a few years ago by clothing manufacturers to address the hazard drawstrings can create on playscapes, etc. But carefully check hand-me-downs and second-hand clothing and jackets. Be sure to remove any drawstrings you find.

### Smart Shopper Tip #1
*Making sense of sizing*

*"I'm confused by all the different sizing I see for toddler clothes—what's the difference between a 2 and a 2T?"*

The difference: clothes that are sized with a T (2T, 3T) to allow more room for a diaper. Sizes *without* a T are for kids who no longer wear diapers. While that is the theory, the reality can be quite different—you may find little or no diaper room in 4T clothes in some cases.

And every catalog or company tends to have its own sizing quirks. Lands End clothing, while high quality, tends to run small. Contrast this with designer brands at department stores—as we mentioned earlier in this chapter, these upper-end clothes tend to be more generously sized than what you see in, say, Target.

Our advice: go to a consignment or second hand store to compare your toddler with the sizing of better brands. That way when you second hand or online at eBay, you have a better shot at correct sizing.

And what about those numbers? Are size 2 clothes for an average two-year old? It depends. With experience, you'll realize your child is probably bigger or smaller than the number size for his age.

### Smart Shopper Tip #2
*Go a la carte*

*"I love those matching outfits in department stores—so cute—but they are so expensive! And now my toddler wants to mix and match her own clothes. Help!"*

Our advice: go a la carte. Invest in a variety of t-shirts and pants/skirts you can mix and match and skip those matching or coordinated outfits (like the mango shirt that only works when paired with the kiwi overalls). Why? Toddlers like to experiment at this age with clothes (some more than others, of course) and for some reason, the perfectly coordinated matching outfit or set never seems to fit into their plans.

### Smart Shopper Tip #3
*Easy on, easy off.*
*"I'd love my toddler to learn how to dress himself, but he seems frustrated with anything that has buttons or snaps."*

Yep, dressing oneself is definitely a major milestone . . . yet parents sometimes unknowingly trip up their toddlers by stocking their wardrobe with toddler-unfriendly items. An example: buttons. Or zippers. Darn difficult to work even for adults! Pull-on pants or pants with slide-in clasps (the Gap sells these) are easier than anything with fancy zippers or buttons.

Does that mean you should NEVER buy clothing with buttons or zippers? Of course not—get one or two items with these features so your toddler can practice. Just don't over-populate your child's wardrobe with them.

For shoes, we bow to the temple of Velcro. The person who invented this should be given a Nobel Peace Prize. The only caveat to Velcro: it can stop sticking after a while. One smart tip: take tweezers and clean the fuzz/lint from the Velcro to make it work like new.

### Smart Shopper Tip #4
*Shoe conundrum*
*"I don't want to buy cheap shoes for my toddler for fear she will have foot problems as an adult. But, hey, $40 for a pair of kid's shoes at Stride Rite? That's highway robbery."*

Yep, it's a struggle for every parent—balancing the desire to get quality shoes that fit your child against the outrageous prices some "full service/full price" stores charge for shoes.

Here's what parents we interviewed advised: invest in good quality "every day" shoes—but then go cheap for special occasion shoes. Many parents we interviewed were willing to invest in better-quality shoes their kids wear every day. But when it comes to special shoes for Easter, a wedding or some other event, the cheaper the better. One mom emailed us she shells out $40 for a pair of tennis shoes at Stride Rite, but then hits Payless for patent leather Mary-Janes at $10.99.

Of course, you don't have to shell out $40 for Stride Rites. We'll discuss ways to slash those prices in half later in this chapter.

**Smart Shopper Tip #5**
*Unisex clothes*
*"We're planning to have another child and I'd like to stretch my clothing dollars as far as they can go. Any ideas?"*

In a nutshell: go unisex. That way you can hand down items no matter what the gender of your next family addition. Colors like green, orange, taupe and red can work for both boys and girls. Avoiding overly boyish or girlish clothes can save down the line.

## Spin Cycle: Laundry Secrets

Here's a scary fact: the average American spends seven to nine hours a week on laundry. And parents of toddlers probably spend more than that. How can you maximize your efforts and minimize the hassle of laundry? Here are our tips:

◆ *When buying pajamas, buy all the exact same style and color;* that way you don't spend time matching up different pieces. Ditto for socks. If you have more than one child, pick a color for each—the older one gets blue pj's and socks with a blue stripe, while the younger child gets green.

◆ *Don't be afraid of hot water.* Many Americans only wash their clothes in warm or cold water for fear of damaging them. But don't be afraid of hot water—the hotter the water is, the better the detergent works.

◆ *Use the web.* Have a stain you don't how to get out of your toddler's clothes? Check out Tide's excellent "Stain Detective" web site (with an entire area for kids and pets): www.tide.com/staindetective.

◆ *Pre-treat stains.* You don't have to buy specialized stain removers; most stains can be removed by simply pre-treating them with your basic laundry detergent.

◆ *Read the directions.* One common mistake: many folks ignore these instructions on laundry detergent boxes, such as how much detergent to use for different size loads. The problem? Put in a big load and not enough detergent, then the soap is diluted, and the resulting clothes may not be as clean as they should be. Most laundry detergents have detailed instructions that need to be followed.

Also avoid white. Sure, these outfits are cute, but they are a magnet for disaster. With our kids, it would never fail—a brand new white t-shirt would fall victim without hours to the heat-seeking missile that was a pepperoni pizza slice.

Speaking of stains, check out the box below for tips and secrets from the laundry room—we've done enough loads of laundry to write a book on this. But we'll keep it to the box below.

◆ *Add clothes after water and detergent.* The correct way to wash clothes: first fill up the washer with water and detergent THEN add clothes. Most folks do their laundry the other way around.

◆ *Consider special fabric softeners.* One of our top picks: Downy Enhancer, which helps keep colors bright and reduces wrinkling during washing. It actually works.

*Figure 3. Got stains? Don't throw away that outfit. Instead, check out Tide.com's Stain Detective web site to get detailed advice on getting out just about anything a toddler can dish up.*

##  Wastes of Money

Just like with baby clothes, toddler clothing and shoe racks are riddled with ridiculous items and other wastes of money. Here are our thoughts on what to avoid:

◆ *Toddler versions of adult brands.* Do toddlers really need a $50 pair of Teva sandals? Or a $58 pair of kid Merrell Jungle Mocks? Are your crazy? It seems like every fancy adult brand of clothing or shoes has rolled out a kid or baby version of their high priced products in recent years. It's absurd to spend that much money on a pair of shoes, sandals or what not.

◆ *Character clothing.* Slap a favorite kid's character on a t-shirt or dress and it seems to be justification for a store to sell the item at twice the price . . . or half quality of plain items. Our advice: steer clear of character clothing and shoes—your money is better spent elsewhere.

◆ *Health Tex.* Sorry, but this discount brand doesn't have the long-term wearability we'd like to see. Parents we interviewed say Health Tex outfits tend to pill after just a couple of washings. Fading is also a problem. After we aired these complaints in our last edition, we should note that Health Tex contacted us to tell us they've made some improvements to the line. John Martin, VP of marketing told us that they use a new process called "Kidproof" which helps pre-vent pilling, fading and staining as well as shrinkage. We're pleased to hear about their improvements but we'll wait for more parent feedback before we recommend this brand.

◆ *Babies R Us toddler clothes.* Moms tell us this chain's store brand, Mini Me, often falls apart after one or two washings.

◆ *Fancy stain removers.* Do you really need to buy a $20 bottle of miracle stain remover? No. In our experience, most stains came out of clothes with simple pre-treating with regular detergent.

##  Money Saving Secrets

**OLD NAVY.** Yes, you can find cheaper clothes at discounters like Target, but moms tell us that Old Navy clothes last

*Figure 4. Our readers say Old Navy is the best bet for affordable, yet quality toddler clothes.*

longer and are better quality. And it's not like Old Navy is super expensive—frequent sales and deals make Old Navy a top bargain. In general, we found Old Navy clothes wash better and shrink less than other discount brands. Ingrid Henden, a reader from Seattle, concurred on Old Navy's quality: "I have not had one single item rip or tear. We live in Seattle and my son wore his Old Navy jacket from October through March and it still looks great! They also have great fleece items, especially hats." Don't forget the clearance section on OldNavy.com for more deals.

**2** **CHECK OUT THE BIG 3 OFF-PRICE DISCOUNTERS: ROSS, TJMAXX AND MARSHALL'S.** Each sells name brands at prices that range from 40% to 70% off retail prices, sometimes even more. Yes, some styles are last year's hip fashion, but will your toddler be able to tell? Bonus: each store sells name brand shoes at half price or more. We love Marshall's and Ross particularly for their shoe deals (you can find Stride Rite among others). Other readers love the name brands (like Ralph Lauren and Tommy Hilfiger) at bargain prices. Among the best bargains we heard: $2.99 for a pair of designer capri pants at Ross snagged by Martha Schaeffer, a reader in Colorado Springs, CO.

**3** **GO SECOND HAND.** Consignment stores are great bargain havens, but don't waste your time—make a beeline to second hand stores in the *richest* part of town. They always have the best designer brands at prices that are usually steals. One example: the Children's Orchard consignment stores (www.ChildOrch.com), a franchised chain with 100 locations nationwide. Another good chain of second hand stores is Once Upon a Child (www.ouac.com). Check Narts.org for locations of consignment stores near you.

## eBay addiction and treatment

Ask any seasoned bargain shopper their secret to great deals on kid stuff and you'll often get a one word response: eBay. The online auction site has transformed the buying of just about everything . . . and kids' clothing and shoes are no exception. Here is a sample eBay success story:

*"I hate to be snobbish about it, but I really have found that the European shoes are of much better quality, especially Elefanten and Brakkies. But I can't afford to spend $50-$60 for each pair of shoes, so I buy most of my daughter's shoes for half off retail on eBay (www.ebay.com)! This works very well for the smaller sizes because kids grow out of the shoes faster than they can wear them out, so there are many bargains to be found. That way I can afford to buy multiple pairs of shoes for my daughter to match all her adorable outfits!"*

So how do you dive into the online auction world? Before you bid, here are our tips to getting the best deals:

♦ **Look for the words "NWT".** That's eBay-speak for "New With Tags." Obviously, the biggest steals on eBay are NWT clothes and shoes that are auctioned off by retail stores at a fraction of retail prices. Why would stores do this? One retailer of posh kid's clothing told us she prefers eBay over a mark-down rack because that way she doesn't upset her customers who paid full price. Other retailers are just over-stocked and need to thin out inventory. eBay offers retailers of better kids' goods a place to quietly sell off overstock.

♦ **Use "My eBay" favorite searches.** You can have eBay send you an email when a new item you're looking for appears on the site. Say you are looking for a particular designer brand—just tell

**4** **eBay.** Yep, one word says it all—check out the box below for more info on the deals and steals on eBay.

**5** **Love Stride Rite shoes but not Stride Rite prices?** Remember that Stride Rite shoes are sold in their outlet stores (see later in this chapter for more details). And those shoes are also sold in department stores, whose frequent sales often mean

eBay to send you an email when that word appears in the item's title or description. You can also set the "favorites" section to email you if a new item appears in a general category you are watching or if a particular seller (say a retailer you know sells an item you are looking for) posts a new item up for auction.

◆ *Do your homework.* Some folks get so caught up in this auction thing that they forget what is a deal . . . and what isn't. Our advice: do your homework and know what things cost at retail. That way you won't over-pay. Don't let emotions rule your bidding decisions.

◆ *Watch out for shipping and handling fees.* Be sure to confirm shipping fees BEFORE you bid. Most sellers list this info in the auction information; other times you have to send an email to the seller to find out details. Our readers in Canada need to be especially careful of this, as cross-border shipping charges can be a killer.

◆ *Combine auctions to save on shipping.* If a seller has several items up for auction, have them hold your purchase to see if you win any other items. Then combine the items into one shipment to save on shipping.

◆ *Watch the seller's feedback.* One of the smart things eBay pioneered was buyer and seller feedback—sellers can rate buyers by how fast they paid; buyers can rate sellers on how fast they shipped, how quickly they responded to emails and so on. Obviously, we'd only deal with sellers who have a good track record; that is, lots of positive feedback.

◆ *Read descriptions carefully.* Most sellers are honest in describing used clothes that might be stained or worn. Be sure to read the fine print in the item description so you know what you are getting.

lower prices than at Stride Rite company stores. Strange but true. One reader found a pair of Stride Rite shoes for sale at Marshall's for $14.99—the exact same pair was going for $45 in Stride Rite's retail stores at the time. Another mom we spoke with discovered Stride Rite are often on sale at JCPenney at steep discounts.

**6** **THE BEST PLACE FOR TODDLER UNDERWEAR?** We vote for Target or Wal-Mart for their affordable selection of underwear basics.

**7** **PAJAMA SAVINGS.** In the summer, why put your kid's in PJ's at all? We just use boxers and t-shirts for our sons. A simple nightshirt for girls is another affordable idea. These cost HALF the price of fancy PJ's. As for the winter, we think Costco has the best deal: $10 for all cotton toddler pajamas. The only caveat: we notice

## Shoe size conundrum

How do you properly size shoes for a toddler? Judging from our email, folks seem mystified at what makes a shoe fit well. Here's our take:

Measure your child's feet later in the day. Statistics show that feet swell as much as 8% larger after a day's worth of walking around. This way, your child won't have too tight shoes.

Measure both feet then ask for a shoe size based on the larger foot. (In case you didn't realize it, no one has a perfectly symmetrical body so one foot is always bigger than the other.)

There should be about a 1/2" space between your child's longest toe and the end of the shoe. Be sure to check this when your child is standing up.

Check to see that the tongue and top edge of the shoe comes just to the ankle. This helps avoid blisters and heal slipping.

Have your child walk then run around the store. Check for any heel slippage. If the heel slips you'll have blistering.

With toddlers, you should check their shoes after three or four months of wear. Yes, they grow that fast. As they approach school age, their growth slows a bit. But you'll still need to resize them at least a couple times a year.

If you're interested in buying shoes via mail order (a risky proposition in some cases), you might want to download a "shoe sizer" like the one we found on If the Shoe Fits Etc (IfTheShoeFitsEtc.com) or on Kids N Feet (KidsNFeet.com).

Costco pajamas tend to shrink a bit, so buy them one size larger than your child would typically wear.

**8 CHURCH SALES.** A cousin to consignment stores are the church sales you see in many areas, especially in the South. Again, the more affluent the area, the better the church sale. "I have snagged three-piece Talbot's outfits for $7, Ralph Lauren Polo t-shirts for $4, Gymboree outfits with tags still on them for just $5. I especially try to hit these sales for Christmas and Easter outfits," emailed reader Debby Moro. One tip: put something in the sale and you often get to shop earlier than the general public! And look for special occasion outfits and Halloween costumes at these events, as they are especially good deals!

**9 GARAGE SALES.** For play clothes and day care outfits, you can't miss with garage sales. Most veteran garage sale shoppers know they can snag a week's worth of clothes for $5 or less. Scope out the suburbs where families live for the best selection and arrive early—the early bird gets the best selection!

**10 END OF SEASON SALES.** In February, look to snare winter gear bargains. In August summer shorts and tops are great deals. One reader in Florida snagged a soft fleece zip up pullover for $3.50 in May at Toys R Us (regular price $15). In recent years, bargain hunters haven't had to wait until spring to find winter gear deals—stores seem to be starting these sales earlier and earlier.

**11 SIGN UP FOR SALE NOTICES BOTH ONLINE AND OFFLINE.** Most major clothing web sites (like Lands End, LL Bean, Baby Gap and Gymboree) let you add your email address to a mailing list. They'll send you announcements of sales and special deals. We snagged a pair of cool tennis shoes for our sons at 50% off from LL Bean during one such sale. Many local kids' retailers have mailing lists as well. And remember that stores like Children's Place, Old Navy and Gap online send out coupons and other special offers (free shipping, anyone?) to customers on their mailing lists.

**12 KOHL'S.** The hip new place to get shoe deals is at Kohl's (www.kohls.com), the Wisconsin-based discounter that recently started expanding nationwide. Now, you can find 420 Kohl's nationwide (although most are east of the Rockies). Barb Mettler, a mom in Atlanta told us the best place for kid's shoe deals is her local Kohl's: "They always have sales and the shoes last. I tried to buy shoes at Target, but they rarely have my son's size in stock . . . perhaps Target sells out quickly." We should note that Kohl's

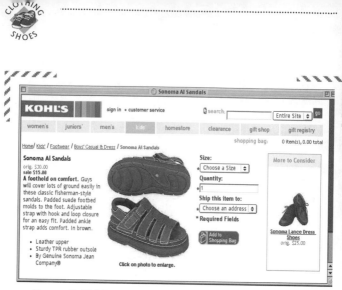

*Figure 5. Kohl's recent national expansion has added to their fan base among parents, who cite their great deals on shoes. Here's a sample deal.*

toddler clothing gets lower marks from our readers, however—one parent in Indiana complained "they have a poor selection and the quality of the clothes is cheap." Others echoed those comments.

**13 SALES AT THE GAP.** Gap Kids stores always have a rack of sale clothes and they regularly mark down items every few weeks. Our best score: a $25 pair of tennis shoes for our son for just $6.97. Another reader emailed us her best sale bargain at Gap Kids: a pair of $36 overalls for less than $10. One mom points

---

### *Boys versus girls:*
### *Where's the selection for little guys?*

Excuse us if we get off on a rant here . . .but as the parents of two boys, we are frustrated with the lack of selection of boy clothes versus what's available for girls. Want color? Don't look at the boy's section, where navy blue is about your only choice. Meanwhile, toddler girl's clothing comes in an amazing variety of colors, patterns and styles. And selection? In many catalogs and in stores, boys are lucky to get a dark corner with a few t-shirts and jeans. Meanwhile, the girl's department sprawls from here to Kalamazoo. So, we have to issue a challenge to kids clothing retailers and catalogs—stop giving boys the short end of the stick! And give us something other than navy blue.

out the Gap offers a $10 certificate for every $250 you spend on a Gap credit card (of course, always pay off your balance each month to avoid finance charges).

**14** **TARGET FOR SHOES AND BASICS.** Many readers find the shoe deals at Target to be fantastic; "you never pay more than $8 a pair for tennis shoes or sandals," one mom raved. Among the better finds: affordable seasonal shoes (water shoes and sandals in the summer; slippers in the winter)—Target's prices on these items are usually excellent. Of course, Target also has affordably priced clothes—we like their simple t-shirts and shorts for summer, as well as winter gear. Yes, they are a bit less trendy than the Gap or Old Navy. One Target tip: read labels carefully. Some Target clothes are polyester blends; others are all cotton.

**15** **BUY FOR NEXT YEAR.** One mom shared her strategy for doing this: "I buy lots of clothes for next year and guess on the size. Don't remove the tags or wash them, because many stores let you return them even a year later as long as you have your receipt." And what if the store doesn't take returns? Sell the items on eBaby—clothes "new with tags" always fetch a premium. One caveat to this tip: while buying next year's clothing is smart, shoes can be tricky—trying to guess your son or daughter's size in six months is tough.

**16** **OUTLET STORE SALES.** The sales at the OshKosh outlets (go to www.outletbound.com for a listing or location near you) are a good example. Big end of winter and summer sales feature clothes marked at 70% off retail—and then the outlets give you another 20% off to boot.

**17** **DON'T FORGET TO CHECK OUT LANDS END'S OVERSTOCK AREA** (www.landsend.com). See the Cyberspace section earlier in this chapter for more details.

**18** **ASK STORES ABOUT THEIR MARKDOWN SCHEDULES.** Every chain (Gap, Gymboree, etc) has certain days when they put items on the markdown rack. "Don't pay full price at any chain store," says one mom. "Almost everything goes on sale sooner or later!" Wednesday seems to be the magic markdown day at the Gap.

**19** **SCOPE OUT WAREHOUSE SALES.** Many local boutiques do "warehouse sales" twice a year to clean out overstock.

*Figure 6. Which factory outlets are near you? Check OutletBound.com for a listing of 14,000 outlets, searchable by location, store, brand and more.*

Sign up on a mailing list to get early word. Keep an eye on local newspapers for other sales. Rachel Wexler of Rochester, NY says this is one her favorite bargains: "We line up for an hour before one local boutique opens for their twice a year warehouse sale—for 50% to 70% off designer brands, it's worth it! Just know your size since there are no returns." Another great warehouse sale: Patsy Aiken's "attic sales" in Raleigh, NC; go to patsyaiken.com for the latest schedule.

**20** **AND THE WINNER FOR BEST SOCKS IS . . .** Old Navy. "They actually stay on their feet," concurs Kalamazoo, MI mom Beth Gregory-Wallis. We have to agree—few other socks can measure up to Old Navy's offerings.

## Potty training-friendly clothes

When your child starts to potty train, the wardrobe needs to adapt—boys needs to have pants with elastic waistbands . . . no zippers, snaps, buttons, etc. Girls need dresses or pull-on pants. The goal is to get the clothes off quickly when they need to go. A major no-no: overalls. Yes, they were cute when your child was a baby, but they'll send you into a fit when potty training time comes.

**21** **FOR SHOES, CONSIDER CANVAS INSTEAD OF LEATHER.** You can save 10% to 20% by choosing canvas. Since toddlers grow out of their shoes so quickly, the quality advantage of leather over canvas is moot.

**22** **KEEP YOUR RECEIPTS.** A shoe box will do. Why? Many stores will give you full credit if the clothes are defective (excessive shrinkage, fading, etc) up to a year from purchase.

**23** **CHECK OUT PAYLESS "BUY ONE GET THE NEXT ONE HALF OFF" SALE.** Several moms tell us they love this sale, as well as Payless' affordable shoes—$10 for kid's character shoes and sandals. Payless.com's web site was running a free shipping special when we last looked (and it offers 360-degree views of their shoes). One negative to Payless: their customer service is light years behind other stores.

**24** **GOT TWINS?** Shop at a store that offers twin discounts and allows exchange items for cash as long as you have the receipt. One example: Osh Kosh B'Gosh outlet stores. Reader Lynn Meshke of Appleton, Wisconsin says that's her favorite place when shopping for her twins: "While I would never pay full price for Osh Kosh merchandise, I find the outlet prices to be very reasonable." Osh Kosh outlets offer a 10% twins discount; that's on top of their regular 30% to 50% discounts (with off-season deals up to 70%).

**25** **EBAY AGAIN**—for selling your clothes! We've heard from several parents who've been successful selling their toddler's outgrown clothes. Of course, designer labels and cute outfits go quickest. Sell items in season for the best prices and consider grouping smaller items together for one auction. One mom we spoke to has been selling on eBay for less than six months and completed over 500 auctions. "It is fun, frugal and I have made a healthy little income on the side, which is great for a stay-at-home mom," she said.

**26** **USE A WEB COUPON.** If you shop online, use web coupons. Find the latest deals at DotDeals.com, CleverMoms.com, FatWallet.com, BigBigSavings.com or eDealFinder. com. These sites list current "web coupons" and discount deals across the web. While these deals aren't as generous as they were in the hey-day of the dot-coms, a deal is still a deal—you can usually snag free shipping or get a percentage off a purchase.

**27** **DON'T RULE OUT THE MALL.** While discount stores have stolen the thunder from mall-based retailers in recent years, don't count out the mall stores all the time. A reader spotted a recent sale on kids' Nikes at a Foot Locker for just $5 a pair.

**28** **SEARS.** Okay, stop laughing. We realize Sears is more associated with power tools than kid's clothes, but things have changed in recent years. Parents rave about the bargains here—like a sun dress for 94¢ that mom Julie Wilson of West Hills, CA scored recently. Or a sales rack that another reader spotted with all cotton t-shirts and light jackets marked down to $1.49. Sears also offers a Kid Advantage discount program—spend $100 on clothes and you get a 15% off coupon for your next purchase. Sears sends out numerous coupons to parents that have their Premier credit card, like $5 off a minimum $5 purchase. And the coupons can be used on sale merchandise, not just the regular-price items. Another bonus: Sears now is selling Lands End kids clothes both in the store and online—if you order from the mail-order catalog, you can return items to the store.

## Outlets

◆ **Stride Rite** (which also makes Keds and Sperry) has three dozen outlets nationwide. You can find them by going to StrideRite.com or check out Outletbound.com. You can get measured at a Stride Rite retail store and then take the little chart they give you to an outlet to get the deals! We've seen deals at 30% to 50% off retail—like leather Keds that retail for $42, just $19 at the outlet. Don't expect much service at the outlet, just great deals!

◆ **Osh Kosh.** With 120+ outlets nationwide, readers say these outlets are good for bargains, especially during frequent sales and clearances. Best bets: seasonal items like shorts in the summer and snow gear in the winter.

◆ **Gap.** Yes, these are the same clothes the Gap sold in their stores at full price last season. We love the deals here and it is worth the effort to check out if you are near a Gap outlet location (search OutletBound.com for an outlet near you).

◆ **Nordstrom Rack stores.** Nordstrom's close-out stores, dubbed the "Rack," have great deals on kid's clothing and shoes. We're talking designer name brands (Teva sandals, Nike tennis shoes) at 30% to 50% off and more. Go to Nordstrom.com to find a Rack location near you. Nordstrom has about three dozen Rack locations nation-wide; most are within spitting distance of their regular department stores. Reader Carolyn Kimball of Pasadena, CA found Stride Rite sneakers on sale at the Rack for $17 (half off the typical $35 retail).

◆ **Rack Room Shoes.** Not related to the Nordstrom Rack stores, the Rack Room Shoes (www.RackRoomShoes.com) is a North Carolina-based chain of 330 stores in 20 states (mostly in the South, Mid-Atlantic and Midwest). "Big brands at big savings" is their motto and our readers agree—the deals are great. A reader in Tampa, Florida scored dress Mary-Janes shoes *and* a pair of Buster Brown athletic shoes for $25 total at a Rack Room store. Another mom in Indiana said she found Nike tennis shoes for her toddler for $20 cheaper here than other stores.

◆ **So Fun Kids** outlets just has 18 locations nationwide (all east of the Mississippi) but our readers rave about their deals. Check OutletBound.com for the latest locations. "If your town has a So Fun Kids outlet, run to it," said Atlanta mom Adrienne Coleman. "The clothes are really cute and different and for the most part, they hold up well in the wash."

*Continued on page 72*

*Figure 8. Looking for shoe deals? Many readers told us their favorite discount stores is Rack Room Shoes, a 330 store chain in 20 states.*

# The best toddler clothing deals in New York City

*What's the best place for toddler clothing deals in the Big Apple? Reader Elizabeth Alcott votes for H&M, the Swedish mega chain (www.hm.com) with 30+ locations in and around New York City and Boston. H&M's flagship store in Herald Square in NYC was where Elizabeth scored these deals:*

"This is the best place for toddler clothes! I bought five pair of pants, eight tops, and a beautiful cardigan sweater for my daughter for $114 total. I suppose I could do the same at Old Navy, but these clothes are WAY cuter, all cotton, generously sized and just plain beautiful. The best part is, they don't look like cheap stuff, or Baby Gap knockoffs. They are unique designs— my favorite piece is a bright yellow, long sleeved t-shirt with embroidered butterflies across the chest... the butterflies are only attached in the center, so the wings fly free—so cute! The t-shirts were $5-8 each; the sweater was $12. I also saw lovely embroidered dresses for $12. They have a baby department, and then toddlers run from 18 months to 6 years."

*Another reader, Debbie Weingand, praised H&M—particularly their special sales:*

"The best bargains for toddler clothes is at H&M stores. The prices in general are not bad, but when they run a sale—the clothes are a steal. We try to go whenever they run their half off the sale price sale. We have bought our son's pants and shirts there for $3.00 and under! You really cannot beat this. We go and buy ahead for the next season and actually get some stuff for the same season. The clothes are good quality and you can buy a ton of stuff for close to nothing."

*A reader in Westchester County, NY chimed in with a vote for another NYC bargain haven, Century 21 (22 Cortlandt St, 212-227-9092; www.c21stores.com)*

"I live in the suburbs of NYC and I have to say that after Sept. 11 many downtown businesses were forced into Chapter 11. But not the old standby, Century 21! If anyone (and everyone should) visits NYC, this designer discount department store reopened after the tragedy to new and improved inventory levels! INEXPENSIVE designer toddler clothing abounds—from Ralph Lauren, QuikSilver, Guess, Sean John, to the Euro stuff: my favorites are Petit Bateau, IKKS, Catamini and there is so much more at drastically reduced prices. This is a must see attraction for kids clothes deals."

*Finally, consider Daffy's: Clothing Bargains for Millionaires. Gotta love that name! With four locations in and around NYC plus stores in New Jersey, Long Island, Philadelphia and even Virginia (www.daffys.com), Daffy's sells overstocks and slightly off-season goods. Andrea Solberg of Sparta, NJ gave us the scoop:*

"My favorite place to buy shoes for them is Daffy's. They sell unique, well made, leather Italian shoes, boots and sandals for anywhere from $13 (on sale) to $35 dollars, with the average price being $23 to $26 for most shoes. They have a terrific selection of both American and European children's clothes which are also reasonably priced (e.g. $12 for a 100% cotton shorts and t-shirt set boys, $14 for an embroidered pair of cotton capri pants and $12 for the coordinating 100% cotton t-shirt)."

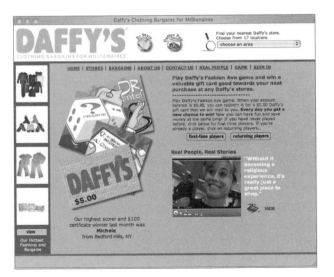

*Figure 9. Looking for European toddler clothes at bargain prices? Daffy's gets the nod from our Big Apple readers for their deals.*

◆ **Children's Place** outlets (www.childrensplace.com) have a killer 99¢ rack, says Florida mom Robyn Tipton. With three dozen locations nationwide, this is one outlet to check out. Watch out for quality, however: several parents gave us mixed reviews on Children's Place. Some thought quality was just fine, while others thought the clothes weren't as durable as other brands.

◆ **A bargain secret** about outlet malls: many centers have coupon books with additional discounts. Go to the customer service counter and ask. Sometimes, you have to show an AAA card to get the coupon deals. One reader, Denise O'Keefe, used this tip to score a coupon for another 15% off at a Stride Rite shoe outlet at her local outlet mall.

## The Name Game: Reviews of Clothing Brands

Judging from our reader email, the top brand for toddlers is *Gap* and their sister brand, *Old Navy*—the clothes and shoes here combine the best quality and value. They are well made and wash well; frequent sales and markdowns make the sale rack at the Gap/Gap Kids/Old Navy a top value spot.

Who's got the best leggings for girls? Parents we interviewed give the nod to *Gymboree*: "They never seem to fade and last forever," said one mom.

While not as popular as their big sister division (Target), *Mervyn's* does merit mention: their Sprockets brand clothes and shoes are good quality, say parents we interviewed. And something is always on sale.

In Canada, we like *Please Mum* (www.pleasemum.com; see next page), the Vancouver-based kid clothing chain with 53 stores from Halifax to British Columbia. Here's what Canadian reader Pamela Winstone said about Please Mum: "I love their stuff—they offer equal quality clothes to Gymboree, but a little less fancy. They sell everything from coats/snowpants, socks, underwear and of course, the typical shirts, pants, shorts and dresses. Their line covers newborn up to ten years old. Please Mum clothes have a generous fit, wash very well and are super durable." One bargain hint about Please Mum: they sell a VIP Gold Discount card for $10 (Canadian) that offers a 35% discount off regular price clothes everyday, with no expiration date.

As for shoes, parents think *Stride Rite* (and its sister brands, Keds and Sperry) are the best, although private label *Gap* shoes are a close second. European brands *Elefanten* and *Brakkies* are also high quality, yet hard to find at a discount (they show up on eBay, however).

What about the clothing brands you see at specialty stores?

Well, the same brands that we liked in our *Baby Bargains* book are also the best bets for toddlers (Mulberribush, Flapdoodles, S.p.u.d.z., Sweet Potatoes, Wes & Willy, Cotton Tale Originals).

## Bottom Line: Our Top Picks

Yes, the average parent shells out $380 to $580 on clothes each year for a toddler. How can you save? First don't waste your money—character clothing is very attractive to toddlers but usually lower quality. In general, avoid toddler versions of adult designer clothes, which are usually grossly overpriced.

Where are the deals? Readers cite eBay, Gap and Old Navy as the best stores, although many readers love the sales at Kohl's and Sears. You can't beat the $1 deals at garage sales, second hand stores and church sales. For shoes, most parents want quality shoes at a decent price—Stride Rite's outlet stores combine the best of both worlds, although deals at Marshall's and TJMaxx are a close second.

Follow the above tips and shop at the outlets listed in this chapter and we estimate you can slash your clothing bills by half—or more.

*Figure 10. Canadian parents voted Please Mum as their favorite toddler clothing source in the Great White North.*

# CHAPTER 4
## Potty Training & Bath

W hat's the best potty seat for your toddler? How can you help your toddler make the transition from diapers to the big potty? We'll answer those questions in this chapter, plus look at other bath items like the best shampoo, skin care products and toothpaste for toddlers.

Remember when you were still pregnant and along with all the terrifying stories of 27 hours of hard labor your friends (and strangers) experienced, you heard tales of miracle babies potty trained at six months? As far as the potty training tales go, we're here to tell you they lied. Big time. The only one who was trained was the parent—trained to put baby on a potty every hour or after every meal. Of course they're going to have "success" when they do that. But babies will never be potty trained that early.

Case in point: our first child. We decided not to push the toilet training since we were pregnant with another baby and we thought our son was having to deal with enough transitions as it was. But then we looked at the calendar and noticed our little guy was about to turn *four*! So we panicked. We told our son we ran out of pull-ups and he'd have to use the toilet. And you know what? He did after a few days of practice. Of course, if you wait till your child enters college it may be just as easy.

But what if you'd like to see your darling young one make it to the toilet instead of the changing table a little earlier? We've got some great tips on that as well as some ideas for help with other grooming and health issues.

Political correctness notice: we will be referring to this process as toilet or potty training. Federal law requires us to disclose the politically correct term for this is now "toilet learning." Yes, we realize we risk the wrath of the email gods by implying that you're going to *train* your child to use the toilet instead of having him *learn* the appropriate behavior. We'll just use the words "potty training" as short hand for this process. Fine with you? Good, let's move on.

## Getting started

So, when can you say bye-bye to those endless diaper changes? Most medical experts say to expect your child to *begin* potty training between 18 to 24 months. In fact, the American Academy of Pediatrics (www.aap.org) states that "children younger than 12 months have no control over bladder or bowel movements and little control for 6 month or so after that." So anyone who claims you can potty train an eight-month-old knows nada about your baby's physiology.

The AAP also noted in their book *Caring for Your Baby and Young Child:*

> *Studies indicate that many children who begin training before 18 months are not completely trained until after age four. By contrast, most of those who start around age two are completely trained before their third birthdays.*

Translation: Start TOO early and, ironically, you'll pay for it! Wait until your child is ready (generally older, about age 2 or 3) and you'll find the going easier, on both parent and toddler.

Here's another interesting fact: in a study by the Medical College of Wisconsin, researchers found that the average age for "graduation from the potty chair to the big toilet" was 35 months for girls and 39 months for boys. Total time to potty train on average: *eight* months. Keep that in mind when your friends brag their child mastered the potty over a long weekend.

Interestingly the fastest learners were girls in single parent homes. Another bit of trivia: African-American children toilet trained earlier than Caucasian children. But the biggest news from this study is that children in daycare were found to potty train at the same time as children who did not attend daycare. Previously, it was thought that daycare caused delays in toilet training.

So when will you know your child is ready to tackle the toilet? Here are some clues for you (your child doesn't have to experience *all* these to be ready). Does your toddler:

1. Have enough bladder control to go three or four hours before she wets?
2. Dislike like a dirty diaper?

3.   Want to watch and emulate you in the bathroom?
4.   Express interest in underpants?
5.   Follow simple directions?
6.   Understand and use words to describe urine and bowel movements?
7.   Pull up and down her pants?
8.   Want to be independent?

Once your child signals he is ready to potty train, what next? The answer: some sort of potty seat, whether a traditional separate potty or a seat insert for the full size toilet is important. Many readers recommend taking your child with you to the store when it is time to buy a seat. Or you can present one as a special gift to your child. This allows you to make a big deal out of being a "big girl" or "big boy." You may also find other training aids helpful and we'll go into that in *What Are You Buying*.

## Parents in Cyberspace

Almost every web site we visited had the same advice for parents: wait till your child is ready. But, if you want a bit more validation you can check out any of the following sites for more tips and tricks to making this a pleasant experience for both you and your child: ParentingTime.com, FamilyDoctor.com, KidsHealth.org, Medem.com. A sample of the potty training advice from KidsHealth.org is pictured on the next page.

Looking for an obscure potty seat? We found a site that just sells potty seats (believe it or not). Check out ThePottyStore.com (www.thepottystore.com) for a great selection of hard-to-find potties, books, videos and other toilet training aids. This site has great prices and offers an additional 10% discount for PayPal orders.

We also found a good selection of potties and training aids on the BabyCenter.com and BabiesRUs.com, as you might expect.

## What Are You Buying

Yes, the key purchase here is a potty seat or a seat insert. But many parents told us they also purchased training pants or underpants, books, videos and sticker charts to help their child with this process.

*Figure 1: Need help and advice on potty training? KidsHealth.org has several good articles and the latest research.*

◆ **Potty seats.** You have three choices here:

1. A traditional separate seat that sits on the bathroom floor.
2. A hybrid (or a combo) seat that works like a traditional floor potty but then has a detachable toilet insert.
3. An insert that fits into a regular toilet, making it easier for a toddler to use the adult potty.

We'll discuss each in detail later in this chapter with specific brand reviews and ratings.

◆ **Training pants/pull ups/underpants.** The co-author of our baby care primer, *Baby 411* (see the back of this book for details) Dr. Ari Brown swears by old-fashioned cloth training pants: "They allow a child to feel wet unlike super absorbent disposable pull ups." On the other hand, disposable pull-ups may be useful at night. Nighttime training often takes much longer and pull-ups can help avoid bedding changes. Some parents go straight to underpants. Their children were emphatic about being able to wear their Scooby Doo underpants, which functioned similarly to training pants allowing kids to feel wet.

One reader recommended trying a few brands of cloth trainers. She liked Nikki's trainers but found them to be rather expensive. On the other hand, Nikki's were soft and seemed more like underwear (www.babybunz.com, $12.95 each). Bummis ($10 to $12), she thought, were cheaper but bulkier under clothing. Dappi's ($5.50) and Gerber are the cheapest, but don't have the soft feel of Nikki's. Both Dappi and Gerber are also easiest to find at stores like Target.

◆ **Books and videos.** Universally, parents recommended the books *Everyone Poops* by Taro Gommi, *Once Upon a Potty* by Alona Frankel and *Toilet Training Without Tears* by Schaefer and DiGeronimo. Video recommendations included "It's Potty Time" and Bear in the Big Blue House's "Potty Time with Bear."

◆ **Rewards.** Like any learning process, rewards can do wonders to get your toddler into this experience. You can make up your own chart with stickers to encourage your child. Or you can buy toilet training "kits" that include a chart and stickers. See below for a few kit options. Other parents have been known to hand out a chocolate chip cookie or two when their kids "did their business." Just remember to phase out rewards as your child gets the hang of this. And hugs, kisses and shouts for joy are free and can work just as well as a cookie.

◆ **Potty Training Kits.** *Flip Trainer* (see www.thepottystore.com) sells their potty seat with several options including sticker charts, books and videos. The Flip Trainer kits range from $15 to $40 depending on which items are included. Other kits have themes like the *Car Potty Training Kit* (also on The Potty Store's site), a kit with a small floor potty shaped like a VW Bug ($45). *Charmin* (www.charmin.com), the toilet paper people offer a free potty training kit. Included is a storybook, a poster, stickers and a roll ruler to help kids figure out how much TP they need (now, that's a good idea). Once they master the toilet, you can also download a free "diploma" from the site to present to your new "big kid."

## Safe & Sound

It goes without saying, but be sure to empty out the potty (or flush the toilet) after Junior has used it. Toddlers are fascinated with *everything*! Also: if you plan to use a seat insert as we'll recommend later in this chapter, you'll need a sturdy step stool for the toddler to climb onto the toilet.

### Smart Shopper Tip #1
Picking a Potty

*"I want to take my daughter to the store to help me pick out a potty seat. But there are so many choices and we don't want her to pick out an expensive model with sounds, lights, lasers and so on. We're just looking for something basic."*

Yes, every parenting expert will tell you to include your child in the selection of a potty. But if you pop into your local baby megastore, even an adult can get overwhelmed with the selection of 57 potty seats. How do you make this work? Since having too many choices can easily lead to a melt down (by both toddler and adult), visit the store yourself *first* and choose a couple seats you think will work. Use our top picks as a starting point. Then revisit the store with your child and give her a choice between two or three options. That makes her feel like she's involved and you get to avoid buying the Star Wars Episode I Galactic Potty & Play Set.

**DISPOSABLE TRAINING PANTS.** We heard you gasp at this one, but hear us out. Remember what you loved about disposable diapers? They were incredibly absorbent, holding the liquid equivalent of polar ice caps without leaking. Well, so are disposable training pants. And that's the problem. If your child feels dry and comfy, why should he/she use the potty?

So give up the disposable training pants and go for either cloth training pants or even real underpants. Cloth training pants are more absorbent than underpants but they still allow your child to feel wet and uncomfortable. There's a bit more risk with leaks and accidents with the underpants, but some parents swear by them. They tell us their children were especially motivated when they got to wear those cool Scooby Doo underpants. Heck, we're wearing Scooby Doo underpants right now as we write this.

We've also had parents recommend allowing your child to run around without any clothes on for a long weekend. They swear it speeds up the toilet training process.

What about pull-ups? These hybrid diapers that look like underpants are fine at night to help stop leaks. Most kids take several more months of training before they can make it through the night dry.

**2** **BELLS AND WHISTLES.** Face it, the fancier the potty, the more expensive it is. We've seen potties shaped like toilets that make a flushing sound when you push the lever, ones that play a song when your guy tinkles, even one with (and we're not making this up) a built in "magazine rack." Baby product makers like to throw in everything but the kitchen sink with their potties to convince parents to part with an extra $10. Yeah, you want this to be a special item that your kids will use, but does it have to be the kiddie version of a Barcalounger?

While we understand potties that offer "rewards" to toddlers for doing their business, we draw the line at anything that requires batteries. Stickers, hugs and kisses should be all that's necessary. A potty that plays Beethoven's 9th Symphony from six Dolby surround speakers is, well, overkill. But you knew that.

---

### E-MAIL FROM THE REAL WORLD
**The Golden Rule of Potty Training**

*Reader Theresa Smead summed up the golden rule about potty training—you must wait until your child is ready:*

"We've experimented with it all: cloth training pants and pull-ups, potty chairs and inserts, sitting with and giving privacy, rewarding with candy and rewarding with toys, planned training and 'letting it happen.' Sadly, I am not sure there would have been any change in the timing or success of our training efforts if we had done none of it at all. They (my kids) seemed to know when they were ready to potty train better than I."

## Money Saving Secrets

**1 CLOTH TRAINING PANTS AND UNDERWEAR.** As mentioned earlier, cloth training pants are a better bet than disposable in helping your toddler learn how to use the potty. But there is also another reason to go with cloth: cost savings.

For example, according to our research, the average toddler takes eight months to potty train. If you use disposable training pants or pull-ups, the total cost for that time would be $585 (assuming four changes a day). On the other hand, cloth training pants cost about $8 per pant—six pants would run $48. Underwear is even cheaper: a seven pack of boys briefs or girls panties at Target runs $7 or so.

Bottom line: using cloth training pants/underwear will save you $500 or more. An added benefit: your child may actually train faster—as much as three months faster!

**2 WAREHOUSE CLUBS.** Want a small supply of Huggies PullUps to use at night? According to a price survey we conducted for this book, the cheapest prices for pull-ups and disposable training pants were at warehouse clubs like BJ's, Costco and Sam's. Runners-up: Wal-Mart and Target. Those sources were often 20% to 30% less than grocery stores.

**3 SEAT INSERTS.** Here's our biggest money saving tip: buy a $10 toilet seat insert and skip the separate potty. Steer clear of those $40 floor potties with the sound and lights. We'll discuss several other great reasons why an affordable insert is a better bet later in this chapter. Your only other cost with an insert: a small step stool (so your toddler can climb on the potty), which you may already have anyway.

## The Best Bets

Here are our top picks for toilet trainers. Detailed reviews of various brands follow this section.

**BEST BET:** All most toddlers need to potty train is a good seat insert and a step stool. Our pick is the **Contoured Cushie Tushie** potty seat by Mommy's Helper (www.mommyshelperinc.com; 800-371-3509). The company used to make a version of this seat without the

"deflector shield" (sounds like a Star Wars toilet seat) but have since discontinued it. If you have a girl and don't want the contour, we've seen similar seats for about $10 to $15 in stores.

To give you an idea of what an insert looks like, we've included the top picture. The Contoured Cushie Tushie is actually pictured below.

Why do we like the inserts so much? First, cleanability. Most kid potties have a separate container you have to clean out. With inserts, your child can flush the toilet herself and save you the clean up. Second, inspiration. When kids get to use the "big potty" just like mom and dad they are often more motivated to give up diapers. Third, transitioning. It will be so much quicker and easier to transition to the adult seat when your child is already familiar with the toilet.

potty/bath

Finally, portability. You can easily pack along a seat insert on trips to grandma's without having to take a whole floor potty.

The only other purchase to consider when using an insert is a step stool. These are necessary so your toddler can climb up on the toilet, as well as to give them a place to push off from when pooping.

When would a seat insert not work? Smaller toddlers may find inserts hard to use if their feet can't reach a step stool. In that case, consider a traditional floor potty (see below for our top pick in that category).

**RUNNER UP:** If you want a traditional floor potty seat, we thought Baby Bjorn had the best bets—the *Baby Bjorn Potty Chair* ($23 on BabyCenter.com) is simple in design but it works. The *Baby Bjorn Little Potty* ($10) is a one-piece potty that is even simpler, but lacks a removable bowl. Hence, the whole thing must be emptied and cleaned.

## Name Game:Potty Brand Reviews

# BABY BJORN

*Regal Lager, Inc. For a dealer near you, call (800) 593-5522 or (770) 955-5060. Web: www.regallager.com.*

### BABY BJORN LITTLE POTTY
**Type**: floor trainer
**Price:** $10
**Pros:** This one piece, molded plastic seat is smooth, lightweight and small with no extraneous parts to clean. Built in splashguard. Good for travel. Carry handle. Good price.

**Cons:** It may be too small especially for older/bigger toddlers. With no cup insert, you'll have to carry the whole potty to the toilet to clean it.

**Comments:** Parents we polled loved this simple seat. It's colorful (available in ocean or red) but uncomplicated. And it can easily be taken with you to Grandma's house or up and down stairs.

**Rating:** B+

### BABY BJORN POTTY CHAIR
**Type:** floor trainer
**Price:** $23 on BabyCenter.com.
**Pros:** High back seat for more comfort, splashguard feature and removable cup for cleaning. Looks nice.

**Cons:** Pricey (about $10 more than Graco's potties).

**Comments:** This seat is a bit bigger than the Little Potty with a few more features, but it's still pretty simple. We liked the removable cup and the bright colors. When potty training, the high back may be a very useful feature to help kids relax.

**Rating:** A

### BABY BJORN TOILET TRAINER
**Type:** insert
**Price:** $30
**Pros:** Soft seat that fits securely to the adult toilet–won't tip over or pinch. Has splashguard built-in.

**Cons:** Expensive—most inserts cost $20 less than the Bjorn! Parents of girls have complained that the splashguard is a bit high for their daughters to climb over. This insert is made of hard plastic (other inserts have more cushioning). As with all inserts, you'll need a step stool to help your child get up and push off from.

**Comments:** This is an award winning design with impressive features. We're partial to the idea of using an insert and parents certainly give this one top marks. The price, however, is too high compared to other inserts which might work just as well for your child.
**Rating:** A-

## FLIP TRAINER

*Available at ThePottyStore.com*

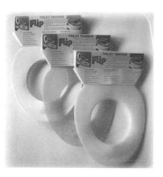

### FLIP TRAINER

**Type:** insert (actually is a "hidden in the lid child-size toilet seat")
**Price:** Starts at $10 for the insert only. Kits start at about $15 and go up to about $40. Kits may include stickers and chart, book and/or video.
**Pros:** No need to take the insert off the adult toilet seat for an adult to use it. You just lift up the Flip Trainer in the same manner as the lid then flip it back down for your child. Very affordable.
**Cons:** No padding. Only available for standard size toilets and only in a contoured shape. Also, you must be sure to have exactly the right type of standard toilet seat to make this work.
**Comments:** What a great idea. Now you can use an insert without having to remove it when the adult uses the toilet. Too bad it isn't padded like soft inserts, but most kids won't mind. There is another, similar seat called the Flip N Flush ($11, www.babyant.com) that comes in a few bright colors instead of just plain white.
**Rating:** A

## THE FIRST YEARS

*For a dealer near you, call (800) 317-3194.*
*Web: www.thefirstyears.com.*

### THE FIRST YEARS 3-IN-1 TOILET TRAINING SYSTEM

**Type:** combination
**Price:** $18
**Pros:** Handles. Includes a storybook and award certificate. Developed in consultation with child development guru Dr. T. Berry Brazelton. Easy to clean. Wide base.

**Cons:** No padding. Removable bowl is easily dislodged and can spill. Difficult to attach and detach to an adult potty.

**Comments:** If you've only got one toilet in the house, this seat will be a bear to use. Parents complained that it is difficult to attach and detach the seat to the adult potty so if you're taking it on and off a lot, you'll be frustrated. Large handles add security for kids along with the wide base. Despite this flaw most parents said their kids liked the potty seat when used on the adult potty, but not when it is used as a floor potty.

**Rating:** C

### THE FIRST YEARS SOFT TRAINER

**Type:** insert
**Price:** $10
**Pros:** Soft, air filled cushion snaps out of the frame for cleaning. The frame has handles.

**Comments:** This insert gives the Cushie Tushie (reviewed below) a run for its money since it adds in the handles for a feeling of security. No bells and or whistles here, just a great basic seat.

**Rating:** A

## FISHER PRICE

*For a dealer near you, call (800) 828-4000.*
*Web: www.fisherprice.com.*

### FISHER PRICE ROYAL POTTY

**Type:** combination
**Price:** $20
**Pros:** Includes a story book, can be used on a toilet seat (when

you remove the legs), plays music.

**Cons:** Requires batteries to get the music to play. Rather expensive.

**Comments:** Can you say overkill? The Royal Potty ($20, although we've seen it for close to $30 on some sites) is a good example of the recent trend where baby product makers try to add every bell and whistle they can think of to convince parents to shell out more money. Case in point: this potty, which has a "two-stage" musical reward system. When baby first sits down, the chair belts out Queen's "Fat Bottomed Girls" (Okay, just kidding—it's actually Sir Mix A Lot's "I Like Big Butts.") Then the chair plays another song, "a royal fanfare with each success." Yes, when your child poops and pees, the engineers at Fisher Price have figured out how to set that to music. So, how does it work in the real world? Reader Michelle McMahon said her toddler loved the seat. Mom was particularly happy that the seat did not leak and the splashguard was removable. Her only complaint: because the music is triggered by an infrared light, just walking too close to the seat can set off the music. And you know how disconcerting hearing Freddie Mercury belting out of your bathroom at 2am can be.

**Rating:** B-

# GRACO

*For a dealer near you call (800) 345-4109 or (610) 286-5951. Web: www.gracobaby.com.*

### GRACO FOLDING POTTY

**Type:** portable insert

**Price:** $10

**Pros:** Folds into a small square size with a zip lock bag to carry with you. The best option for parents who want to keep kids toilet training on the road.

**Cons:** Ugly! Couldn't Graco have come up with a better color for this than brown? Also doesn't fit elongated toilet seats, which are common in public restrooms.

**Comments:** One parent told us she used the Folding Potty as a regular seat insert at home. She thought it worked very well and made transitioning to a regular toilet easy. Detractors of this seat say it doesn't work well in public restrooms with elongated toilet seats (unfortunately quite common).

**Rating:** B

### GRACO POTTY SEAT & STEPSTOOL

**Type:** floor trainer
**Price:** $12
**Pros:** Low price. Separate bowl to empty. Converts to a step stool
**Cons:** Seat is hard plastic. Non-skid feet.
**Comments:** This basic model is okay, but the all but non-existent splash guard will make some parents of boys wish they bought a different brand.
**Rating:** C

### GRACO SOFT SEAT POTTY TRAINER

**Type:** combination seat/insert
**Price:** $20
**Pros:** Both a toilet and seat insert. Close the lid and it's a step stool. Cushioned seat.
**Cons:** Insert seat doesn't work well—slides around on potty; splash guard comes off too easily. Hard to clean.
**Comments:** Not a bad price for a combo potty chair and seat insert. But like most Graco products, quality is disappointing—some parents say the insert slips on the toilet, making it frustrating to use in the real world. Parents also complain the splash guard comes off too easily, often falling into the toilet. This seat also is hard to clean—urine gets into crevices.
**Rating:** C

### GRACO SOFT SEAT POTTY SEAT

**Type:** insert
**Price:** $11
**Pros:** Low price. Carry handles. Splash guard.
**Cons:** Same problems as mentioned above (insert slips, slash guard comes off too easily).
**Comments:** While the carry handles are nice, their position on the side of the seat might be more of a hindrance than a help. This seat's tendency to slip on the potty and that problematic splash guard make us hesitant to recommend it.
**Rating:** C

### GRACO TRAINING REWARDS SOFT SEAT POTTY/STEPSTOOL.

**Type:** combination
**Price:** about $20
**Pros:** Same as the Soft Seat Potty Trainer, but includes 48 reward stickers.

**Cons:** Same as above.

**Comments:** Graco basically took its Soft Seat Potty Trainer and added 48 stickers to "reward toddler's success." But the same problems that dog the basic Soft Seat Potty Trainer are here as well.

**Rating:** C

potty/bath

# MOMMY'S HELPER INC.

*To find a dealer near you call 800-371-3509. Web: www.mommyshelperinc.com*

## CONTOURED CUSHIE TUSHIE

**Price:** $10 to $15.

**Pros:** The best toilet seat inserts on the market. Mommy's Helper used to make a basic Cushie Tushie for about $10, however, they now only make the Contoured Cushie Tushie (pictured at left). This seat includes a deflector shield and lifting handle. (We've also seen a musical version of the Cushie Tushie on BabyAge.com—the seat plays 30 seconds of music when your child sits down).

**Comments:** Each seat has little characters that glow in the dark just in case your toddler gets lost in the bathroom at night and can't find the toilet. The price is now a bit higher for the Cushie Tushie contoured version, but it's still a nice seat.

**Rating:** A

# SAFETY 1ST

*To find dealer near you, call (800) 926-7233 or (781) 364-3100. Web: www.safety1st.com.*

## SAFETY 1ST 3-IN-1 POTTY 'N STEP STOOL

**Type:** combination

**Price:** $10

**Pros:** Low price. Removable trainer seat for full size toilet. Base becomes stepstool.

**Cons:** Minimal splashguard. No padding on the seat—hard plastic.

**Comments:** This simpler potty scored better with parents than other Safety 1st potties, but its hard plastic seat and rather narrow base (which could tip over) don't make this model the best choice. The minimal splash guard will make parents of boys unhappy.
**Rating:** C+

### SAFETY 1ST COMFY CUSHION POTTY SEAT
**Type:** insert
**Price:** $12
**Pros:** Soft seat you use on a regular toilet.
**Cons:** No carry handle. Might slip.
**Comments:** A basic toilet seat insert, but the design here isn't as good as brands like the Cushie Tushie. It slips on the toilet, which will frustrate parents and toddlers alike. Hard to find, Safety 1st may be eliminating this seat in favor of their One Step Trainer Seat (see later in this section).
**Rating:** C+

### SAFETY 1ST EASY LEARN POTTY TRAINER
**Type:** combination
**Price:** $20
**Pros:** Includes targets to encourage kids to make it in the bowl, as well as reward stickers and a diploma. Can be used on a full size toilet. Has handles and parents empty the bowl by sliding it from the back of the base.
**Cons:** Same cons as the 3-in-1—hard plastic seat, minimal splash guard, too narrow base.
**Comments:** Safety 1st basically took the 3-in-1 Potty 'N Step Stool and added a slightly different top (this one has a lip and different color handles), as well as reward stickers and a potty training guide. But the same cons we noted with this potty's sister model apply here as well.
**Rating:** C+

### SAFETY 1ST MUSICAL POTTY & STEP STOOL
**Type:** combination
**Price:** $25
**Pros:** Plays music and flushing sounds when baby pulls a handle. Reward stickers. Non-skid feet. Converts to step stool.

**Cons:** It leaks!

**Comments:** No potty we researched drew the ire of parents like this one—its tendency to leak (especially with boys) has driven parents bonkers, understandably. Safety 1st has quietly offered replacement potties to those who complain, a clear sign they realize this one is a loser.

**Rating:** F

**SAFETY 1ST MY POTTY**
**Type:** combination
**Price:** $18
**Pros:** Flushing handle plays parent's reward message. Reward stickers. Top lid has a frame for child's picture or artwork. Built in shield. Converts to a step stool.
**Cons:** Needs 3 AAA batteries.

## 5 Secrets to Potty Training

Yes, we've potty trained two boys and lived to talk about it. Here's our list of top tips:

1. *Be sure your child is ready, not you.* But how do you know? Check out our list earlier in this chapter for signs of readiness and don't be shy about talking to your child's doctor about it either.

2. *Never scold for accidents.* You don't want your child to withhold going to the bathroom due to stress.

3. *Let your child observe other family members.* This is no time to be modest. The more people your child has to model behavior after, the better.

4. *Start on a long weekend.* Reader Erik Powers of Atlanta, Georgia recommended parents "start the training when (they) have time to focus attention on the trainee—we used the long Memorial Day weekend."

5. *STAY CALM!* Kids are great at figuring out when you're uptight. And a test of wills over potty training could spell disaster with more accidents, withholding or an extra long training period.

**Comments:** This is a new potty, so we don't have much feedback on it yet. The concept of personalizing the potty with pictures or artwork is an interesting idea. And the parent reward message is great. Of course, most parents know they should be around when their kid uses the potty, so they could just give them the message in person. If you have a child who isn't able to hear from a parent at work, the message might be nice encouragement.
**Rating:** C

### SAFETY 1ST ONE STEP TRAINER SEAT

**Type:** modified insert (attaches to hinges on adult toilet)
**Price:** $10
**Pros:** This insert lifts up like the lid of a toilet making it easier for adults to use. Also, your little one can't just walk away with the insert. Has built in splashguard.
**Cons:** No padding. Can't easily take it to Grandma's house or another toilet in your house.
**Comments:** This seat is similar to the Flip Trainer (reviewed above). It works fine and they've dropped the price a bit.
**Rating:** B

### SAFETY 1ST
### POTTY 'N STEP STOOL

**Type:** combination
**Price:** $15
**Pros:** Comes with lid and handles. Seat attaches to full size toilet and base becomes step stool.
**Cons:** Poorly made. Useless splash guard. Hard to empty—bowl slides out from front. Seat isn't padded.
**Comments:** Again, Safety 1st designs a potty that isn't bad in theory but awful in practice. Little things annoy parents about this seat—the lid that doesn't stay up, the splash guard that comes off way too easily (often falling into the potty), etc. The bowl slides out from the front (instead of lifting out of the top), making it easy to spill. Parents of girls seem to be less critical of this potty, which does have a detachable insert that fits on a regular potty.
**Rating:** D+

# Totco, Inc.

*For a dealer near you, call (814) 398-2209. www.tot-co.com.*

### Toilet Trainer
**Type:** combination
**Price:** $40 to $49.
**Pros:** Lightweight design with a seat insert that can fit over a regular toilet as well. Designed to look like a real toilet with flush handle and flush sound, tank and toilet paper holder. Top holds wipes.

**Cons:** Expensive. Large footprint won't work for those with small bathrooms.

**Comments**: Yes, it's the only toddler potty that really looks like the real thing, but we found the flush feature (press the handle and hear a flush sound, thanks to a sound module and 9-volt battery) to be a bit of overkill. On the other hand, at least you get a potty with a detachable insert that can fit over an adult potty seat. And the toilet paper holder and places for wipes is a nice touch. So it's a mixed review for this potty—nice design, but the hefty price tempers our recommendation.

**Rating:** B

## Grooming and Bath Items

As your child leaves babyhood behind and enters her active toddler years, you'll need more than a bottle of baby shampoo to get you through bath time. And there is no shortage of shampoos, de-tanglers, soaps, toothpastes and moisturizers marketed to toddlers and parents alike.

◆ *Hair care.* Baby Magic and Johnson & Johnson baby shampoos seemed to work for everyone. But now you're asking, do I need a shampoo with conditioner or fruity scents? What about a de-tangler or kiddy conditioner? And is all this stuff irritant free?

Good news: almost everything made for kids is safe if it gets in their eyes (the exception are some all-natural products, which usually note this fact on their packaging). What about additives like dyes and fragrances? If your child is allergic to these additives, we'd recommend shampoo by Johnson & Johnson's Aveeno brand. This product includes oatmeal extract and "cleans without drying." Great stuff for about $4.

If you don't mind dyes and fragrances, shampoos by L'Oreal Kids and Suave for Kids are excellent buys. At $3.50 a bottle, L'Oreal offers fruity scents with a combo of shampoo and conditioner. Their new "Fast Dry" shampoo solves the problem many parents face after bath—putting their child to bed with a head of wet hair. This new shampoo dries quicker than other brands. They've also added "no-static" shampoos and conditioners.

Suave's knock-off line of similarly fruity shampoo is only $2.50 a bottle, but the smell is generally a bit stronger than the L'Oreal options. Both manufacturers also offer conditioners and detanglers in their line. Johnson & Johnson still make their detangler (I can remember my mom using it on me years ago) as does White Rain.

The options for kids' shampoo will stun you. We've only hit on a few major brands, but a quick search of the Internet will lead you to an abundance of all natural products, high-end foaming shampoos and more. Our recommendation: get something your child will like that doesn't break the bank. And be sure to smell it first before you buy it. That Cherry Blast may seem like a good idea, but after a while you may balk at the strong scent.

◆ *Skin Care.* Skin care may mean as little as finding a good soap to caring for a serious dry skin problem. In general, your best bet is to stick with liquid soaps. They are less drying and easier to use. Kids also seem fascinated by the foaming soaps, so if you want to encourage hand washing, check them out.

What about anti-bacterial soap? Be careful how much you use. While this seems like a smart product for toddlers, we found the chemicals used in these soaps can irritate skin. And in the case of our child, it actually aggravated his eczema. Washing frequently with a regular soap will accomplish all you need when it comes to avoiding germs.

Moisturizers can be useful and once again we'd recommend the Aveeno line. They make a great bath treatment (see picture) as well as moisturizer with oatmeal. If you're looking for a bit less expensive alternative, Suave also offers a cheaper oatmeal bath additive. Serious skin care products from Eucerin and Aquaphor are amazing when treating eczema topically.

And what discussion of kids bath items would be complete without a nod to bubble bath, that quintessential bath item? Walk into any grocery store and you'll see bottles of this stuff, adorned with cartoon cartoons and more. But we say don't waste your money on the fancy stuff. Simple Ivory dish soap makes great bubbles and is gentle to the skin—at half the price. Another caveat: kids with eczema or other skin conditions should AVOID bubble bath. It tends to aggravate these problems. And remember this safety tip: keep all adult bath items (oils, soaps) away from the tub on a high shelf.

potty/bath

◆ **Toothbrushes and toothpaste.** This has always been a struggle around our house. It just seems so "inconvenient" to our kids. But we highly recommend the character toothbrushes from Barbie to Scooby Doo. Just be sure to choose a brush for your child's age. Stay away from hard bristles since they can be uncomfortable and damaging to tooth enamel. Some parents recommend finding a non-character brush if you don't want to commercialize their lives yet.

We recommend the kids flavored toothpaste, not the adult spearmint stuff. You'll know why the first time your kids asks to taste your Crest—the screaming can be heard for miles when that minty stuff starts burning their little taste buds! You may have to try a couple different flavors from favorites like Colgate and Crest. Another idea: our kids love Tom's of Maine's all natural kids toothpaste in Silly Strawberry ($4). Better than the bubble gum options from the big guys but certainly more expensive.

For parents who reject the commercialism of the cartoon character toothpaste and ultrasweet flavorings, one parent emailed us her tip—*start* your child with tiny amounts of adult toothpaste. That gets them used to the taste and you can hopefully avoid any of the kid's stuff as a result. In the end, however, you want to encourage kids to brush. Don't consider yourself a failure if your toddler won't use the adult minty toothpaste.

## Money Saving Tips: Bath

1 **BUY IN BULK.** Check out warehouse clubs. We've found six packs of toothbrushes, triple packs of toothpaste and tons

of lotion options including Lubriderm and Nivea. Keep an eye out for gift packs that let you sample different items from a line. Prices are 30% to 40% less than grocery stores. The pharmacies at warehouse clubs are another source for deals for "special order" (not necessarily prescription) health items. Sample: we ordered a quality sunscreen brand via Costco's pharmacy for 35% less than the retail price.

**2** **CHECK THE WEB.** Specialty items like Aveeno or Aquaphor may not be available at warehouse clubs or discounters. However, you'll find them competitively priced online at sites like DrugStore.com (www.drugstore.com) and DermStore.com (www.dermstore.com). Once again, buying several may save you on shipping. Many sites offer free shipping when you order a certain dollar amount of product.

**3** **MAKE BATH TIME FUN—FOR PENNIES.** Throw in a few drops of non-toxic liquid food coloring into your toddler's bath and whamo! A fun bath for pennies. Make it educational—combine blue and yellow food coloring to teach your child about colors.

## Safe & Sound

As your child exercises more independence, she may want to brush her own teeth and wash her own hair, not to mention check out all the personal care products mom and dad use. Keeping your child safe at the same time you encourage her independence is a delicate balancing act. And don't forget that hygiene doesn't stop at your bathroom. Daycare may present some of its own safety issues.

**1** **SLIP AND SLIDE.** Your little one is ready for a bath in the big tub, but what to do about slippery surfaces? We recommend considering either a tub mat or no-skid stickers for the bottom of your tub. And make sure rugs in the bathroom have a no skid backing so little feet don't go flying out from under little bodies. Also: have a family rule against running in the bathroom to prevent such falls.

**2** **BATH SEATS.** We strongly encourage parents to avoid bath seats for toddlers. They can be very dangerous as they offer a false sense of security. Small children should never be left alone in the tub regardless of whether they are in a bath seat or not. When can you leave a child in the tub alone? We don't recommend it until the child is at least school age. And you'll still want to check on him frequently because he may still need help getting clean and climbing in and out of the tub.

**3 TOILET TROUBLE.** Yes, they get curious. But here's your dilemma: you want to encourage them to use the toilet, not play in it. How to do that? First, avoid those colored chemical disks that deodorize and clean your toilet. The color is an enticement itself, and storing those strong chemicals around can be another danger. Second, pick one "practice" toilet that you leave unlocked—keep toilet locks on other toilets in your house.

By the way, you'll have to address the "how much is too much" toilet paper question at some point. Be very clear about what toilet paper is for and how much they can use in the toilet. We experienced the "stuffed toilet syndrome" several times with our toddler and it can be both dangerous and damaging to your home. A related problem: stuffing items down the toilet. This is a huge discipline issue for many parents. Be clear about what can go down the toilet and what can't. Our kids stayed away once they realized that what goes down never comes back!

**4 TOOTHPASTE ETIQUETTE.** Kids love to put lots of bubble gum flavored Crest on their nifty new PowerPuff Girls toothbrush. Encourage them to use only a small amount (about the size of a pea), and rinse well rather than swallow their spit. Doctors tell us that ingesting too much fluoride can be a health problem. You may even want to keep toothpaste in an upper cabinet to avoid potential ingestion.

**5 ENCOURAGE HAND WASHING.** Yes, that is the safest way to stop the spread of germs. Teach your child to wash their hands with soap EVERY TIME she uses the potty.

**6 LOOK OUT FOR LICE.** The word strikes fear in the hearts of parents everywhere. And it used to be something to worry about only once your child started kindergarten. But today as kids head off to daycare and preschool earlier and earlier, it becomes an issue for toddlers. So how do you avoid it or treat it once your child gets it?

◆ *Remember, kids with lice aren't "dirty."* Lice actually prefer clean heads to dirty ones. And no one should be blamed for spreading lice—in most cases you simply don't know who "had it first."

◆ *Consistently check your child over at bath time* especially if lice are discovered at his school or in the neighborhood. Nits can usually be found at the base of the hairline.

◆ *Keep hair short.* Short hair makes it a bit more difficult to get lice and easier to identify it.

◆ *Don't allow your child to share clothing and hats with other children.* In fact, encourage your daycare/preschool to get rid of dress up clothes. Yes, we know that can be an unpopular stance to take, but lice are spread from child to child via shared clothing, towels and bedding. If your child naps at school, make sure you provide bedding or the school washes its bedding every day.

◆ *If your child gets lice, talk to your doctor first.* You may not need to go in for a visit, but your pediatrician will have excellent advice on treating lice. Most will prescribe an insecticidal shampoo as well as combing to remove nits. Follow the prescribed treatment exactly.

◆ *Wash all bedding and towels in hot water as well as any clothing your child wore*. Keep your child at home until the doctor tells you it's OK for him to go back to school.

◆ *If your child gets lice, inform everyone who has come in contact with him—including the school and neighbors.* Parents will thank you for the warning.

## Bottom Line: Our Picks

The best potty for a child who's learning to use a toilet isn't a potty at all, but an insert. These products make an adult size seat friendly to a toddler, but be sure to get a step stool so the child can reach the potty (and has a place to put his feet). The best insert is the Cushie Tushie from Mommy's Helper.

If you want to try a separate potty, the simple yet effective Baby Bjorn Potty Chair ($22) is our top pick. It doesn't have any fancy bells and whistles but it works fine.

Our pick for the best toddler shampoo is a tie between L'Oreal's Kids line and Suave for Kids. For skin care, the Aveeno line from Johnson & Johnson is a best bet. Their bath treatment line is great for toddlers with dry skin.

# CHAPTER 5

## Meal Time!
### Booster seats, cups & more

### Inside this chapter

*A*fter your toddler outgrows a high chair but doesn't quite fit in a regular chair, what is the next step? Answer: a booster seat. We'll rate and review the best options in this chapter. And what about those toddler meals? We'll discuss this topic, as well as give our picks for the best cookbooks and lunchboxes for toddlers.

## Smart Shopper Tips

### Smart Shopper Tip #1
*Beware boosters that don't work for toddlers.*

*"I got a booster seat that says it can be used from six months to age four. But my two-year-old is clearly too big for the thing!"*

Blame over zealous baby product makers for promising the moon and delivering far less. The latest example are booster seats that promise use from birth to college (okay, age four). The reality: most are too small to use for any child over three (or even two, if you have a large toddler).

The biggest trend in boosters is what we call the "high chair replacement" pitch: you don't have to spend $100+ on a high chair, when our Super Dooper Booster will work for just $20! To make boosters work better for infants, baby product makers have added seat reclines, different height adjustments and closer fitting trays. Then you are supposed to remove the tray and just use the seat for older toddlers.

The problem: many boosters don't work well for babies. And then toddlers grow out of them too quickly. First, a wide high chair tray will always beat the skimpy booster seat trays. Second, the too-tight seats (especially with trays) make the booster unworkable for larger toddlers.

So, are boosters good for anything? Yes—first, consider them as a great high chair substitute for grandma's house. Most fold up for storage and are perfect for occasional use. Second, consider a booster WITHOUT a tray—when your toddler is old enough to sit at the table and not launch food into low Earth orbit, this option is great. Bonus: boosters without trays are cheaper, of course.

So, let's sum up our thoughts:

◆ *Don't fall for the "birth to age 12" pitch on these products.*

◆ *If your toddler is mature enough, get a booster without a tray for longer use.* Older toddlers may find the "cushy" boosters more comfortable than hard plastic seats (more on these later).

◆ *For restaurants, consider a hook-on chair.* We'll also discuss these chairs later. Note: some restaurants don't permit the use of hook-on chairs if their tables have narrow bases or other hazards.

### Smart Shopper Tip #2
*Keep the receipt.*

*"I have had a heck of a time finding a booster seat that is stable, fits underneath my table, and so on. Is there one perfect booster out there that works for all situations?"*

Yep, finding the right booster seat for a toddler can be challenging. The three variables involved here—your child, the chair, the table—can make it frustrating to find one booster that works. And it is hard to eye ball this in a store or from an online picture; you have to get the thing, strap it to your chair, and put your child in it to judge how well it will work. A word to the wise: keep the receipt and don't throw away the box and packaging. And buy a booster seat from a store or online site that has a good return policy, as you might find yourself trying out more than one booster before you find one that works. Another hint: try it in the store with your toddler. Many baby stores have booster seats set up on store shelves.

# Wastes of Money

### Waste of Money #1
*Toddler Meals: Convenience or a joke?*

*"I have noticed many baby food companies have come out with toddler meals, like Gerber Graduates or Finger Foods. And juices. And fruit cups. And so on. Are these good for baby or a sinister plot to pad the earnings of baby food companies?"*

After realizing growth in the baby market was slowing several years ago, baby food companies like Gerber hit upon the idea of selling parents on "toddler foods." Gerber now has an entire line of "Gerber Graduates," cereals, juices and so on.

Gerber defends these foods by claiming that small children don't get enough nutrition from table foods. In an effort to "help" parents, Gerber's offerings are extra fortified. Take their apple juice, for example. Gerber has added extra calcium that regular apple juice lacks.

The only problem with this argument? Toddlers don't need extra-fortified foods if they eat a balanced diet. Example: there's a great calcium supplement out there. It's called *milk*. Kids don't need special calcium-fortified apple juice if they drink enough milk each day (at least 16 ounces of milk, preferably skim after age two). Pediatricians also recommend against giving small children lots of juice since it can fill them up and keep them from eating other, nutritious foods.

The bottom line is: you pay extra for that Gerber apple juice. A 32 ounce bottle of Gerber's "special" apple juice costs 16% more than the same size bottle of Mott's apple juice. In general, we found Gerber foods priced 10% to 30% more than similar non-baby foods.

Yes, we'll grant you that Gerber's diced fruit and vegetables are a great convenience—but most grocery stores sell sliced/peeled FRESH fruit and vegetables today . . . at prices that are as much as 30% lower than Gerber's. And fresh fruits and vegetables are better for toddlers than canned/jarred alternatives.

As always, consult with your pediatrician regarding your child's diet—your doctor should be able to give you guidelines for how much milk and other foods your toddler needs. The bottom line: toddlers don't need special foods (at high prices) as long as they eat a balanced diet.

## Name Game: Kitchen Booster Seats

You're toddler has outgrown his high chair, but doesn't quite fit into the adult chairs at the kitchen table. What to do? Consider a booster. There are three types of booster seats on the market today:

**1** **HOOK-ON CHAIRS.** As the name implies, these seats hook on to a table, instead of attaching to a chair. Pros: Lightweight; yet most can hold toddlers up to 35 to 40 lbs. Very portable—many parents use these chairs as a sanitary alternative when they dine out since many restaurants seemed to have last cleaned their high chairs during the Carter administration. Cons: May not work with certain tables, like those with pedestal bases. Fear of tipping an unstable table leads some restaurants to prohibit these chairs. Hook-on chairs do not recline, a feature you see on regular boosters.

**2** **BOOSTER SEATS WITH TRAYS.** These boosters strap to a chair and usually have a tray. Pros: Most fold flat for travel. Some have multiple seat levels. Can use with or without a tray. Cons: Child may not be sitting up at table height. Some brands have too-small trays and difficult to adjust straps make for a loose fit.

**3** **PLAIN BOOSTERS (NO TRAY).** These chairs are just boosters— nothing fancy, no trays. Pros: Better bet for older toddlers (age four or five) who want to eat at the table. Cons: No restraint system or belt, so this isn't a choice for younger toddlers.

Here's an overview of what's out there, with our picks:

## HOOK-ON CHAIRS

**CHICCO HIPPO**
**Booster type:** Hook-on chair
**Web:** www.ChiccoUSA.com
**Price:** $50.
**Weight limit:** 37 lbs.
**Pros:** More padding and feels more solid than Graco Tot-Loc. Weighs just six pounds. Comes with nylon travel bag. Seat cover is removable for washing.
**Cons:** Expensive. No tray. Not easy to set up. Seat is a tight fit for older toddlers. Yes, seat cover is removable for washing, but it's not easy.

**Comments:** This seat is more cushy than the Graco Travel-Lite, but it's limitations (washable seat fabric is a pain to take off, difficult set-up) make it not worth the extra price. And the too small seat (which is tight for bigger toddlers) limits the usefulness of this product. So, if it is a hook-on chair you want, save nearly $20 and get the Graco.
**Rating:** C

### GRACO TRAVEL-LITE TABLE CHAIR

**Booster type:** Hook-on chair
**Web:** www.GracoBaby.com
**Price:** $33
**Pros:** Simple, safe, affordable. Baby is up at table height. Very portable—weighs just 10 lbs. Has tray.
**Cons:** Padding on vinyl seat isn't overly cushy. Tray (14.5" wide) is rather small, but workable.
**Weight limit:** 37 lbs.
**Comments:** Parents tell us this chair is a winner, especially for eating out. The Traval Lite does the job, whether at home or out on the town. It is our top pick for a hook-on chair. Toddlers love being up where the adults are and this chair is easy to use. The only caveat: tables that aren't flat underneath and certain pedestal tables won't work with this chair. FYI: this chair used to be called the Tot-Loc. Graco didn't change it much, just a new name and fabric.
**Rating:** A

### ME TOO! PORTABLE HIGH CHAIR

**Booster type:** Hook-on chair
**Web:** found on www.BabyCenter.com
**Price:** $45
**Pros:** Simple adjustable clamps attach seat to table. Very portable—weighs just 2 lbs and folds to 1" thick.
**Cons:** No tray and no padding.
**Weight limit:** 40 lbs.
**Comments:** Parent Corey Derrenbacher turned us on to this seat. She loved the portability and easy installation of this hook on chair. It's very basic and easy to clean also.
**Rating:** B

## BOOSTER SEATS

### ESPECIALLY FOR KIDS BOOSTER

**Booster type:** Booster with tray.
**Web:** www.BabiesRUs.com
**Price:** $13.

**Pros:** Lowest price booster on market. Three height levels. Very simple design. Rubber feet on base keep seat from slipping.

**Cons:** No frills. Not a great high chair replacement for infants.

**Comments:** This is Toys/Babies R Us private label brand booster. It's OK; yes, it is cheap, but it does the job. The only complaint we hear: parents who want to use this as a high chair replacement at grandma's house find it doesn't work well for the youngest toddlers (there is no seat recline; the tray can be kicked off too easily, etc). Yet, since this book focuses on older toddlers, this seat would be a fine no frills selection.

**Rating:** B

### 1ST YEARS 4 STAGE FEEDING SEAT (A.K.A. RECLINING FEEDING SEAT)

**Booster type:** Booster with tray.
**Web:** www.TheFirstYears.com
**Price:** $30

**Pros:** Two height positions, three position recline. Vinyl cushion removes for cleaning. Tray has one hand release. Can plop the whole thing in a dishwasher.

**Cons:** A bit of overkill for older toddlers—the reclining seat feature is better for infants.

**Comments:** Parents give this seat good marks; many like it as a high chair substitute for grandma's house. But this seat is overkill for older toddlers (2 and up), since they won't get much out of the seat recline feature. More caveats: the height adjustment can be tricky and some parents say their toddlers learn how to remove the tray too easily. Despite these drawbacks, this is still an excellent booster.

**Rating:** A-

### 1ST YEARS SWING TRAY PORTABLE BOOSTER

**Booster type:** Booster with tray.
**Web:** www.TheFirstYears.com
**Price:** $20

**Pros:** Tray swings out using only one hand and is lightweight. 100% dishwasher safe for easy cleaning. Can be used up to 50 lbs.

Three height adjustments.

**Cons:** May not fit older/bigger children as well as some seats.

**Comments:** Great seat for anyone with a smaller or younger toddler. Doesn't seem big enough to make it to 50 lbs. as the box promises. Ease of use and clean-ability make this a great seat.

**Rating:** A-

### SAFETY 1ST ON THE GO FOLD-UP BOOSTER (ALSO CALLED FOLD N GO)

**Booster type:** Booster with tray.
**Web:** www.Safety1st.com
**Age:** Six months to four years.
**Price:** $20
**Pros:** Good price. Safety straps retract. Folds up and has handle for portability. Storage compartment.

**Cons:** Tray is smaller than 1st Years boosters and somewhat more difficult to remove. No seat padding. Seat base isn't as stable as 1st Years models, in our research.

**Comments:** Parents we interviewed knocked this seat for several obvious and not so obvious flaws: the lack of any seat padding is a major negative. And we heard complaints about the tray, which is somewhat smaller than rival brands and a pain to remove from the seat. On the other hand, the cool storage compartment is a nice plus, as is the carry handle. Overall, however, parents gave better marks to the 1st Years 4 Stage seat and so will we.

**Rating:** B-

### SAFETY 1ST FOLD-UP BOOSTER SEAT

**Booster type:** Booster with tray.
**Web:** www.Safety1st.com
**Price:** $20
**Pros:** Two height positions. Very basic design.

**Cons:** Hard plastic seat (no padding). Smallish tray.

**Comments:** This is an earlier version of the On the Go Fold-up booster (see above); it has some of the same drawbacks, including a difficult to remove tray.

**Rating:** B-

## PLAIN BOOSTERS (NO TRAYS)

### 1ST YEARS
### ON THE GO BOOSTER SEAT
**Booster Type:** Booster, no tray.
**Web:** www.TheFirstYears.com
**Price:** $20 on BabyCenter.com
**Weight limit:** 20 lbs.

**Pros:** Lightest booster seat—it inflates! Weights just 2 lbs. When folded less than 2″ inch. Safety harness has thick crotch restraint, not just a strap (see picture)—best at keeping wiggly toddlers in their seat.

**Cons:** It inflates? What if you get a puncture? Doesn't sit as high as other boosters. Very low weight limit.

**Comments:** This funky booster has a self-inflate valve—yes, it actually inflates to give your child a cushy seat. While that sounds great in theory, a few parents complain the seat doesn't stay even when their child shifts his weight from one side to the other. And the low height of this booster won't work for many parents either. On the other hand, how many booster seats are just 2″ tall when folded? Bottom line: this is a great booster for travel—if you have a small toddler (under 20 lbs).

**Rating:** B+

### BABY BJORN BOOSTER SEAT
**Type:** Plain booster without tray.
**Web:** www.BabyBjorn.com
**Age recommendation:** 30 months to five years.
**Price:** $35.
**Pros:** Simple design.
**Cons:** $35 for this?

**Comments:** Bjorn's molded plastic booster seat is nice enough, but just doesn't justify the $35 price tag. And the hard plastic seat is a bit small to fit the five-year-olds Bjorn claims in their age limit guidelines. (Note: Bjorn also sells the seat with a "safely bar;" the booster seat without the bar is pictured here).

**Rating:** C

### BabySmart Cooshie Booster

**Type:** Plain booster without tray

**Age guidelines:** 12 months to four years.

**Price:** $30.

**Pros:** Only soft, foam booster on market. Non-slip surface. Weighs under 2 lbs.

**Cons:** No safety harness—toddlers must be mature enough to sit in seat without restraint. Tote bag isn't very durable.

**Comments:** This is our recommendation for older toddlers—the Cooshie Booster's super comfortable foam design is a winner. No, there isn't a safety harness, but older kids don't really need it. How old? The manufacturer says this seat would work for babies as young as 12 months, but we think that is a stretch. The optimum time to use this booster would be for ages three to five, in our opinion. Yes, we think some toddlers as young as two would be mature enough but any younger would be pushing it. We used this booster with our youngest son and it got raves.

**Rating:** A+

### Ikea Agam

**Type:** Toddler high chair.

**Web:** www.ikea-usa.com

**Age guidelines:** For ages 18 months and up.

**Price:** $35.

**Pros:** With a price that can't be beat, these chairs look more like dining chairs than high chairs. Made of beech wood.

**Cons:** You'll have to assemble it. Ikeas aren't everywhere, so you may have to order online. No tray. Very barebones.

**Comments:** A reader turned us on to this Ikea toddler chair. She couldn't believe the price (neither could we!) and her child loves it. It's very basic, but at that price, you could buy more than one (parents of twins take note). A chair pad is available for a mere $10.

**Rating:** B

### STOKKE KINDERZEAT

**Type:** Toddler high chair.
**Web:** www.stokkeusa.com
**Age guidelines:** 18 months & up.
**Price:** $200 at RightStart.com and other independent retailers.
**Pros:** Cool looking toddler chair from Norway. Seat and footrest adjust to any size child. Strap included. All wood. 11 colors. 5-year warranty. Beech wood construction.

**Cons:** Did we mention it is $200? And the seat cushion is extra? Have to use a screw driver to change the height.

**Comments:** Leave it to those wacky Norwegians to come up with a stylish toddler chair that solves a problem those $20 boosters can't avoid—dangling feet. Stokke says without a footrest, a child gets fidgety and has a poor reach. The KinderZeat can adjust to fit kids from 18 months through—and we're not making this up—15 years. The chair includes a safety strap and an optional back and seat cushion (machine washable) is available at an extra cost. So is this seat worth $200? Well, it's so new we don't have much feedback on it from parents. But we think it is a great idea and well designed. Yet, as the authors of a book with BARGAINS in the title, we know if we recommend this seat, our email box will get flamed. So let's put it this way—if money is no object, then go for the KinderZeat.

As a side note, there is a cheaper knock off of the KinderZeat on the One Step Ahead web site called the Euro Chair. It sells for $100 including cushion and looks quite similar. We haven't had feedback from readers on this option, but it is a good buy.
**Rating:** A

## HIGH CHAIR/TODDLER CHAIR

### SVAN

**Type:** Infant high chair morphs into a toddler chair.
**Web:** www.scandinavian.com
**Age guidelines:** For ages six months and up with infant kit. 18 months and up for basic chair.
**Price:** $220 with infant kit; $170 for just the basic chair.
**Pros:** Swedish version of a universal toddler chair. This one can accommodate babies as young as six months with an optional infant kit. Seat and footrest adjust to any size child—cushion is extra. All wood. Three wood finishes and three cushion colors. Unlike the Stokke chair, you can adjust the seat and footrest without unscrewing anything.
**Cons:** Ultra modern styling won't appeal to everyone.

**Comments:** If you're looking for another ergonomic option for your toddler, Svan has entered the market to compete with Stokke. It's a bit less expensive for the toddler only chair but there are no straps. Once again, the pads are extra and we recommend them—that's going to be one hard seat to stay in during Passover seders or Thanksgiving feasts. We like how this chair is easier to adjust than the Stokke. But there aren't as many color options to go with your kitchen décor as the Stokke.

**Rating:** A-

## *Best Bets: Kitchen Booster Seats*

◆ *Booster Seat* (under 3): 1st Years 4 Stage Feeding Seat (www.thefirstyears.com) features two height positions and a three position seat recline. It is a good buy at $30. *A runner-up:* the 1st Years Swing Tray Portable Booster ($20) is great for small or young children. Easy to get them in and out with the swinging tray.

◆ *Booster Seat (over 3):* BabySmart's Cooshie Booster ($30) is an excellent soft foam booster. Nothing fancy, but does the job. Can they make these for adults?

◆ *Hook-on Chair:* The *Graco Travel-Lite* ($33) is a great solution for parents who want to take their toddler out to eat, but don't trust those restaurant high chairs. This hook-on chair ain't much to look at, but it does the trick. *Runner-up:* the Chicco Hippo Hook-on Chair ($50) is better looking than the Travel-Lite, albeit for $17 more and no tray.

◆ *Toddler Seat* (when money is no object). Yes, *Stokke's KinderZeat* is $200, but it is one of the very few "toddler chairs" on the market. We liked the numerous height levels and adjustments, which give your toddler a place to rest their feet. And the 11 available colors means it can fit into any decor. Very cool. *Runner-up:* Ikea's toddler chair, the Agam. Cheap, basic and maybe all you need.

## Best Bets: No-Spill Cups

What's been the best invention for parents since the babysitter? Well, besides disposable diapers that can hold the water equivalent of Lake Erie, we'd vote for the No-Spill Cup. These marvels of science have saved countless car interiors, kitchen floors and other surfaces from being coated with sixty-four ounces of junior's Big Gulp Apple Juice.

Last time out we touted a cup from *1st Years* called the Clean & Simple Spill-Proof Cup. Well, we have egg on our face. It seems that while you could turn one of these cups over and nothing would spill out, if your child knocked the cup on its side it would leak. And in fact, the company admitted that the cups are made that way intentionally. Now, as Sam Lehman, a bright reader of our book asked 1st Years, "Aren't spills and leaks synonyms?" They are in our book, so we're not recommending these cups any longer.

Yes, we're back to recommending the cups with the separate valves. *The Playtex Big Sipster Sprill Proof Cups* ($7 for a two-pack; pictured) is one winner. Gerber also makes a great cup, the *Fun Grips*, with a separate valve ($7 for a two-pack). They also sell the valves separately for those folks with carnivorous dishwashers. Munchkin (www.

munchkininc.com) makes a spill proof cup called *My First Cup* ($3). We liked the "no slip grip." Although it uses a valve, Munchkin sells replacements. Munchkin also has character cups like Blues Clues and Sponge Bob.

What about *Avent's Magic Cup*? Well, it was a bear to clean (four separate parts to wash), so we weren't very excited by it in our last edition. However, reader Gabrielle Lynas noted that the no spill spouts will fit on any regular Avent bottle (not disposable).

So, you say, who cares? But just think of all those baby bottles you have that can now be converted to spill proof cups! You can buy the spouts separately for $4 per two-pack.

Now for a new idea in no-spill: the *Snack Trap* (pictured). We tend to concentrate on keeping liquids in the cup, but what about snack foods? The Snack Trap

(www.snacktrap.com) makes a two-handled cup with a specially designed plastic lid ($5). The lid is see through and allows your toddler to reach into the cup for some of those goldfish crackers. But as soon as she takes out a handful the lid closes behind her. And the same manufacturer also makes a no spill lid for water bottles ($8.50).

## Cookbooks

You can't turn on the TV today without hearing some new, scary food warning. *Potato chips cause cancer! Kids are too fat! Obese alien kids take over Albania!*

Every parent starts out with the best of intentions—we *do* want our children to eat healthy, balanced meals. And, yes, we realize McDonald's french fries do not count as a serving of vegetables.

But even the most diligent parents can be challenged when trying to feed a toddler. And it's easy to run out of ideas when you have to plan a week's worth of meals.

Our solution: cookbooks designed with kid friendly meals. Basically, Emeril for the toddler set.

We like these cookbooks for more than just recipes—sometimes it is the creative presentation that makes all the difference. Or a fresh spin on an old favorite.

Here's our top picks:

◆ *Healthy Food for Healthy Kids* ($12, by Bridget Swinney, Meadowbrook Press, 1999). We've always been fans of Swinney, a nutritionist who combines real-world sensibility with her smart nutritional advice. The sub-title of this book sums it up: "A Practical and Tasty Guide to Your Child's Nutrition." We loved the menus, recipes and dishes here, all designed to be quick and easy to prepare. You get a nutritional breakdown for each recipe but purists beware—Swinney doesn't shy away from ketchup or salad dressing. This is *not* the book if you are looking for vegan, low-fat, dairy-free recipes. Favorite section: Ten Tricky Ways to get Your Kids to Eat Their Veggies.

◆ *Brown Bag Success: Making Healthy Lunches Your Kids Won't Trade* ($13, By Sandra Nissenberg and Barbara Pearl, John Wiley & Sons, 1998). Tired of the same old standbys for kids lunches? Now that you're sending them off to preschool, its time for an upgrade. And you'll find plenty of ideas here. Not only are there recipes but also tips and lists to help you organize yourself.

These books are out of print, but still valuable—see if you can track them down at a local library:

◆ **The Book of Children's Foods** ($12 by Lorna Rhodes, HP Books, 1992). Well-known cookbook author Rhodes takes the reader on a colorful journey to Kid Food Land, with creative presentation ideas and easy to execute recipes. Each recipe features a full-color photograph, as well as pictures of prep and other details. Over 100 recipes.

◆ **Healthy Yummies for Young Tummies** (14.95, by Ann Schrader, Rutledge Hill Press,

## Toddlers: Care & Feeding

Yes, it may seem like an epic struggle—getting a toddler to eat something more than french fries. We feel your pain. As parents of a certified "Picky Eater," we can understand. Here are our survival tips:

◆ *Feed them what you eat.* Real food is so much better than canned toddler stuff. And don't be afraid to give her sauces and other condiments. You'll be surprised at how adventurous a two-year-old can be.

◆ *Mix it up.* Breakfast is fun to eat at dinner—and vice versa. Changing up the routine can make a picky eater more excited about meals.

◆ *Don't sweat the daily details.* Focus on what your child eats over an entire week, not each meal. Just like adults, toddlers' appetites ebb and flow. Don't fret if your child doesn't each much for lunch one day, he'll make it up later.

◆ *Forget the dessert-as-a-reward trick.* It's a bad habit. On the reverse side, we do withhold the "bed time snack" for our children when they refuse to touch dinner. Instead, we morph the snack into a dinner redux.

1993). Colorful, well-designed book has emphasis on low-fat, low-sodium, low sugar recipes.

◆ *The Penny Whistle Lunch Box Book* ($11, by Meredith Brokaw, Fireside, 1991). Over 100 ideas for that vexing challenge that faces every parent—what to do for lunch? Easy to make recipes with common ingredients.

## Lunch Boxes

Now that you have an idea of what to feed your child, it's time for the next challenge—what to put that lunch *in* when your toddler goes off to daycare or preschool. The search for the perfect lunch box can leave most parents scratching their heads. Where to start?

Call it the Holy Grail of Lunch Boxes: a container that keeps

◆ *Keep to a schedule.* Make dinner the same time each night. Yes, you as an adult can wait until 7pm or 8pm for dinner—but a toddler can't. And make healthy snacks a regular part of their diet. Their tummies are smaller so they get hungry between meals.

◆ *Monkey see, monkey do.* If you skip breakfast, what will your toddler think about this meal? Set a good example by eating a wide variety of foods yourself—yes, including fruits and vegetables.

◆ *Go on a grocery safari.* Have your toddler come grocery shopping to show him/her the ways to select nutritious foods.

◆ *Stay away from highly allergenic foods.* Your child shouldn't eat shellfish until he's at least five years old. Yes, fish is fine, but you don't want to introduce a life threatening food allergy that will remain with your child forever. And allergists also recommend staying away from nuts until your child is at least three or four years old (five if you can manage it). Yes, that includes staying away from peanut butter! We know this is a tough one for folks who think peanut butter is the ultimate kid food, but as parents of a peanut allergy kid who can literally die after eating one peanut, we urge you to stay away from it as long as you can.

cold items cold, is easy to clean, lightweight, easy to carry and—most of all—still looks cool.

Here's our shopping guide to the best lunch boxes for toddlers and preschoolers.

## Smart Shopper Tips

### Smart Shopper Tip #1
*Plastic/metal or soft side?*

*"Which is better for lunch boxes: plastic or soft side?"*

There are two basic choices when it comes to kid's lunch boxes: plastic or metal options and those "soft side" lunch boxes. Cost-wise, both are similar in price. Here are the differences.

Hard plastic/metal lunch boxes are easier to clean and very durable. Most stand up well to normal wear and tear. The downside? Most are heavier than soft side boxes. And given the rigid frame, you don't have as much flexibility when it comes to storage here.

Soft side lunch boxes tend to be lighter and easier to stuff things in. You can more easily mark your child's name on a soft side box than a hard plastic one. The downside? These can be a bear to clean. Look for ones with a removable liner for easier cleaning. Or get a soft side that is machine washable.

### Smart Shopper Tip #2
*Best features to look for*

*"Most lunch boxes seems to be sold based on what cartoon character is on the front. What are the best features to really look out for?*

Here's our checklist of what to consider:

**1** **MICROBAN.** This special coating inhibits odors, stains and mildew. The better quality lunch boxes have it; the cheap ones don't.

**2** **INSULATION.** The best lunch boxes have insulated sections to keep drinks cold, etc.

**3** **SURPRISE SNACK POUCHES.** Gotta love a secret place to stash cookies, little notes or other surprises.

**4** **WASHABILITY.** Can the lunch box go into the dishwasher? Is there a removable liner than can be washed?

**5** **CHARACTERS.** Yes, we realize many toddlers and parents choose their lunch box based on the character on the outside. While we understand that, remember you often pay a premium for the character theme. Don't forget to check for quality features. Some character lunch boxes are sold strictly on the cartoon on the outside, not what's inside.

**6** **EASE OF USE.** Remember, you can't rely on your daycare or preschool staff to help your child master his lunch box. The best lunch boxes are toddler friendly, with easy clasps or closures.

**7** **SPILL PROOF.** Thermos/cups can be the cause of major frustration. Our sons always had problems with thermos tops that had to be screwed tightly shut to avoid leaks . . . inevitably, the top would not get screwed on tight, causing a leak. A better bet: cups with flip top lids or straws. These seem easier for kids to close than screw-top lids. One tip: check out the PecoWare (www.pecoware.com) line of kid's lunch containers (sandwich containers, canteens, lunch boxes). We've found them to be among the more kid-friendly lunch accessories on the market.

## Best Bet: Lunch Boxes

What's the coolest lunch box we've ever seen? The Lunch Pack line from *California Innovations* (which, ironically, is based in Toronto; www.californiainnovations.com). This maker of innovative coolers has a lunch box line that includes Microban, Therma-Flect insulation, and lots of other useful features. The M Series Lunch Pack (available on TheOutdoorWorld.com) runs about $8.

California Innovations also makes exclusive lunch boxes for wholesale clubs. We spied one such example recently at Costco: the "Cool Dome." It has lots of pockets, including a zippered inside pocket and outside storage pockets. It comes with a microwave safe lunch container and a separate drink compartment. This dual compartment feature (each part is insulated) is a great way to separate foods that need to be kept at different temperatures. We love the removable liner that you can easily clean. A rugged carry strap and overall cool look make this one a winner. A steal at

$10. Check the California Innovations web site for more locations and web sites that carry their boxes.

## Bottom Line: Our Top Picks

When shopping for a kitchen booster seat, look for one big enough to accommodate your growing toddler—some of the boosters pitched to parents as lasting from baby through age six won't cut it. Keep the receipt and make sure the booster works with your kitchen table and chairs.

As the best booster seat for toddlers under three, we pick the 1st Years 4 Stage Feeding Seat. For toddlers over three, we liked BabySmart's Cooshie Booster. If money is no option, the Stokke KinderZeat at $200 is pricey but very cool.

What's the best spill-proof cup? Spill proof cups from Playtex, Gerber and Munchkin got the best reviews from parents. And if you have lots of old Avent baby bottles lying around, consider buying Avent spill proof spouts to turn those old bottles into new spill proof cups.

The best toddler lunch boxes are made by California Innovations. Keep an eye out for their exclusive lunch boxes designed for warehouse clubs like Costco (they're also available online and in stores).

# CHAPTER 6

*Car Booster Seats*
*Picking the best seat for your toddler*

### Inside this chapter

N *ow that your toddler has outgrown her convertible*
*seat, what's the best booster? We'll review and rate*
*the best options, plus give you advice on how to get the best*
*fit, the low down on seat belt adjusters and the new hybrid*
*seats on the market.*

What is it with driving today? Every time we hit the road here
in our hometown of Boulder, Colorado, we get the feeling we're
in some sort of bizarre demolition derby—SUV's driven by suicide
bombers, insane bicyclists who think stop signs are "not for them"
and kamikaze pedestrians so engrossed in their cell phone conversations they don't have time to look for traffic. Forget get-rich-quick
schemes on the Internet—the real money to be made in the next
decade must be body shop repair.

But seriously, motor vehicle accidents are a major threat to
everyone today, children included. Sadly, traffic crashes are the
leading cause of deaths for children six to 14, according to the federal government. And a big reason: most kids aren't properly
restrained. Only six percent of children of booster seat age actually use booster seats.

Most parents know they have to put an infant or toddler into a
car seat. What some folks don't realize, however, is that child passenger safety doesn't end when baby outgrows that convertible
car seat—any child from 40 to 80 pounds and less than 4'9" (generally, kids age four to eight) should be restrained in a booster seat.

And in some cases, booster seat use is mandated by law.
Numerous states (including such populous places as California)
have passed laws requiring the use of booster seats. And more
states are following their lead. Here's our look at the best and worst
booster seats on the market today.

## Getting Started:
## When do you need a booster?

Your child needs a booster seat when he outgrows his convertible seat. This happens when he exceeds the weight limit (typically 40 pounds) or when he is too tall for the harness (his shoulders are taller than the top slots in the seat). For most children, this happens around ages three or four.

## Sources

Like most other car seats, booster seats can be found both online and in chain stores. The best bets are Babies R Us and Baby Depot. Both carry a decent selection in their stores and online (babiesrus.com and coat.com). As for cyber sources, we'd suggest sites like BabyUniverse (which sells the Britax boosters among other brands) as well as BabyCatalog.com. Who has the lowest prices? WalMart.com and Target.com have great deals, although their selection is a bit slim.

## Parents in Cyberspace

*We found several booster seat info resources online. Here are a couple to check out:*

◆ *SafetyBeltSafeUSA* (www.carseat.org) has three good reports on booster seats (click on the button, Booster Seats) that explain proper installation and offer other tips. Another great site is *CarSeatData.org*.

◆ *The National Highway Traffic and Safety Administration* has an excellent online brochure on booster seats: "Boost 'em Before You Buckle 'Em." http://www.nhtsa.dot.gov/people/injury/childps/Boosterseat/index.html.

Also cool: the NHTSA now rates and reviews booster seats for ease of use and other factors. Go to : http://www.nhtsa.dot.gov/CPS/CSSRating/

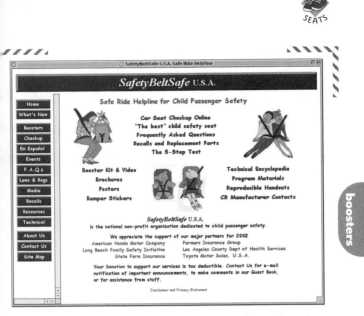

*Figure 1. SafetyBeltSafeUSA.com has several good articles on booster seats, including lists of models and advice on installation.*

## Smart Shopping tips

### Smart Shopper Tip #1
*Booster Laws*

*"My daughter just turned 4, and my state doesn't require her to use a carseat anymore. She just uses the seat belt now."*

A number of states have recently enacted stiffer carseat laws, usually requiring children to use "appropriate restraints" until age six or 60 pounds. But most states still only require carseat until a child turns four, (some even just two) years old. So why should you continue to hassle with a carseat or booster after this time?

We like to remind parents that there is the law and then there is the law of physics. Car belts are made for adults, and children (as well as some short adults) just don't fit well, and don't get good protection from those belts. Lap belts used with 4-8 year old children routinely cause such severe injuries and paralysis that they even have their own name: "lap belt syndrome." Children using lap/shoulder belts often put the shoulder belt behind their back (since it is so darn uncomfortable), giving them no more protection than a lap belt alone. Ejections are another common problem with young children in adult belts, even if they are using both the lap and shoulder belt.

Booster seats (and of course regular carseats) work very simply to eliminate this problem. Boosters properly position the lap part of the belt on a child's strong hips, not their soft internal organs. They elevate the child and include a special adjuster so that the lap shoulder belt fits right on the strong shoulder bones. Booster seats should be used until a child fits the adult belts like an adult. Try out the 5 Step Test (later in this chapter) to see if your child is ready yet.

### Smart Shopper Tip #2
#### Different seats, lots of confusion?

*"When I was shopping for a booster seat, I was confused with all the types of seats out there. Why isn't there just one type of booster?"*

Good question. We've noticed that buying a booster seat can be a bit more complex than buying another car seat. For example, an infant car seat is, well, an infant car seat. But a booster can come in several versions: shield boosters, high back boosters, backless boosters, combination seat/boosters, and more.

In this chapter, we'll try to simplify things a bit. Any time we refer to a *booster*, we mean a seat that uses the lap/shoulder belt to secure the child. Most other car seats (like convertible seats) use an internal harness to hold the child, while the seat itself is attached to the car with the seat belt or the new LATCH system.

What's made this so confusing is that car seat makers have blurred the lines between convertible seats and boosters in recent years by coming out with multi-purpose models—Cosco's Alpha Omega, for example, is a convertible seat that can be used for infants rear-facing 5 to 35 pounds, forward-facing harnessed from 20 to 40 pounds and THEN it becomes a booster to 80 pounds. Other makers, like Britax, have debuted models that use a five-point harness for children up to 65 pounds—these seats are not boosters but new hybrid convertible seats, which used to have weight limits at 40 pounds.

Confusing, yes we know. But we want this chapter to cover all the options for older children who've outgrown their traditional convertible seat . . . so you'll see a variety of options in this chapter.

Let's break down what's out there:

 ◆ **Shield boosters:** These are what boosters USED to look like (see picture left). Most car seat companies stopped selling shield boosters in the mid 1990's when tougher crash standards were enacted. For some reason, however, Cosco continues to sell one

shield booster (the Grand Explorer pictured at left). Frankly, we think shield boosters are dangerous. "Cosco has been sued at least seven times because of injuries or deaths with its shield boosters, court documents show," reported *USA Today* in a 2001 story. Yet Cosco says these shield boosters are needed for children who outgrow a convertible seat because of height but not weight (Cosco just recommends the shield booster for children between 30 and 40 pounds). Bottom line: we don't recommend shield boosters. If you have a child who is less than 40 pounds, keep him in a harnessed seat.

◆ **Combination (combo):** These are probably the most confusing "booster" seats because sometimes they are a booster, and sometimes they aren't. They come with a 5 point harness, which can generally be used to 40 pounds. Then the harness comes off, and the seat can be used as a belt positioning booster, usually to 80 or more pounds. They get the name "combination" or "combo" for short from the two jobs they do. What's great about these seats is that most of them have higher harness slots, so tall children can stay in a harness to a full 40 pounds even if they've outgrown their convertible height-wise. And then, after 40 pounds, the seat is still useful, converting to a booster that might be the last seat your child needs. Yes, there are a few combo seats with harnesses that can be used past 40 pounds, like the Safety Baby Airway (more on this seat maker later) with a harness that goes to 50 pounds, becoming a booster to 80 pounds—but these seats are hard to find. Combo boosters are great for children that have outgrown their convertible seats but aren't mature enough to sit in a belt-positioning booster (the types described below). The five-point harness provides that extra measure of safety and security while they are still young (typically, a child has to be three or older to be mature enough to handle the belt-positioners). Some combo seats start at just 20 pounds.

◆ **High back boosters (HBB):** These seats have often been called "small person's captain's chairs", which they kind of resemble. They are really simple, but provide vital safety features for children who've outgrown the harnessed seats. These boosters properly position the lap belt on a child's strong hip bones, rather than letting it ride up on the soft internal organs. And they provide correct positioning of the shoulder belt, so the child can comfortably wear it and get critical upper body support. The high back also protects the child's head from whiplash if there are no head restraints in the vehicle, and the high back may also give some side sleeping support. ALL of these boosters require a lap and shoulder belt.

◆ **Backless boosters:** These work the same way as high back boosters— they just don't have a back. Safety-wise, these can be a bit better than a high back booster, since the child sits right against the vehicle seat. They do the same job positioning the lap belt, and usually include some sort of strap to adjust the shoulder belt. But they don't provide head support if you have low seat backs, and they don't give any side or sleeping support. On the other hand, they are often popular with older kids, since they can be quite inconspicuous. All of these also require a lap/shoulder belt.

◆ **Special/Hybrid Seats:** There are a few seats on the market now that don't really fit into any category. One is the Britax Husky (pictured; formally called Super Elite). It is a huge seat that uses a harness forward facing from 20 to 80 pounds, so it fits most kids until age 8-10. It isn't a booster since is always uses the harness. It is a terrific option for children who reach 40 pounds before they are three or so, and really need the protection of a full harness, or for families with vehicles that only have lap belts in back. Britax also sells the Marathon and Wizard seats that can be used up to 65 pounds with a five-point harness.

### Smart Shopper Tip #3
*Avoid Seat Belt Adjusters*

*"The shoulder belt was bugging my son's neck, so I bought a lit- tle adjuster thing. Is that as good as a booster?"*

Several companies make inexpensive adjusters ($10 or so) which help to properly position the shoulder belt on your child. Sounds good, right? Wrong. Look closely at the pictures on the box. In order to pull the shoulder belt down, and make it more comfortable for a short passenger, virtually all of these devices also pull the lap part of the belt UP, right back onto the tummy. Marketed to kids 50 pounds and up, these devices are also packed with statements that confuse even the most safety conscious parents, like "designed to meet FMVSS 213," a reference to a federal safety standard in crash testing. What's wrong with that picture? That federal standard doesn't even apply to items marketed for children 50 pounds and up! Worse yet, crash tests showed that a three year old dummy was less protected when using one of these adjusters compared to using the regular safety belt. When crash tested with a six year old dummy, the seat belt adjusters didn't improve crash protection either. So, bottom line, if your child doesn't fit that adult belt, get a booster.

### Smart Shopper Tip #4
#### Cars with only lap belts
*"What if my car has only lap belts in the back seat?"*

While lap belts are just fine with infant and convertible seats, they are a no-no when it comes to boosters. If your vehicle doesn't have shoulder belts, check with your vehicle's manufacturer to see if they offer a retrofit kit. If that doesn't work, consider buying a newer vehicle with lap/shoulder belts in the back seat. In the meantime, there are a few seats that can be used with a lap belt for kids over 40 pounds. The Britax Husky, can be used up to 80 pounds, though it requires a tether after 50 pounds. The Britax Marathon and Wizard seats can be used to 65 pounds. The Safety Baby Airway has a harness rated to 50 pounds.

### Smart Shopper Tip #5
#### LATCH system and boosters
*"I have a car with the new LATCH attachments. Do booster seats work with this system?"*

First, just what is LATCH? In a nutshell, LATCH is an easier way to attach a car seat to a vehicle—it is a series of buckles and hooks that latch onto metal loops installed in the seat back of all new vehicles. All car seats manufactured after September 1, 2002 must have LATCH attachments. So do booster seats work with LATCH? Yes and no. Basically, LATCH is only for seats using an internal harness. Some "combo" seats DO have LATCH attachments for you to use when using the internal harness; then you convert the seat to a booster (removing the internal harness) and secure your child with the vehicle lap/shoulder belt. Boosters without an internal harness (hence, most belt-positioning boosters) do NOT have LATCH—they don't need it. Check the seat's instructions before purchasing the seat to confirm LATCH compatibility.

### Smart Shopper Tip #6
*Back Harness Adjuster*

*"I loved our combo seat—until the day I discovered its fatal flaw. When it was cold, my daughter's thick coat required me to loosen the belts on her five-point harness. I discovered this could only be done from the BACK of the seat! What a pain!"*

More and more booster seats are adding five-point harnesses so they can be used at younger ages/weights (some seats start at as little as 20 pounds). The problem? The cheapest combo boosters do NOT have upfront belt adjustments. You must adjust the belts from the back of the seat, which is a pain especially in cold weather. A word to the wise: if you get a combo seat, make sure the belt adjustments are UP FRONT and easy to access.

The question of coats/snowsuits and car seats comes up frequently—we should stress that most safety advocates suggest that a child in a safety seat wear a coat that is no thicker than a polar fleece (the Land's End Squall gets good reviews for this job). Big bulky coats are a hazard. Why? In the event of a crash, the coat will compress, creating a gap between the child and the restraint (and possibly ejecting the child from the seat).

### Smart Shopper Tip #7
*Shoulder belt guides*

*"I read in* Consumer Reports *that some booster seats have dangerous belt guides. Which is best? My son is tall—do we need to use the belt guide at all?"*

In a recent article, *Consumer Reports* pointed out that booster seats come with three different types of belt guides (the part on the booster that positions the vehicle shoulder belt for the child). The best choice is "open loop" guides that allow the belt to slide freely— and retract snugly against the child. Britax, Jupiter, Graco (TurboBooster) and one Cosco booster (the Summit) use these types of guides. The next best choice is a "locking guide" like those seen on the Century Breverra seats. This clip holds the belt tightly, but can introduce slack into the belt (which is dangerous). You should always check to make sure the belt has no slack with these seats. Another bummer with locking guides: it can be difficult for a child to buckle their own seat belt when using a booster that has a locking guide.

Finally, the third type of belt guide is used by most Cosco and Evenflo boosters—these seats use a plastic strip along side the seat to hold the belt. *Consumer Reports* recommends steering clear of these seats—in their tests, these guides could cause the belt to jam or derail, creating dangerous slack in the belt and compromising the safety of the seat. We asked a number of parents with this third kind of seat if they've seen this problem. Most responded that they had not but some had. So if you have one of these, or buy one, make sure that your vehicle's particular belts don't allow this kind of slack. And if your car has adjustable shoulder belts in the back seat (or your child is tall enough to use the booster without any adjuster), just skip using it.

FYI: *Consumer Reports* updated their booster seat ratings in May 2003. We have adjusted this chapter to reflect their latest crash test results; unfortunately, CR still doesn't review many popular booster seat models on the market today (including the Jupiter line).

### Smart Shopper Tip #8
#### Too Tall for a Convertible

*"My daughter is too tall for her convertible car seat but is only 32 pounds. Now what?"*

Many children outgrow their convertibles by height before weight. Most convertibles say that they are good to 40" tall, but a better measure is to make sure the child's shoulders are no higher than the top harness slot. If this happens well before a child is 40 pounds, the next step is a combo booster seat. Most have higher slots (17" or so inches, vs. about 15" for the convertibles). The exception are combo seats from Cosco. None of their combo booster seats have this feature, so unless you know you've got a very short torso child, skip the Cosco combo.

### Smart Shopper Tip #9
#### Booster Testing—Do they Really Test it to 100 lbs?

*"I just bought a booster rated to 100 pounds. What kind of testing is done to make sure that my booster really works for a child that heavy?"*

Little notice has been given to the fact that current regulations only require booster seats to be tested with the three year old (33 pound) and six year old (47 pound) dummies. In fact, current regulations only apply to seats made for children smaller than 50 pounds. So how can so many seats have an upper limit of 80 or even 100 pounds? It all comes down to how the company thinks their product will perform. We contacted several companies that offer boosters rated up to 100 pounds. Britax uses "all dummies on the market appropriate for the rating of the restraint", including the 10 year old, 4'6", 76 pound dummy. Jupiter tests with the 105 pound 5th percentile female dummy. We didn't get any response from Cosco. So it appears that some companies are voluntarily using the appropriate weight of dummies to test their products, but we thought that you should be aware that this is not required.

Frankly, this appears to be a case of where the market is outpacing safety regulations. More and more states are now requiring children to ride in safety seats (that is, boosters) until six years of age and manufacturers are quickly rolling out new seats to the meet the demand. While that's great, we urge the federal government to catch up with its safety regulations on this matter—if a booster claims to be effective to 80 pounds, we expect the federal government to REQUIRE that seat to be crash tested to 80 pounds! Having seat makers voluntarily test their seats and assign a weight limit based on what they "think" is the seat's limit sets a dangerous precedent.

## Safe & Sound

**1 CHECK YOUR VEHICLE'S OWNERS MANUAL.** We're amazed at the detailed info on installing child safety seats you can find in an owner's manual, especially for newer vehicles. All car seats also include detailed installation instructions. Unfortunately, some parents don't read these manuals and attempt to "wing it" during installation.

**2 ALWAYS USE THE LAP/SHOULDER BELT WITH THE BOOSTER**—this provides crucial upper body protection in the case of an accident. NEVER use just the lap belt.

**3 DON'T EXPECT TO USE THAT BOOSTER ON AN AIRPLANE.** FAA rules prohibit the use of booster seats on airlines. Why? Booster seats must be used with a shoulder belt to be effective—and airplanes only have lap belts. Our advice: a child under 40 pounds should ride in a convertible or combo seat on a plane; over 40 pounds, just use the airplane seat belt (no booster). Just make sure to take the booster for the rides to and from the airport. Gate checking (or storing in an overhead bin) will insure that your boosters arrive at your destination with you.

**4 AVOID SHIELD BOOSTERS.** See earlier in this chapter for more detailed info. In short, they are dangerous.

**5 BE CAREFUL OF HAND-ME-DOWN AND SECOND-HAND BAR-GAINS.** Most old booster seats are of the "shield" variety or don't meet current safety standards. Older combo seats usually have the rear harness adjustment, which is a pain to use, as we discussed previously. If you do find a newer used booster, make sure you ask the original owner if it has been in a crash, and then check the seat for recalls (Safety Belt Safe has a great recall list at www.carseat.org). And if the seat has been in a crash, is over six years old or missing its proper labels, stick it in a black garbage bag and throw it away.

**6** ONLY USE CARDBOARD CUPS IN BOOSTER SEAT CUP HOLDERS. You'll note that some seats now come with cup or juice box holders. These are a great convenience, but most manufacturers only recommend cardboard cups or juice boxes be put in such holders. Anything harder (plastic, etc.) is more likely to become a dangerous projectile in a crash.

boosters

**7** WHEN IS A CHILD BIG ENOUGH TO JUST USE THE AUTO'S SAFE-TY BELT? When a child is over 4'9" and can sit with his or her back straight against the back seat cushion (with knees bent over the seat's edge), then he or she can go with just the auto's safety belt. Still have doubts? Try this 5 Step Test from Safety Belt Safe, USA:

◆ Does the child sit all the way back against the auto seat?
◆ Does the belt cross the shoulder between neck and arm?
◆ Is the lap belt as low as possible, touching the thighs?
◆ Can the child stay seated like this for the whole trip?
◆ Do the child's knees bend comfortably at the edge of the auto seat?

If you answered no to any of these questions, your child needs a booster seat, and will probably be more comfortable in one too.

## Money Saving Secrets

**1** COUPONS. If you want to buy online, always check for coupons. Many web sites have coupons deals, but they sometimes forget to tell you. The deals? Well, they aren't as good as they were in the great dot-com giveaway days of 1999 and 2000. But you can still find $10 to $30 off and other deals that are 10% to 20% off. While that isn't a big steal, it might pay for shipping. Find the latest deals with coupon web sites like edealfinder.com and amazing-bargains.com. Both have complete lists of "baby" store coupons.

**2** SHOPPING 'BOTS. Web sites like mySimon.com let you compare prices for booster seats across several sites. You can search for specific brands or models, or look at all booster seat prices.

**3** **DISCOUNTERS.** Stores like Wal-Mart, Target and K-Mart don't have a wide selection of boosters . . . but prices are often lower than stores like Babies R Us, especially if you check their weekly sales. Just make sure that you'll be getting the same features, since some similar seats may lack important things like a front harness adjuster.

**4** **EXPENSIVE BOOSTERS AREN'T NECESSARILY BETTER OR SAFER.** The same rule for car seats applies to boosters: the SAFEST and BEST booster is the one that fits your child, can be correctly installed in your vehicle, and is easy for you to use, every single time. Sometimes the cheapest $25 backless boosters work just as well for your child as the more expensive versions. Letting your child help decide which booster to buy (within a pre-selected list) may also help keep your child happily using the booster until he or she truly fits the adult belts.

## The Best Bets

Here are our top picks for boosters. Detailed reviews of various brands follow this section.

**BEST BET:** Yes, we have a new winner: the *Graco TurboBooster* ($50 to $60) is now our top pick for boosters. This seat can be used from 30 to 100 pounds and offers impressive features for a low price—you get a back that reclines, built-in cup holders and more. Best of all, it features an open loop design that has performed well in crash tests. FYI: Graco sells the TurboBooster in two versions—a backless model ($20) for vehicles with high backrests and a model with the back ($50 to $60). For the latter, there are two pad versions, a basic $50 one and a more plush $60 version. Coming out by the time you read this: Graco will introduce a TurboBooster with reversible pad for $70 to $80. It will have a winter side (fleece) and a summer side (cotton). The only downside to the Graco TurboBooster? It offers little head support for sleeping toddlers. And seats like the new Britax Bodyguard offer better side impact protection (we review this seat in-depth later in this chapter). Nonetheless, we think the Graco TurboBooster is the best bet overall in this category.

**RUNNER UP:** The *Britax BodyGuard* is the latest booster seat from Britax, replacing the previous Starriser/Comfy. This $120 booster's big feature is side impact protection. The wraparound headrest looks like something out of NASCAR. The only problem with this seat? The high starting weight (40 pounds) and stiff price (twice the TurboBooster) make it a tough sell for some parents. And a few parents complain  their kids feel confined in the headrest, limiting their view out the window. Bottom line: this is a great seat, but have your kid sit in it first before buying. And if your car already has side-curtain airbags in the back seat (many new models do), then the BodyGuard may be overkill. Instead, consider the TurboBooster.

Another runner-up: Jupiter Industries *Komfort Kruiser LX100* ($90). Yes, it looks like something NASA might design for future toddler missions to Mars, but the Komfort Kruiser is a great seat and our runner-up choice in this category. It works with kids 33 to 100 pounds—yes, that's 100 pounds. It weighs a mere seven pounds and has deep "side wings" to provide head sup-  port for napping toddlers and side impact protection. The cons? The Kruiser is a bit bulky and wide compared to other seats (it is four inches wider than the Britax BodyGuard), which means it might not work well in cars with tight back seats. It also lacks a five point harness, which parents of younger toddlers may see as an important safety feature. And it is pricey at $90. Not to mention hard to find—only specialty stores and some web sites sell it. Yet we think it is worth the effort to seek out; the Komfort Kruiser is a winner.

**OTHER GOOD CHOICES:** Need a combo seat? The *Cosco Summit High Back Booster* ($100) is a good choice if your child has outgrown their convertible seat, but isn't mature enough to sit in a belt-positioning booster like the Graco TurboBooster. This seat's best feature: a five point harness that can be used for kids 22 to 40 pounds. After that, the seat can used as a belt-positioning booster to  100 pounds. This seat has an excellent shoulder belt adjuster—an open loop that allows the shoulder belt to pull out and retract smoothly. This model also has a front harness adjuster, a two-piece

boosters

harness retainer clip, armrests and cup holder. The Cosco Summit is the only combo seat that *Consumer Reports* recommended in their May 2003 report. FYI: The similar Safety 1st Vantage Point is also made by Cosco, but omits some of the features of the Summit. We'll discuss the differences later in this chapter.

Finally, we should mention the backless version of the Graco TurboBooster—at just $15.74 at Wal-Mart, this is the best value for a backless booster. A great choice for kids over 40 pounds if you've got

head rests and if your child doesn't nap anymore. This is such a terrific price you might want to buy an extra as a spare!

## Name Brand Reviews: Car Booster Seats

### BABY TREND

*1567 S Campus Ave., Ontario, Ca. 91761. For a dealer near you, call 800-328-7363. Web: www.babytrend.com. Customer support: ceciliav@babytrend.com.*

### RECARO START
**Booster type:** high back booster
**Weight Range:** 30 to 80 pounds.
**Price:** $349.99
**Pros:** Very comfortable, many adjustments.
**Cons:** Price! Shoulder belt lock off makes older children feel confined, adjustments hard to use.
**Comments:** Talk about pricey! This seat is off the chart when it comes to the price. So why would someone part with that much money just to get a child booster seat? Well, this seat is made by Recaro, an internationally renowned company that makes high quality racing seats, trucking seats, and car seats. And by car seats, we mean for adults. They've turned this expertise to making a booster seat, and this thing is impressive. It is made like a nice ergonomic office chair. According to our child testers, that translates into fantastic comfort. It also has more adjustments than most carseats, (height, shoulder width, and seat depth adjustments) and it has one of the highest high backs on the market. The deep side wings provide nice sleeping support and possibly side impact support. But the adjustments are cumbersome, so this is not a good seat to share between siblings. And it is a lousy choice for carpools

at a hefty 18.1 pounds. The shoulder belt lock off MUST be used on this booster, for all ages, which can feel very confining for older children. In Europe, this seat is marketed for children 9 months to 12 years, but since it is just a booster, we only recommend it for children at least three years old and 40 pounds. (Note: the Recaro Start is imported to the U.S. by Baby Trend.)

**Rating:** A-

**Dimensions.** Back height: 29", Outside width: 16.5"

## BASIC COMFORT

*445 Lincoln St., Denver, CO, 80203 For a dealer near you, call (800) 456-8687 or (303) 778-7535. Web: www.basiccomfort.com.*

### GALAXY 2000 (HIGH BACK)

**Booster type:** High back (#961)
**Weight range:** 30 to 70 pounds
**Price:** $49 at www.babyabby.com.
**Pros:** Kids like it.
**Cons:** Not good for long trips. High back is not very tall—which means a child will outgrow the seat too quickly.
**Comments:** We couldn't see much point to this seat as a high back booster. The back is so short that most children will outgrow it long before they are done with boosters. The back does give some side sleeping support, but not much. The back is easily removable, and we did like the seat as a backless booster (reviewed below), but if you need a high back booster, choose a taller one or one with better sleeping support.

**Rating:** D

**Dimensions.** Back height: 23", Outside width: 15.5".

### GALAXY 2000 (BACKLESS)

**Booster type:** Backless (#960)
**Weight range:** 40-75 pounds
**Price:** $19 at www.babyabby.com.

**Pros:** Price, kids like it.

**Cons:** Not good for long trips. Can't be used until 40 pounds.

**Comments:** Our child testers gave this backless booster their highest marks. We filled a van with backless boosters and let kids try them all. Over time, the Galaxy 2000 proved to be the favorite. So even though this is a pretty obscure brand (it is hard to find in stores and is mainly sold online), it warrants a closer look. Made entirely of EPS foam, the backless version weighs just two pounds and is covered with a purple quilted material. Children can easily tote the booster with them for carpools, though like most seats made from EPS foam, it is a bit chunky. The shoulder belt adjuster is easy to use: a Velcro sleeve that sits on the child's chest. The inside width of the seat is roomy enough even for older/bigger children. The cons? We didn't like the thick armrests, which may position the lap portion of the belt on the child's thighs not hips. And we found that our child testers couldn't bear to use this seat for long trips, but they sure love it around town and for short (less than an hour or two) trips.

**Rating:** A

**Dimensions.** Outside width: 16.25″, inside width: 12″.

## BRITAX

*13501 South Ridge Drive, Charlotte, NC 28273. For a dealer near you, call (888) 4-BRITAX or (704) 409-1700. Web: www.britaxusa.com*

### BRITAX BODYGUARD

**Booster type:** High back booster.

**Weight range:** 40 to 100 pounds.

**Price:** $120 to $130.

**Pros:** Enhanced side impact protections, built-in lock-offs on base for seat belt (prevents tipping), optional headphones, all cloth spine, adjustable base goes to 13.8″ seat width, back reclines to better fit vehicles with sloping back-seats. One hand height adjustment.

**Cons:** High starting weight (40 pounds). No five-point harness for younger kids. Twice the price of Graco TurboBooster. Wrap-around headrest provides extra side impact protection, but at a cost of visibility—child will not be able to see out of the window as easily.

**Comments:** Britax's brand new booster replaces the previous StarRiser and adds a major new feature: enhanced side impact protections. Basically, these are side wings that wrap around a child's head. Cool, yes, but some parents say their kids complain the seat is too "confining"—and the children can't see out the car window, etc. A word to wise: make sure your child sits in this seat before buying. On the plus side, we like the adjustable base, all cloth spine and a back that reclines to better fit vehicles with sloping backseats. But the price of this seat ($120 to $130) is going to be a deal breaker for some parents. And the tight seat width (13.8″ versus 16″ for the TurboBooster) means larger kids may outgrow this seat too soon. Our take: if your car HAS side curtain air bags in the back seat, then the BodyGuard is redundant. Instead, we suggest the Graco TurboBooster (reviewed later). If your vehicle does not have such side

impact protection, then the BodyGuard may be a good investment.
**Rating:** A
**Dimensions:** Seat weight:12.8 lbs. , 34"H x 17" (backrest width).
Seat width: 13.8". Seat depth: 14.5" *Not certified for use on aircraft because it is a belt-positioning booster.*

### BRITAX HUSKY (FORMERLY THE SUPER ELITE)
**Booster type:** Not a booster, just a harnessed seat.
**Weight range:** 22 to 80 pounds.
**Price:** $230.
**Pros:** The first, and only, 5 point harness seat for kids up to 80 pounds.
**Cons:** Did we mention it is $230? It is also quite wide and heavy.
**Comments:** Britax first released this seat, originally called the Super Elite, in May 2001. Unfortunately, demand for this seat far outstripped the limited supply Britax manufactured, despite the steep price. So, what's all the fuss about? This seat really does fit children from a year and 22 pounds, up to 8 or 9 year olds and 80 pounds—with a five point harness. It is the ONLY seat on the market to have a five point harness for kids up to 80 pounds. So, what's to not like about this seat, except for its hefty price tag? First, the seat will also take over your backseat and is, at 23 pounds, way too heavy to move between cars. Second, it is still very hard to find. Britax promises to make more of them when it renames the seat the "Husky" and adds a recline bar and more padding, plus LATCH attachments (the Husky will be out by the time you read this). The Husky is perfect for children who have hit 40 pounds but aren't ready (or their parents aren't ready) for the lap/shoulder belt and a booster, mostly kids three and under. A few big kids like this seat fine, but most will probably prefer buckling themselves into a regular booster. The other down side to this seat is that it *requires* the tether past 50 pounds. So if you have an older car that didn't come with tether anchors, you'll have to get them retrofitted (tether anchors can be added to most 1989 and newer cars. Call your dealer— many will do it for free). Yet another con: if you think this seat will be just as nice as the Britax Roundabout or Freeway, but will just last longer, think again. This is a nice seat, but doesn't have all the amazing features of the Britax Roundabout.
**Rating:** B
**Dimensions.** Seat weight: 23 pounds, 22"W x 22.5"D x 30.25"H. Top Harness Slot: 20", Back height: 29.5", Seat width: 21.5".
*Not certified for use on aircraft because it is too wide.*

### BRITAX LAPTOP

**Booster type:** Energy absorbing restraint
**Weight Range:** 30 to 65 pounds.
**Price:** $49.99
*This seat is now discontinued.*

### BRITAX MARATHON AND WIZARD

**Booster type:** Not a booster, a convertible
**Weight range:** birth to 65 pounds.
**Price:** $230 for the Marathon; $250 for the Wizard.
**Pros:** Harness goes to 65 pounds.
**Cons:** Price. Children will probably reach height limit before 65 pound weight limit. Probably won't look very cool to kids that are five or older.
**Comments:** Okay, so what's a convertible seat doing in this chapter? Well, good question—the Marathon is the first (and so far only) convertible seat to use a five point harness up to 65 pounds. (Britax's Husky, by contrast, goes up to 80 pounds but is a forward only seat). The Marathon can be used rear-facing for infants to toddlers, five to 30 pounds. Then it can be used as a forward facing seat from at least one year old to six or seven years of age, 20 to 65 pounds. So if you've got a young child (under three years of age) who has reached 40 pounds and outgrown their convertible seat but you don't want to go without a five-point harness (as with a traditional belt-positioning booster), this may be a good choice for you. It certainly is expensive, but has all the amenities of the Britax Roundabout PLUS having a higher weight limit and a higher back. So, unlike the Super Elite/Husky, this seat should fit in most cars, even if you have more than one child in your backseat. The Marathon has a harness adjuster that always moves easily to tighten and loosen the harness, a tether that can be used forward and rear facing, and more. We anticipate most families choosing this seat from the start, or when their baby outgrows the infant seat, banking on wanting the higher weight limit down the road, rather than purchasing this seat when a child reaches 40 pounds at age three. The Wizard is very similar Marathon, but one big difference: while the Marathon has four harness slots; the Wizard has a sliding mechanism to position the harness anywhere between the lowest

slots and the highest slots (like the Britax Advantage compared to the Britax Roundabout). Hence, the Wizard makes it easier to adjust the belt heights; whether this convenience is worth the extra $20, is a toss-up. Another difference with the Wizard: it has enhanced side-impact protection (basically deep side wings) that the Marathon lacks. As with the BodyGuard, however, the side wings get mixed reviews from parents—some say their kids feel too confined in the seat and give the Wizard a thumbs down, despite the added side impact protection.

**Rating:** A

**Dimensions.** Top Harness Slot: 17", Back height: 24.5"

### BRITAX STARRISER COMFY

*The StarRiser Comfy has been discontinued, replaced by the BodyGuard (see earlier for a review). But you might still see this seat for sale online, so here is a review.*

**Booster type:** High Back and backless

**Weight Range:** 30 to 80 pounds as a high back and backless booster

**Price:** $100.

**Pros:** Very narrow, very tall back, back is removable.

**Cons:** Not as cushy as some others. Height adjustments tricky.

**Comments:** Britax's StarRiser Comfy has lots of adjustments, including seat width (which is unusual in this category). The base starts at a mere 13" wide, which is terrific for narrow spaces. As the child gets bigger, the base expands to 15" wide. The headrest is unique too. It looks rather space-age, but does gives some support to sleeping children as well as head support if your vehicle doesn't have head rests. This seat has one of the tallest backs (equal only to the Jupiter Komfort Rider GTX and Baby Trend Recaro Start), great if you've got a tall kid. The backrest, comes off, leaving a backless booster you can pop into a carpool or take when traveling. *Consumer Reports* gave it excellent marks in their recent crash tests; the design of the belt guide for the StarRiser was considered superior to competitors. So overall, this is a perfect choice if you need head support even for an older child, plus sleeping support, or have a very narrow spot for your booster. The only downside to this seat? It isn't quite as plush or padded as others, like the Komfort Kruiser by Jupiter. The StarRiser Comfy also lacks a five point harness, which some parents might prefer for younger toddlers that have outgrown their convertible seats. And the height adjustments are a bit tricky, according to parents we interviewed. Yet, overall, this is our great choice for a booster—if you can still find it.

**Rating:** A
**Seat weight/dimensions:** 8.8 lbs. 19.25″ x 26.5″ x 25″ Back
height: 29″ totally extended, Outside width: 13″-16″.
*Not certified for use in airplanes.*

### BRITAX STARRISER

*The StarRiser has been discontinued,
replaced by the BodyGuard (see earlier
for a review). But you might still see this
seat for sale online, so here is a review.*
**Booster type:** backless
**Weight Range:** 30 to 80 pounds

**Price:** $45
**Pros:** Very narrow but expandable for older children. Versatile, well
designed and can be used starting at 30 pounds.
**Cons:** Price. Not very cushy. Fabric choices not that exciting.
**Comments:** What's the difference between the Britax StarRiser
Comfy and the plain StarRiser? The Comfy has the back/headrest;
the Starriser is just the base. Again, this is the perfect booster for
those really narrow spots. Nothing beats its 13″ footprint, which can
be expanded wider as a child grows. The padding on this base is
adequate, but nothing special. And the price is high, compared to
the backless version of the Graco TurboBooster. The shoulder belt
adjuster is unlike any other, but isn't too difficult to use. Later versions of this seat have a crotch strap to keep children from sub-
marining down in the seat. Like all backless boosters, this seat
requires a lap/shoulder belt, head rests in your car, and gives no
sleeping support. But it is also very safe, easy to use, and inconspicuous. If you can find it, the StarRiser would be make a good
choice for a backless booster.
**Rating:** A
**Dimensions:** Weight: 5.4 lbs. 15.5″W x 9″H x 16.5″D
Outside Width: 13″-16″

### BRITAX ROADSTER

**Booster type:** High Back and backless
**Weight range:** 40 to 65 pounds as high
back booster, 40 to 100 pounds (56″) as
backless booster
**Price:** $75 to $80
**Pros:** Can use it up to 100 pounds.
**Cons:** Starting weight is 40 pounds, and
high back can only be used to about 65 pounds.
**Comments:** Britax's cushiest booster—we like the multiple adjust-
ments, although the seat does look like one of those creatures on

Mystery Science Theater. The back just slides up and down to the proper position, and the shoulder belt adjuster is that open loop kind the *Consumer Reports* liked in their tests. You use the base with back up to 65 pounds; after that, you use the base alone from 65 to 100. The backless base is safe for use with children who are over 40 pounds (as long as they have head support in the vehicle), but this is pretty pricey if you only want a backless booster. The weight of this seat (7 pounds) makes it car-pool friendly. It also comes in some great prints, like Big Cat and Cowmooflauge, and has more padding than the StarRiser Comfy. It is also wider and deeper. Like most Britax seats, this is well-made but very expensive. Even though the Roadster and StarRiser Comfy look alike, the latter is a better buy—the starting weight on the Roadster is 40 pounds (versus just 30 for the StarRiser Comfy) and you can't use the back beyond 65 pounds (the StarRiser Comfy goes to 80).

**Rating:** A-

**Dimensions:** 7 lbs. 18" x 19"x 27.5"

Back height: 23.5" totally extended, Seat width: 16".
*Not certified for airline use.*

## CENTURY

*See Graco for contact info.*

### BREVERRA ASCEND
**Booster type:** Combo
**Weight range:** 30 to 40 pounds with harness, 30 to 80 pounds as booster
**Price:** $80
**Pros:** Affordable. Five point harness (30 to 40 pounds) with a front harness adjuster; regular belt-positioning booster to 80 pounds. Higher harness slots than other seats. Cool cup holder.

**Cons:** Shoulder belt adjuster clip locks belt in place, which makes it difficult for young ones to buckle themselves in. Doesn't always fit well in cars, some kids find it uncomfortable, and older kids may outgrow it before 80 pounds.

**Comments:** The Breverra Ascend was one of the first combo seats to come out, and has the most important features: a front harness adjuster and higher harness slots. But if your kid still falls asleep a lot in the car, this seat will be a real trial, as it doesn't give much side support. The seat isn't very tall, either, with a back height of just 24", and kids may outgrow this by height before they are ready for adult belts. The shoulder belt adjuster does lock the belt in place, keeping your child from introducing slack. *Consumer Reports* recommends using this type of adjuster "with care" to make sure the belt is always tight. The big bummer with this type of clip: when it locks the belt, kids may find it difficult to buckle themselves in to the booster by themselves—which is a big pain, from a parent's perspective, of course. The seat does include armrests, a two-piece harness retainer clip, a cup holder, and the all-important higher harness slots. In a previous edition of this book, we recommended the Breverra Ascend as our top pick—it was one of the first combo seats out there and still has some great features. But newer models (see our best bets) have out-shined this seat. And the locking shoulder belt adjuster makes it a pain to use.

**Rating:** B

**Seat weight:** 12 lbs.

**Dimensions. Top Harness Slot:** 16.8", Back height: 24", Seat width: 17".

### Next Step

**Booster type:** Combo

**Weight range:** 20 to 40 pounds with harness, 30 to 80 pounds as a high back booster.

**Price:** Used to come in several versions, but now there is just one—it sells for $90 to $120.

**Pros:** Can use starting at just 20 pounds (and one year of age). Higher top harness slots, some models have front harness adjuster, armrests pivot to allow for growing child. Rated "Excellent" in *Consumer Reports* crash tests.

**Cons:** Recline is a joke; no front adjustment for harness belts in SE version. More expensive than similar seats without many extra features.

## What is EPS foam?

You'll note more and more boosters (and other car seats) are now using EPS foam. So what is EPS foam?

EPS (expanded polystyrene) is the foam you see in bicycle helmets and other safety equipment to protect the head from injury. EPS foam is also used in packing to prevent damage during shipping. As a closed-cell, rigid plastic, EPS is dense but very lightweight. Hence it provides protection without adding to the weight of a seat—one booster seat we'll review in this chapter, the Komfort Kruiser by Jupiter, is made entirely of EPS foam. The seat weighs a mere seven pounds, yet can safety protect a 100 pound child from injury in an accident.

**Comments:** Introduced in 1998, the Next Step was a revolutionary combination of a toddler seat with five-point harness (for babies older than a year and weighing 20 to 40 pounds) and a belt-positioning booster (30 pounds to 80 pounds). This sounds like a great idea since you can eliminate the need for a convertible seat, right? Wrong. Babies need to stay rear facing to at *least* 12 months old, but most can stay rear facing much longer, which is far safer. So the idea of going from an infant seat to a Century Next Step usually doesn't work in practice: a regular convertible is still going to be needed to keep babies rear facing to 18-24 months, and then can be used forward facing, giving much more side and sleeping support than a seat like the Next Step. And forget about the Next Step's alleged recline feature; it's a joke! Small infants who nap will find this seat very uncomfortable, in our experience, since it provides little head support and sits rather straight up. The best use of the Next Step is for children who outgrow their convertible by height before they reach 40 pounds, or families who need a replacement seat for an already-forward-facing toddler. One bonus: it does have a front adjuster (some earlier versions of the seat lacked that feature). Aside from all this criticism, we should note most parents we interviewed who have the Next Step seem very pleased with it. But what was revolutionary in 1998 now is showing its age.

**Rating:** B+

**Dimensions:** 14″ x 18″ x 30″h. Top Harness Slot: 17″, Back height: 25.5″, Seat width: 17.5″.

# Cosco

*2525 State St., Columbus, IN 47201. Call (800) 544-1108 for a dealer near you (or 514-323-5701 for a dealer in Canada). Web: www.djgusa.com.*

### COSCO ALPHA OMEGA (AKA, THE EDDIE BAUER THREE IN ONE)

**Booster type:** convertible and combo

**Weight range:** birth to 35 pounds rear facing, 20 to 40 forward facing with harness, 30 to 80 as booster.

**Price:** $129 to $149. The Eddie Bauer version is $160.

**Pros:** Multi-purpose seat, from infant to toddler and beyond.

**Cons:** Twisty straps, Cosco's abysmal safety record, low top harness slots, shoulder belt adjuster may allow dangerous slack.

**Comments:** This seat tries to do everything, holding children from birth to 80 pounds. Basically, this seat morphs from a convertible seat to a booster; one of the few on the market. Occasionally, this works out. The seat has some very nice features, like a no-thread harness with 4 positions, several recline settings, a removable base for installation in smaller spaces, and a selection of good-looking fabric covers. But the Alpha Omega really falls down when children hit about three years old. Lots of kids outgrow the seat height-wise, with their shoulders getting taller than the top harness slot. There is, in fact, a 5th "slot", but it can only be used in booster mode. So families are stuck buying a combo seat with higher harness slots for the child from 30 to 40 pounds. And of course, some parents just graduate the child to the booster too early. When a child gets to 40 pounds and at least three years old, they can move back into the AO. As a booster, this seat has a number of failings. It has the poorly designed shoulder belt adjuster that concerned *Consumer Reports* in a recent report—the adjuster can introduce dangerous slack in the belt. This is the only booster we've seen that has failed to properly position the lap/shoulder belt on a child – perhaps because it encouraged the parents to use it on a young child, and perhaps because it lacks armrests to keep the lap portion of the belt low. On the plus side, the massive base must be removed for booster seat use, which helps it fit in smaller spaces.

Despite all the criticism of this seat, it remains a best-seller . . . so Cosco keeps rolling out new versions of it. The latest version, the Alpha Omega Elite ($150), now can be used up to 100 pounds and features a new front harness adjustment, narrower base and three-position crotch strap adjustment. Those refinements do address some of our criticism, but we still don't recommend this seat for the above-mentioned reasons.

**Rating:** C

**Dimensions.** Top Harness slot: 15", Back height: 24.5 inches in booster mode, Outside width: 18".

### Cosco Auto Booster Seat & High Rise Auto Booster Seat

**Booster type:** backless booster

**Weight range:** 30-100 pounds. Kids must be 52" or less.

**Price:** $17 to $39

**Pros:** Cheap backless booster. Cup holder.

**Cons**: None.

**Comments:** These very simple and affordable seats are backless boosters. Both versions have padded armrests and a fold-down cup holder. The "High Rise" version adds a mesh storage pocket. Both are very similar in dimension and design.

**Rating:** B

**Dimensions:** 16"D, 17"W, 9.5"H.

### COSCO GRAND EXPLORER

**Booster type:** shield and backless booster

**Weight range:** 30-40 pounds with shield, 40-80 as backless booster.

**Price:** $19 for the regular version to $30 for the Eddie Bauer padding.

**Pros:** Cheap.

**Cons:** Dangerous to use as a shield booster; no shoulder belt adjuster

**Comments:** Cosco makes the only shield booster still on the market. The rest failed the new test limits in the mid-1990's, but this seat still passes the crash tests. Numerous reports have linked this shield booster to severe injuries and death in real world crashes, but Cosco persists in saying that it is safe when used for kids in the 30 to 40 pound rage. Bottom line: we suggest you steer very clear of this seat as a shield booster, or any other shield booster. This seat CAN be used quite safely as a backless booster from 40-80 pounds. The Grand Explorer does the same job as any other backless booster by properly positioning the lap portion of the belt on the child's hips, not stomach. As backless boosters go, this one is quite minimal. The Grand Explorer is fairly narrow; many children will find it uncomfortable as they grow older. It doesn't have any shoulder belt adjuster, so it may leave the shoulder belt uncomfortably resting on a child's neck. So if you've got one of these seats, throw away the shield and use it for kids over 40 pounds as a backless booster. It is a good choice to stow in the trunk for a booster emergency.

**Rating:** D

**Seat outside width:** 16.5″

*Not certified for use on aircraft because it has no rigid seat back.*

### COSCO HIGH BACK BOOSTER
### (AKA THE COMMUTER, VENTURA, EDDIE BAUER VERSIONS)

**Booster type:** combo

**Weight range:** 22-40 with harness, 30-80 as belt positioning booster. A new version of this seat (to debut in late 2002) will be certified up to 100 pounds.

**Price:** Three different versions, $39 to $199

**Pros:** Inexpensive, fits great in cars, five-point harness option from 22 to 40 pounds, headrest, armrests, storage bag, cup holder.

**Cons:** Straps twist, rear harness adjuster in most models, Cosco's abysmal safety record. Seat belt guide can cause belt to jam, creating dangerous slack. *Consumer Reports* did not recommend this seat for that reason.

**Comments:** Like Century's Breverra, Cosco's High Back booster comes in several versions. At $39, the regular high back booster (02-200) is the cheapest combo seat on the market. It does the job, providing a five point harness from 22 to 40 pounds, then working as a booster from 30 to 80 pounds. But this seat has cut corners at every turn. First and foremost, the top harness slots on this seat are the same as Cosco's convertible, the Touriva, meaning that lots of kids get too tall for this seat before they reach 40 pounds. Second, the only way to adjust the harness is in back, an almost impossible feat on a daily basis. Third, the tether strap is also a total pain to adjust and get tight.

Cosco plans to debut a slightly revised version of the high back booster, which should be out by the time you read this. The 22-208 model will add a two-piece chest clip, cup holder and front belt adjuster for $49.

The Ventura (02-240) is the next step up at $50, just adding armrests. The first significant improvement comes in the Commuter (02-239 pictured at right), which sports a front harness adjuster as well as the cup holder and armrests, and goes for about $59.

The Eddie Bauer versions of this seat use exactly the same shell, just with the Eddie Bauer covers, both the more traditional beige colors and the new "sport" look in blues, yellows and blacks. The basic Eddie Bauer version, sans front harness adjuster, starts at $59, with the deluxe version with front adjuster going for $79. For a whopping $199 you can get this seat with a leather cover and front adjuster.

While this seat does fit terrifically in cars, and some models do feature the front harness adjuster, we don't give it high marks. The expensive versions cost as much as other brands' combo seats that have higher harness slots and will last most kids longer. And Cosco's safety track record gives us pause. Quite frankly, Cosco has had so many safety recalls in the past several years for their car seats that we just don't feel comfortable recommending anything made by them. We also note that parent reviews of Cosco's boosters have been mixed. For every parent we interviewed who liked their Cosco booster, another gave it a thumbs down—some gripes were minor (Cosco's light tan fabric on some of the boosters stains too easily), while other frustrations were more series (quality complaints, straps that twist and are hard to adjust, etc.). And, most importantly, we should note that *Consumer Reports* did not recommend this Cosco booster seat due to a poorly designed shoulder belt adjuster clip which the magazine claimed in its tests could jam or derail the safety belt.

*(Note: Cosco has since released the Summit, reviewed below, with*

*a safer, open loop shoulder belt adjuster).*
**Rating** (for the Commuter, 02-480 pictured above): C
**Dimensions.** Top Harness Slot: 15.3", Back height: 25", Seat width: 17.3".

### COSCO COMPLETE VOYAGER AND VISTA
**Booster type:** high back booster
**Weight range:** 30-80 pounds.
**Price:** 8 different versions, $29 (Complete Voyager) to $39 (Vista)
**Pros:** Inexpensive, fits great in cars, armrests (Vista), cup holder.
**Cons:** Cosco's abysmal safety record. Seat belt guide can cause belt to jam, creating dangerous slack. No five-point harness.

**Comments:** The Complete Voyager is the cheapest high back booster out there. And it does the job, positioning the lap belt correctly on the child's hips, as well as raising the child up to fit the shoulder belt. If the shoulder belt is still too tall for the child, the adjuster on this seat iis helpful. Unlike the Cosco high back booster versions listed above, the plain booster has the shoulder belt guide molded right into the shell, which may help it work properly. The parents we polled found that this adjuster worked OK. For an additional $10, you can get the Vista, which adds armrests. Your child might like these, and they help keep the lap belt nice and low on the hips. If you don't have a problem with the shoulder belt adjuster (try it in your car with your child), then this may be a good, inexpensive booster choice.
**Rating:** B
**Back height:** 25", Seat width: 17.3".

### COSCO SUMMIT
### (AKA SAFETY 1ST VANTAGE POINT)
**Booster type:** combo
**Weight range:** 22-40 lbs. with harness, 30-100 lbs. as belt positioning booster.
**Price:** $79 for the Safety 1st Vantage Point, $99 for the Cosco Summit.
**Pros:** First combo seat to have an open shoulder belt adjuster, neat look, armrests that raise and lower. 100 pound weight limit.
**Cons:** Top harness slots no higher than most convertibles, Cosco's abysmal safety record.
**Comments:** This is the first combo seat to provide an excellent

shoulder belt adjuster – an open loop that allows the shoulder belt to pull out and retract smoothly. Cosco matched this feature with a 100 pound limit on the booster, a front harness adjuster, a two-piece harness retainer clip, armrests and cup holder. Sounds perfect, right? Well, not quite. The big disappointment with this seat is that top harness slots are no higher than an average convertible, about 15". So some kids can use this seat to a full 40 pounds, but many will outgrow it by height before weight. It also comes with the fussy Cosco tether adjuster, and Cosco's dubious track safety record. But if you think that your child is average or short in the torso, then this might be the seat for you. The Summit and the Safety 1st Vantage Point share the same shell, but the Summit sports more features, including a base that reclines (though the completely upright position gives more crash protection), one-hand adjustment for the harness, swiveling armrests, and some extra inserts. The Safety 1st Vantage Point is more bare bones, omitting all those features.

**Rating:** B+

**Dimensions.** Top Harness Slot: 15", Back height: 27", Seat width: 18".

# EDDIE BAUER, SAFETY 1ST, NASCAR

All of these seats are made by Cosco; see the above reviews for more details. The Eddie Bauer high back booster (02-880 MBP, pictured at right, for $79) has the same features as the Commuter High Back Booster, model 02-880 WAL, but costs $10 more. Frankly, we don't see why anyone should buy the EB models. All Cosco does is put some tan fabric on their seats, slap the Eddie Bauer name on top and then raise the price. Of  course, the Eddie Bauer name has more cache than Cosco, but what's the point? It's the same product. The Eddie Bauer seats cost an extra $10 or more for the very same thing. And that light tan fabric? It's a stain magnet. We say skip it. We realize that some kids might get jazzed by the NASCAR cover or the Eddie Bauer look . . . and that might get them to buy into the booster seat concept in general. Some parents may think that is worth $10; and we see their point. But since the goal of our books is to save money, we say skip these brands.

## EVENFLO

*1801 Commerce Dr., Piqua, OH 45356. For a dealer near you, call (800) 233-5921 or (937) 415-3300. In Canada, PO Box 1598, Brantford, Ontario, N3T 5V7. Web: www.carseat.com.*

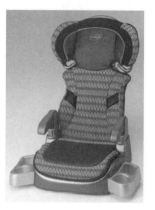

### EVENFLO BIG KID

**Weight:** 40 to 80 pounds.
**Booster type:** Belt-positioning
**Pros:** Low price.
**Cons:** Not out as of this writing, so no parent feedback yet.
**Price:** $39-59; a backless version will sell for $19.
**Comments:** This seat will be available by the time you read this; we did get a sneak peak of this booster at a recent trade show. Basically, this is Evenflo's answer to the Graco

Turbo Booster—this belt-positioning seat has a unique feature: the company promises it will be "fully adjustable" both in height and lap depth. The latter is unique, as most boosters just adjust in height. The back removes as kids grow bigger, adding a discreet boost to older kids without having them look "uncool." On the plus side, it is less expensive than the Graco Turbo Booster (a $40 version in Target is especially affordable). On the downside, the padding is a bit more skimpy than the Graco, making this seat less comfy for longer trips. A backless version of the Big Kid will be sold later in 2004; this will replace the popular Right Fit (reviewed later in this section).
**Rating:** B

### EVENFLO COMET

**Weight:** 20-80 pounds; 20 to 40 pounds with harness. 30-80 pounds as belt positioning booster.
**Booster type:** Combo
**Price:** $70 to $90
**Pros:** First combo to offer extras: EPS foam in the head rest, harness adjustment knob, padded armrests, nice color fabric choices (five muted grays, blues).
**Cons:** Doesn't offer much in the way of sleeping support, adjusting the

harness is tricky. Shoulder belt adjuster is the kind that locks belt in place, possibly creating slack in the belt.

**Comments:** This seat started out as the Apollo, Evenflo's first attempt at a high-end booster to compete with the likes of the Britax Starriser. We liked the seat's features, but the price—it sold for $100—was too high and it quickly disappeared from the market. Evenflo decided to scale back the Apollo and drop a few features and extra padding. The result: the Comet, which now sells for as little as $70 at Wal-Mart. Yes, the seat still has some nice pros: EPS foam and a "height right" feature. EPS foam is that stuff you find in bike helmets, and we like the idea of that relatively soft foam behind a child's head. The up front knob to tighten the harness (called "tension right") is a great feature too. The "height right" feature to change the harness slot heights from the front of the seat was a little tricky to figure out, but once you master it, you can avoid re-threading the harness as your child grows. So, why did we lower this seats rating? *Consumer Reports* crash tests, for one. In May 2003, CR reported that in their crash tests, the shoulder belt disengaged from the Comet . . . and that the seat's belt guide may prevent the belt from retracting. As a result, we believe this seat is not the best choice among combo seats on the market. Another problem: this seat is a loser when it comes to sleeping children. The wings just aren't deep enough, and the seat is just too upright, to keep a sleeping child from slumping. That's a problem when Evenflo pitches the seat to parents of toddlers who weigh has little as 20 pounds. 20 pound toddlers may be as young as six months to one year—still prime napping time, of course. And the Comet (in booster mode) still features those shoulder belt adjusters that allow a child to put slack in the belt, but don't allow the belt to properly retract. Like the Breverra, this makes it more difficult for a toddler to buckle themselves in when the seat is in booster mode (when you use the vehicle safety belt). So if you use this seat, keep an eye on your child until you find out if this is going to be a problem for you.

**Rating:** C

**Dimensions.** Top Harness Slot: 16.8", Back height: 27", Seat width: 17".

### EVENFLO CHASE COMFORT TOUCH

**Booster type:** Combo

**Weight:** 20-80 pounds; 20 to 40 pounds with harness, belt-positioning booster for 30 to 80 pounds.

**Price:** $80

**Comments:** This seat is very similar as the Express (see review below), but it adds fancier padding (the Comfort Touch), armrests and a cup holder. For this, you pay an extra $20. Also new: the "Chase

Combo" seat will be similar to the Express Comfort Touch, but will add armrests and cup holder.

**Rating:** B

### EVENFLO SIGHTSEER COMFORT TOUCH

**Booster type:** high back booster

**Weight:** Belt-positioning booster for 30 to 80 pounds.

**Price:** $49

**Pros:** Low price, Comfort Touch padding, arm rests

**Cons:** Shallow sides and upright design give minimal sleeping support. Back height won't support older kids. Ugly fabrics.

**Comments:** Basically, this seat is like the Express Comfort Touch, but without the five-point harness (hence it is just a belt-positioning booster). The Comfort Touch padding on this booster gets a big thumbs up. And parents like the price tag. *Consumer Reports* didn't like the shoulder belt adjuster, noting that it allowed slack in the belt, but most parents we talked to didn't actually have this problem. And Evenflo's designers picked some ugly fabrics for this booster, including a hideous blue check pattern called "blueberries."

**Rating:** C

**Dimensions.** Back height: 25.3", Seat width: 17.5".

### EVENFLO RIGHT FIT

**Booster type:** Backless booster

**Weight:** 40-80 pounds

**Price:** $25

**Pros:** Low cost; good option for kids who are too cool for boosters.

**Cons:** Only works if your car's back seat provides adequate head support, doesn't give any sleeping support. Can't be used until 40 pounds.

**Comments:** (This is scheduled to be discontinued in 2004, but limited quantities may still be for sale through out the year. A similar seat, the backless Big Kid—reviewed earlier—will be its replacement). In a previous edition of this book, we dismissed this seat as an inferior choice. Since then, we've had a change of heart. Child safety seat techs pointed out this seat fits a good niche in the market; we also noticed the Right Fit scored well in *Consumer Reports* recent crash tests. Note: in order to use the Evenflo Right Fit, your vehicle

must have a back seat that supports your child's head and neck. (Certain vehicles with very low seat backs would NOT be acceptable). And if your child still takes naps in the car, you probably want to skip this seat and pick a high back booster with sleeping wings. The Right Fit does include a shoulder belt adjuster, which properly positions the belt on your child's neck, but it is kind of a pain to use. Perhaps this booster seat's best feature is its anonymity—the Right Fit is wide enough to comfortably fit small 10 or 12 year olds, yet discrete enough to keep them from getting teased for riding in a "baby seat." The pad seems thin, but kids find the seat comfortable. Unlike most other backless boosters, you can probably find this one at a local store, so your child can give it a nay or yeah before you buy it. Overall this is one of the best backless boosters on the market (next to the backless Graco TurboBooster and the Britax Starriser).
**Rating:** B+

### EVENFLO VISION (AKA EXPRESS)
**Booster type:** Combo
**Weight:** 20-80 pounds; 20 to 40 pounds with harness, belt-positioning booster for 30 to 80 pounds.
**Price:** $59
**Pros:** Low price for a combo with front harness adjuster and higher harness slots. Great padding.
**Cons:** Twisty straps and fussy harness adjuster can be a nightmare. Not much sleeping support.

**Comments:** This low-price booster is a scaled down version of the Express, a similar model it replaced. The differences? The Vision has armrests and front harness adjustment. A cup holder attaches to the front of the seat. Basically, that's it—there is no Comfort Touch padding. And like some other cheaper carseats, there is a trade off between price and ease of use. Many parents we interviewed liked the harness straps, but others find them twisty and hard to use. The front harness adjuster (located on the harness, below the harness retainer clip) works well and fits nicely on most kids, but may not give a snug fit on smaller children. The padding of this seat passed the kid testers with flying colors, but the shallow side wings and upright seating position don't give much sleeping support, much like our criticism of the Evenflo Comet. *Consumer Reports* gave this seat a thumbs down because of the shoulder belt adjuster, used in booster mode. However, we asked many parents about this, and most said that it wasn't a problem—the shoulder belt was able to retract properly through these belt guides, perhaps because they are molded into the shell. We recommend that you try this out in your own car right away so you know if you are going to have a problem when your child is using the seat as a booster. So overall, we like this seat, but some folks will find it frustrating.

**Rating:** B

**Dimensions.** Top Harness Slot: 17.3", Back height: 25.3", Seat width: 17.5".

## FISHER-PRICE

*636 Grand Ave., East Aurora, NY 14052. For a dealer near you, call (800) 828-4000 or (716) 687-3000. Web: www.fisher-price.com*

Note: Fisher Price announced in 2001 they will no longer make car seats. So why include them in this chapter? Well, you might still see a few of these booster seats on eBay or on discount store shelves as retailers sell through their inventory. Though the Fisher Price Grow With Me was an excellent combo seat, beware that many "new in box" Grow with Me seats sold on eBay come from Canada. These seats are illegal to use in the U.S. Why? Canada tests the seats to different standards than the U.S. (Canada requires all seats tested with a tether strap) and that can mean different weight limits. This is not to say the Canadian standards are inferior to the U.S. rules; they are just different. As a result, federal law forbids the use of car seats manufactured for Canada here in the U.S.

## GRACO

*P.O Box 100, Elverson, PA 19520. For a dealer near you, call (800) 345-4109, (610) 286-5951. In Canada, call (800) 667-8184. Web: www.gracobaby.com*

### GRACO CARGO: TREASURED, ULTRA, AND PLATINUM

**Booster type:** Combo

**Weight range:** 20-40 pounds with harness, 30 to 80 pounds as high back booster.

**Price:** $59 to $99

**Pros:** Good price; starts at 20 pounds, upfront belt adjustment on some models, narrow.

**Cons:** Skimpy padding, mediocre shoulder belt adjusters.

**Comments:** Graco's first attempt at a booster, the Cherished CarGo, has give way to a whole line of CarGos: the Treasured, Ultra and Platinum. The Cherished CarGo felt flimsy, and the harness adjuster clip (paper-clip style) often broke. But these newer models all have the nice two-piece harness retainer clip and also have a handy cup holder. The Grand CarGo has the front harness adjuster right on the harness, like the Evenflo Express, while the Ultra has a traditional A-lock front adjuster. Graco really missed the boat with their Treasured CarGo—it has that rear harness adjuster that will likely keep even the most diligent parent from keeping the straps tight every day. If your pre-schooler still naps in the car, the Ultra and Platinum models are a good choice since they have the up-front adjuster and nice deep wings that gives some sleeping support. The top-of-the line Platinum CarGo adds a two-position recline, more plush padding and extra storage pockets—nice, but it runs a whopping $99. This version might be best for younger kids that are still napping in their car seats. The Graco CarGos are also the narrowest combos on the market . . . great if you've got two or three kids to squeeze next to each other. The biggest problem with all the CarGo is their mediocre shoulder belt adjuster. Like the Century Breverras, these clips tend to lock the belt into place, which might introduce dangerous slack in the belt. And they may make it difficult for your toddler to buckle themselves into their seat, a major pain as we discussed earlier in this chapter. We'll give these seats separate grades since their different features make the Ultra and Platinum CarGos clearly superior to the Treasured CarGo.

**Ratings:** Treasured CarGo: C; Ultra Cargo: B, Platinum CarGo: B
**Dimensions.** Top Harness slot: 17", Back height: 26.5", Outside width: 16".

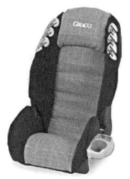

### GRACO MY CARGO

**Booster type:** High back booster
**Weight Range:** 30 to 80 pounds.
**Price:** $49
**Pros:** Deep side wings, narrow.
**Cons:** Shoulder belt adjuster, skimpy padding. No five point harness.
**Comments:** The My CarGo is just the booster part of the CarGos listed above. If you don't need the five point harness (hence your child is over 30 pounds and

mature enough to sit in the seat with just the auto safety belt), save the $20 and go right for the plain booster. Compared to other high back boosters, this one is adequate. It does have deeper sides than most, which may give your child more sleeping support. It is on the narrow side, but not nearly as narrow as the Britax Starriser Comfy. The shoulder belt adjuster, just like with the other CarGos, is mediocre (see the previous review of the CarGos for more details).

**Rating:** B
**Dimensions.** Back height: 26.5", Outside width: 16"

### GRACO TURBOBOOSTER

**Booster type:** Belt-positioner
**Weight range:** 30 to 100 pounds as high back booster (backless, it is 40 to 100 lbs).
**Price:** $50 to $60, depending on the fabric. Backless version runs $15.74 at Wal-Mart.
**Pros:** Top choice in booster market—both affordable and well-designed.
**Cons:** Doesn't have as much side impact protection as Britax Bodyguard.
**Comments:** This is our top pick as a great, affordable booster seat. We love the sharp design and open loop belt adjuster, which does away with all our previous complaints about belts that jammed. Graco did this one right: you get padded armrests that are height adjustable, EPS foam, hide-away cup holders and more. The seat pad removes for cleaning and there is an easy one-hand adjustment for the headrest. By the time you read this, Graco will debut a version of the TurboBooster with a reversible pad (fleece for winter/cotton for summer). Heck, Graco even does this seat in cool looking fabrics. Our kid testers gave this seat a thumbs up, even for long rides. So, what are the drawbacks? Well, Britax's BodyGuard does have more side impact protection than this seat; but that's about it. And if your vehicle already has side curtain airbags in the back seat (many new models are now offering this as an option), then the TurboBooster should be all you need. Another note: Graco sells a backless version of the TurboBooster at Wal-Mart for just $15.74. If your child doesn't nap any more and you have a vehicle with headrests in the back seat, this would be a good choice.
**Dimensions.** Back height: 27", seat width: 16".
**Rating:** A

## JUPITER INDUSTRIES

*1399 Kennedy Rd. #22, Scarborough, Ontario, Canada, M1P2L6. 800-465-5795. Web: www.jupiterindustries.com, sales@jupiterindustries.com.*

### KOMFORT KRUISER

**Booster Type:** High back

**Weight Range:** 33 to 100 pounds; 37" to 60" in height.

**Price:** $89; available at USA Baby and other stores.

**Pros:** Very comfortable and yet supportive.

**Cons:** Wide seat, bulky but light. No five point harness.

**Comments:** Yes, it looks like something NASA might cook up for future toddler missions to Mars, but the Komfort Kruiser is impressive. This seat is a great improvement on Jupiter's first version of this seat, dubbed the GTX (it is a bit wider, although a touch shorter).The Komfort Kruiser still sports the Dupont Jaguar fabric, but now has a very dark look. There are several improvements over the GTX: the KK is much firmer and will keep kids in position – no more worries about slumping. Yet it doesn't sacrifice any comfort, according to our child testers. While both the GTX and the KK are made of EPS foam, the KK uses molded pieces, which are much stronger. So even though this seat is admittedly large and bulky, it weighs a mere 7 pounds. We like the EPS foam construction of the Komfort Kruiser; contrast this seat to boosters made of hard shell plastics. In our opinion, EPS foam is better.

Jupiter has kept the same 100 pound weight limit on this seat even though it is two inches shorter than the GTX. The 27" back height will have no problem accommodating children up to a seated height of 28" (the height limit stated in the manual) but will be less of an obstruction in the rear view mirror than the 29" high GTX. The shoulder belt adjuster is simple, but works just as well as other open loop belt adjusters. The base is wide and covered with a grippy material that resists tipping. And unlike the previous model, this seat has "arm buds" to keep the lap belt down, low and in place. Jupiter has also provided deep side wings, adjustable with superstrong Velcro, to give your child sleeping and side impact support. They've even added a few extras: a mesh cup holder on each side and a mud flap to protect your car. So if you've got the space, the Komfort Kruiser should please both parent and child. We give this seat a runner-up recommendation, behind the Graco TurboBooster and Britax BodyGuard.

New this year is a "special edition" of Komfort Kruiser (also called the LX 100). Basically, this has a deluxe cover and is an inch shorter than the original model—Jupiter had a few complaints that the original version was too tall for shorter parents to see over in their rear view mirror. The LX 100 version also has "memory foam" that conforms to the child's body. Also new: the price on this seat is lower, coming in at $90 (it used to sell for as much as $120 in stores). Jupiter lowered the price to better compete with the Graco Turbobooster.

**Rating:** A

**Dimensions.** Back height: 27", Outside width: 19.5"

## KOLCRAFT

(773) 247-4494. Kolcraft had a couple of booster seats on the market a couple of years ago (the Prodigy was one), but has since withdrawn from the booster market.

## LAROCHE BROTHERS

*158 1/2 Rear Main Street, P.O. Box 95, Gardner, MA 01440 (978) 632-8638. Web: boosterkids.com*

This small Massachusetts company makes three basic belt-positioning boosters. No, you won't see them in any chain stores, but they are for sale in some specialty shops and online on LaRoche's web site. While the designs are good, the prices are on the high side (and probably explains their very limited distribution). All of the seats have the same foam shell and side wings that provide additional crash protection.

### TEDDY BEAR
**Booster type:** belt-positioning
**Weight range:** 30-80 lbs; 33"-57" in height.
**Price:** $109
**Comments:** LaRoche's basic booster includes side "wings" for head and neck support, plus side storage pockets. Nothing fancy.
**Rating:** B-

### GRIZZLY BEAR
**Booster type:** belt-positioning
**Weight range:** 40 to 100 pounds; 36" to 57" in height.
**Price:** $119
**Comments:** Basically, the same as the Teddy Bear but it is two inches wider. And can be used up to 100 pounds (instead of the 80 lb limit on Teddy Bear).
**Rating:** B

### POLAR BEAR
**Booster type:** belt-positioning
**Weight range:** 30 to 100 lbs. 33" to 57" in height.
**Price:** $129.
**Comments:** LaRoche's most versatile booster—can be used for children as small as 30 pounds up to 100 lbs. Similar to the Grizzly, but has the seat belt adjuster on the outside of the shell.
**Rating:** B+

## OSH KOSH
These seats are made by Evenflo. See their review earlier for details.

## SAFETY BABY/ NANIA (TEAM TEX)
*(803) 980-1555. Email: dorontal@compuserve.com Web: www. team-tex.com.*

Remember Renolux? The France-based maker of car seats was a big player in the US market in the 1980's and early 90's—until a string of recalls forced their withdrawal from the market in 1993. Now, Renolux is back. Renolux's former owner, Yves Nania, has introduced seats in the U.S. under the name Safety Baby/Nania. The company's French-based parent, Team-Tex, has released a slew of booster seat products and plans other models in the near future. Here's an overview.

### AIRWAY
**Booster type:** combo
**Weight range:** 33 to 50 pounds with harness, 33 to 80 pounds as booster.
**Price:** $80
**Pros:** Harness goes to 50 pounds.
**Cons:** May be hard to find.
**Comments:** Safety Baby's newest offerings aim to compete with Cosco's line of inexpensive seats, yet with a few new twists. Case in point: the Airway. Due out by the time you read this, the Airway will be the first combo seat with a harness that goes beyond 40 pounds (Safety Baby says it will be rated to 50 pounds). The extra 10 pounds may not seem like much, but the difference will probably keep many children in a harnessed seat to a full four or five years old. So, what's not to like about this booster? Well, Safety Baby/Nania's behavior in the past few months has given us reason to worry about their stability. First, the company promised a

slew of new models in 2001 to be sold in a joint venture with Combi, the stroller maker. Then Combi withdrew from the venture when it became clear that Safety Baby/Nania failed to have the seats safety certified by their launch date. So when (if?) this model should ever appear on U.S. shelves is a big question mark.

**Rating:** C

### HIGHWAY

**Booster type:** backless
**Weight range:** 33 to 80 pounds
**Price:** $25
**Pros:** price, nice shoulder belt adjuster
**Cons:** Narrow, thin pad
**Comments:** The Highway came out after the Polo/Uno (reviewed below) and features a wider base, apparently in response to parent feedback. The Highway *is* wider, by about an inch. But the armrests got smaller, and the front of the seat (on either side of the child's knees) got built up, which made our child testers less comfortable than the Polo. And the thin pad is a loser.

**Rating:** D+
**Dimensions.** Outside width: 14.5"

### POLO/UNO

**Booster type:** backless
**Weight range:** 33 to 80 pounds
**Price:** $25
**Pros:** Price, nice shoulder belt adjuster
**Cons:** Narrow, thin pad
**Comments:** Found in many USA baby stores, this backless booster is definitely adequate. It has nice deep armrests, which will position the lap part of the belt low on the child's hips. The shoulder belt adjuster sits on the child's chest, attaching around the belt with Velcro. The price is right. The pad is nothing special, but does the job and stays in place. The big down side to the Polo/Uno is that the seat is quite narrow inside, so children may find it uncomfortable as they grow older and wider. And that could be a fatal flaw for a booster pitched to kids as heavy as 80 pounds—many might simply outgrow this booster width wise before they are ready to ride in an adult belt. So what's the difference between the

Polo and the Uno? The Polo has a partial cover, while the Uno padding fully covers the seat.

**Rating:** C

**Dimensions. Outside width:** 13.5"

### SPEEDWAY

**Booster type:** combo

**Weight range:** 22 to 40 pounds with harness, 33 to 80 pounds as a high back or backless booster.

**Price:** $50

**Pros:** Narrow outside width; converts to high back AND backless booster.

**Cons:** Narrow inside width, fits badly in many cars, short back.

**Comments:** The Speedway is an innovative concept. Safety Baby/Nania started with the Polo booster and added a back to make it a high back booster. The back also has a harness that can be used from 22 to 40 pounds. The harnessed seat has a one-pull front adjuster, which we liked. But the top harness slots are low, and the belt path is high, making for difficult installations. This seat is narrow as well. As a result, we think it won't fit children in the harness to a full 40 pounds. So despite the multi-purpose aspect of this seat, we give this one a thumbs down. Nice concept, bad execution.

**Rating:** D

**Dimensions.** Top harness slot: 15.5, Back height: 23.5", Outside width: 15".

*Update for 2004:* Safety Baby plans to debut a couple new models this year, including the "Nuevo" ($79 to $99). This combo booster works from 22 to 40 lbs with a five-point harness and than up to 80 lbs as a booster. The same seat comes with less-fancy fabric (called the Solo, $59) and as a backless model ("Ola").

## SAFETY 1ST

See Cosco.

◆ *A note of thanks.* Before we wrap up this chapter, we'd like to thank a car seat expert who helped in writing the above reviews. Toby McAdams is a certified Child Passenger Safety Technician and a parent. She is co-community leader for Parents Place's car seat web site (www.parentsplace. com—go to message boards and then car seats) and the primary car seat expert on our web site's message boards (www.toddlerbargains.com—go to the message boards). Toby also maintains the only listing of which car seats fit in which cars, at www.carseatdata.org. We appreciated Toby's insights, reviews and advice in selecting the best booster seats to recommend to parents.

## Bottom Line: Our Top Picks

What's the best booster seat on the market? Before you can answer that question, you must look at your child—his/her weight, height and maturity (ability to sit in an auto safety belt) are the key factors to consider. Smaller/younger toddlers might be better off with a combo seat that has a five-point harness up to 40 pounds (and then is a belt-positioning booster thereafter). In that category, we liked the Cosco Summit best.

Older toddlers (above 30 or 40 pounds) that are mature enough to sit in a booster with the auto safety belt would be best off in a high-back booster. Our top picks here are the Graco TurboBooster and the Britax Bodyguard.

And remember the best advice is to use a booster until your child is big enough to be secured correctly with the auto safety belt (see the five point test earlier in this chapter to answer that question).

So now you've got your toddler safely bucked up, what do you do for a stroller? Funny you should ask—the next chapter on that topic awaits!

# CHAPTER 7

## On the Go Gear
### Strollers, joggers, bike trailers

**strollers**

Y ou've long ago cast off that big, bulky infant stroller, so now what? Should you buy a lightweight umbrella stroller? One of those fancy all-terrain models? What if you want to actually get out and exercise, God forbid! Which strollers are best for serious runners? After you get all your gear, where do you go? We'll discuss some tips for smoothing out the bumps when traveling with a toddler—and review one of the more popular destinations to take a toddler in the summer . . . the waterpark. We'll show you which water parks we think are best and why.

We'll answer those questions and more in this chapter, including taking a look at bike seats, trailers and tag-alongs. Our "Best Bets" section will highlight picks in several categories such as the best indoor/mall stroller, best all-terrain stroller, best jogger and more. Along the way, we'll review and rate 28 stroller brands (yes, there are actually that many different manufacturers of strollers for sale).

If buying a single stroller wasn't complicated enough, what about a double? We'll go over the pros and cons of tandems versus side by sides, including detailed reviews of the best picks in each category. Then let's discuss safety with bike trailers and bike seats.

But first, let's go over some smart shopper tips for finding the best stroller for you and your toddler.

**Smart Shopper Tips: Strollers**

### Smart Shopper Tip #1
*Magic Bullet?*

"I'm looking for a full-featured stroller that will work from new-born up to age six, is lightweight and that converts from a stroller to a regular size toaster oven, all for under $100. What model would you suggest?"

Okay, we're kidding with that one, but we get emails all the time from parents who ask for the "perfect" stroller that will do everything but make toast. Moms and dads, in describing their perfect stroller, will tick off a long list of desired features and then top it off with something like, "and oh, it would be great if it cost under $100."

Well, folks, bad news—there is no "magic bullet" stroller that will do it all, lasting from newborn up to college. Most parents go through more than one stroller as their child grows; some collect several strollers along the way. That's because while there has been an explosion in the number of stroller models today with more strollers being built for specific niches (jogging, the mall, airplane travel, etc.), a jogging stroller with air-filled 20" tires and a fixed front wheel that is perfect for use while running isn't going to work in the tight spaces of a shopping mall.

Here's our advice: go for one good stroller for indoors, another for outdoors, if you want to exercise. If you are a serious runner, a jogging stroller can double as a good outdoor model for hikes, etc.

What if you have another bun in the oven? Adding a second child into the mix complicates things. That's because the choices for double strollers are narrower and, until recently, inferior given the current offerings on the market. We'll discuss the options later in this chapter, including several new doubles that have debuted recently.

### Smart Shopper Tip #2
*What to look for*

"Okay, smarty pants, there isn't one magic stroller. But what do I look for when shopping for a stroller for a toddler?"

Here's our checklist of what to consider when shopping for toddler strollers (that is, a stroller for a child age 2 to 5).

◆ **Wide seat.** Strollers that are built for newborns may be uncomfortable for toddlers—check the seat width to make sure your child will fit comfortably. And that there is room to grow.

◆ **Tall backrest.** It's important to take your toddler with you stroller shopping so you can evaluate the height of a stroller backrest. Also check the shoulder width.

◆ **Foot rest.** Cheap strollers omit this feature, but it's important for a toddler's comfort. Make sure the stroller's footrest is properly placed for your child.

◆ **Weight capacity.** Some strollers have a weight capacity of just 40 pounds; others go up to 100 pounds. Obviously, the higher the better.

◆ **Lightweight.** You might have been willing to live with a bulky, full-featured stroller for your newborn, but now weight is critical— the lighter, the better.

◆ **Other smart features.** While not critical, a compact fold is an important feature for most parents. This is especially true for folks who take the subway or public transportation; a compact fold is critical to getting around. Another good feature to consider: one-hand steering. If you have another baby on the way, one hand steering is a plus, since one hand may be occupied with baby #2. A versatile model may also allow you to snap in an infant car seat (again for child #2) while the older toddler walks.

### Smart Shopper Tip #3
*The Test Drive*
   *"What are the key points to keep in mind when you test drive a stroller?"*

   If you are lucky enough to have a store nearby that carries different stroller brands, give the models a test drive. Look for the following:

◆ **Maneuverability.** How well does the stroller turn in tight spaces? Try to maneuver the stroller down a narrow aisle.

◆ **One hand steering.** As mentioned above, this is important especially if you have two children (or are planning to have another child soon). So, will the stroller really push straight with just one hand? Give it a try.

◆ **Is the handle height comfortable?** Most strollers are designed for the average woman (about 5′6″); if you or your spouse are taller, look for a stroller with a height adjustable handle. That way you can push the stroller without bending over or kicking the back of it.

◆ *Do the fold.* Don't just admire the stroller set up; try folding it. Some models have one-hand or simple folds. Others require two hands and lots of effort. Once the stroller is folded, try carrying it for a short distance. Or lifting it onto a shelf—this will approximate what it is like to put it in a trunk. This point is important particularly for double strollers and joggers . . . these strollers are especially bulky and hence the hardest to fold. Some joggers have a simple one-step fold; others require the removal of pins and other contortions by the user.

◆ *Now unfold it.* Again, the best strollers have a one-step or easy set-up.

◆ *Check the storage.* Is it adequate? Can you access the basket when the seat is in the recline position? This is a problem with some double strollers—when the rear seat is reclined, the storage basket can be inaccessible. Some stroller makers get around this problem by having the basket slide out on a track.

◆ *How adjustable is the canopy?* Many strollers have skimpy sunshades that don't block much sun. The best strollers have adjustable canopies with full coverage.

### Smart Shopper Tip #4
*The Serious Runner*

   "I want to get back to running my usual four miles a day. I keep seeing these ultra-cheap jogging strollers in discount stores—will they work?"

   Most folks who buy a jogging stroller don't actually use it to jog or run—they simply go on walks in the neighborhood and perhaps pack it in the car for a hike on a gravel road out in the country. For simple walks or other light duty, low cost joggers (we'll review them later) are fine.

   However, serious runners (see the box on the next page) need a better quality stroller—you want it to glide smoothly without any wobbling or tracking problems. You also need 16" or 20" wheels (cheaper joggers have smaller, 12" wheels). The lightest weight (and hence easiest to run with) joggers have frames made of aluminum. Unfortunately, these are also more expensive than the ultra cheap models you see at discount stores, which are typically made of steel.

   In order to get those features, better quality joggers for serious runners usually start at $200 and can go up to $350. Sure, those

## What the heck is a "serious runner"?

So, what's the difference between a stroller that's best for walking versus jogging or running? Walkers (who have a 20-minute per mile pace; or just take the occasional neighborhood jaunt) can get by with a jogging or sport stroller with 12" wheels. Zooper, Mountain Buggy and Baby Jogger's City Jogger are examples of brands that have that feature.

We define joggers as those who run three or more times per week, typically doing two or more miles at a time. A typical pace would be ten minutes per mile. Folks who fit into that category should consider a jogger with at least 16" wheels.

What about true serious runners? These folks run five or more miles at a time, often three times a week (or more). They might hit a 6-8 minute per mile pace. These folks need joggers with 20" wheels for the best performance; the new Baby Jogger III even has 24" wheels, which would be fine as well.

cheap $100 steel jogging strollers may look like a deal, but most serious runners find they are more trouble then they are worth.

### Smart Shopper Tip #5
### Reach the beach

*"We want a stroller to go to the beach. What should we look for? Any special problems with the salt air?"*

Most jogging strollers will do just fine at the beach, but watch out for two things: rust and sand. Get a model that is rustproof—that is a frame made of aluminum and wheel rims that are made of polymer or alloy. The Baby Jogger Twinkle is an example of a model that combines those features.

Be aware: most joggers have steel wheel rims and these can rust out in salty air. Ditto for cheaper joggers with steel frames you see for sale at discount stores. Also: make sure the wheels have sealed bearings. This prevents sand from gumming up your stroller.

The best strollers for the beach are those with 20" wheels. They are the easiest to push in the sand. While 16" wheels might work, we think 20" is a better bet. Which brands make joggers with alloy or polymer wheels with sealed bearings and aluminum frames? Kelty, Dreamer Design (all models, except the suspension version), Mountain Buggy and Baby Jogger (most models except the 16" have alloy wheels). We'll review these brands later in this chapter.

### Smart Shopper Tip #6
*Jogging stroller savvy: shocked or not shocked?*

*"I noticed lots of jogging strollers now feature shock absorbers. Is that important?"*

Yep, it's the latest hot feature for jogging strollers—shock absorbers or suspension to give a smoother ride for baby. BOB started this trend with their Sport Utility Stroller (reviewed later in this chapter) a few years ago and now other brands are busy adding them to keep up (Dreamer Design has its Suspension model, etc.).

So, is it necessary? Probably not. All joggers, by their very nature and design, have built-in suspension. The bicycle-type, air-filled tires smooth out most bumps that just about any toddler would feel. So, is the extra suspension and shock absorbers overkill? Yes, probably for most folks.

The exception: parents who run, jog or hike on "washboard" roads (dirt or gravel roads where erosion has created a bumpy surface). In that case, suspension or shock absorbers might be a good thing.

Of course, some parents WANT their toddlers to feel the ups and downs of a rough road—the bumps put some toddlers right to sleep!

### Smart Shopper Tip #7
*Stroller for two?*

*"I have a three year old and another baby on the way. What is the best double stroller option?"*

Picking the right stroller for one child can be tough enough; deciding the best way to transport two is downright tricky. That's because the choices are much more limited and until recently, inferior quality-wise compared to single strollers.

There are basically five solutions:

**1** **THE TANDEM (FRONT/BACK) STROLLER.** The baby usually rides in back; the older child in front. As a result, the back seat fully reclines, while the front may only offer a partial recline. This is the best choice when you have an older child/newborn situation. ***Pros:*** Can fit through narrow aisles/doors. Some models allow you to attach an infant seat. ***Cons:*** While tandems may work fine for an infant/toddler combo, most parents switch to a side by side when their children get older. Why? Weight—many tandems weigh 30 lbs. empty . . . as a result, these strollers can be very difficult to push when fully loaded. And they turn with all the agility of the Queen Mary. Most tandems are made by Graco and Cosco, two of the lower-quality stroller brands.

**2** **SIDE BY SIDE STROLLERS.** Both kids get a front row seat, but that can be a plus and a minus—there is more of a chance the children can fight when sitting side by side. *Pros:* Lighter weight than most tandems. No fights over who gets the front seat. Better quality brands than tandems. *Cons:* Some models too big to fit through narrow doorways or aisles—make sure the model you pick is 30″ wide or less. Narrow seats can squeeze larger toddlers. Some side-by-side strollers lack fully reclining seats, making them less ideal for newborns.

**3** **THE PUSH CART.** Baby Trend's Sit and Stand is an example of this popular stroller concept imported from Europe. The younger child rides in front; the older one stands in back. This is a good option when you have an older toddler (at least two and half; better if they are three or four) who doesn't want to sit in a stroller but may get tired of walking at some point. *Pros:* Most models of infant seats can snap into the front of a push cart. Some models have jump seats for an older child to sit in back. *Cons:* Front seat doesn't fully recline. Older child may not like riding facing backward on the jump seat. Limited brand choices—basically Baby Trend, not one of the better quality stroller makers out there.

**4** **KIDDY BOARD.** Lascal's "Kiddy Board" and "Buggy Board" ($60 at DmartStores.com; $70 at BabySuper Mall.com) attach to the rear bar of a stroller so an older child can ride along. The Kiddy Board attaches to the center axle of a stroller; the Buggy Board attaches to the side rails above the rear wheels (see pictures). The boards hold kids from age two to five, up to 65 pounds. *Pros:*

Great for older toddlers who aren't interested in riding in a stroller, but still get tired of walking. ***Cons:*** Pricey. Won't work with umbrella-fold strollers.

**5** **SKIP THE DOUBLE STROLLER.** If you have an older toddler (four or five when your second child arrives), our best advice is to skip the double stroller. That's because older children often are not interested in riding in strollers, preferring to walk instead. With the huge expense of double strollers (the better brands run $300+), it might be better to carry a newborn in a front carrier or sling for the first few months and use a single stroller for the older child if needed.

## Money Saving Secrets

**1** **WAREHOUSE CLUBS.** In the past, clubs like Costco, Sam's and BJ's used to carry off brands of strollers—if they carried any at all. Lately, we've seen better brands and some amazing buys. The best bet: Costco. Costco has sold Peg Perego Pliko strollers online at 40% off (non-members can buy off their web site, costco.com for a 5% surcharge). And the best steal of all: jogging strollers. For a while this year, Costco offered an exclusive Bell/Co-Pilot aluminum 16" jogger for just $119—about half or one-third the price of similar joggers. Like anything at the clubs, however, you've got to act fast: if you see it, snap it up because it probably won't be there for long!

**2** **YARD SALES.** Yes, we consistently hear of parents who found steals on strollers at yard sales—hit them early for the best selection. And do your research before hand: study the brands we review in this section. That way you'll know which are quality and which are junk.

**3** **DON'T OVERBUY.** Do you really need a $300 jogger for the occasional spin around the neighborhood? No, a low-cost jogger that runs $100 will probably do the trick just fine. Most folks who buy joggers or sport strollers (those with air-filled tires) don't actually jog with them! If you are not a serious jogger or hiker, a low-end model will do the trick.

**4** **LOOK FOR WEB DEALS.** Our message boards (ToddlerBargains.com—hit the message board link at left) are constantly buzzing with parents who've found great deals on strollers online and offline. Look for coupon codes that are posted on our boards. Also look for sale notices as web sites often clear out "last year's" models at great prices.

**5** **FACTORY SECONDS.** Both Combi (combi-intl.com) and Baby Jogger (babyjogger.com) sell factory seconds from their web sites. Most models are reconditioned and are great deals—you can save 50% or more!

## Name Brand Reviews: Strollers

In our previous book, *Baby Bargains*, we have in-depth reviews of stroller makers in Chapter 8. Since we realize some readers of this book may not have read our first book, we wanted to give a quick run down of the major players in the stroller biz. These reviews focus on what these brands offer for toddlers (as well as double strollers). We also have reviewed several new brands of strollers that aren't yet in our *Baby Bargains* book. Here are the brands, in a nutshell:

**Aprica** (www.apricausa.com). This Japanese stroller maker sells very pricey lightweight strollers running $200 to $500 (most are about $300). Used to be a bigger player in the U.S. market, but high prices, quality woes and little innovation have made Aprica an also-ran in recent years. And the brand has just about disappeared from stores. ***Rating: B***

**Baby Trend** (www.babytrend.com). Innovative strollers, lousy quality is how we'd sum up Baby Trend. These imported strollers (made in Asia) are often innovative (the Sit N Stand, mentioned earlier; the Snap & Go recommended in our *Baby Bargains* book) and there are lots of double strollers to choose from. Baby Trend is also big into low-cost joggers, sold at Babies R Us among other chains. Prices are reasonable ($100 to $150 for joggers, under $200 for doubles), but quality often leaves much to be desired here. Baby Trend also makes strollers under the name Swan; these are the same as Baby Trend's models, just different fabrics for a different market (specialty stores). ***Rating: B-***

**Baby Jogger** (www.babyjogger.com). Yes, this is the company that practically invented the jogger category 20 years ago (and has since sold over 1 million strollers). Baby Jogger's success was built on their quality and a plethora of models—they have strollers with 12", 16" or 20" wheels, double strollers, triple strollers, strollers with swivel front wheels, etc. Their latest: the Baby Jogger III, an amazing jogger with optional 24" back wheels, shock absorbers, reclining seat and a 100 lb. weight limit. Price: $340 to $400, depending on the wheel size you choose. And that's one of Baby Jogger's bigger problems: price. In the past few years, Baby Jogger's success has spawned a raft of new competitors. Most of these new jogger brands manufacturer their strollers in Asia (Baby Jogger is the only one that still assembles joggers in the U.S., although parts are made in Mexico and China). As a result, Baby Joggers tend to be priced higher than comparable models from other brands. Another drawback: Baby Jogger's seats tend to be narrower compared to competitors' models. That might not be a big deal for an infant, but we hear complaints from parents of toddlers and older children that the seat is too tight. (That might be why the new Baby Jogger III features a wider, deeper seat; but that's the only model that has it). And other joggers have a complete line of accessories (bug canopies, full sun covers, etc) that the Baby Jogger lacks. So it is a mixed review for Baby Jogger. Quality is excellent, but the prices are high and the seats (and most models) are too narrow—making this brand tough to recommend for toddlers. And other brands are now out-flanking the Baby Jogger with more convenience features (storage pockets, sippy cup holders, etc). It's no surprise that this company had to declare bankruptcy in 2002, as sales shrunk in half from their '90's peak. On the upside, the company did find a buyer in 2003 and now appears to be headed for better times with new models and accessories. An example: a $59 infant car seat attachment bar. Weight capacities: 50-100 lbs., depending on the model. ***Rating: A-***

***Bell*** (a.k.a. Co-Pilot). Better known for its helmets, Bell jogging strollers have shown up in warehouse clubs recently. Marketed under the name CoPilot, these strollers feature aluminum frames, 16" wheels, canopy, rain cover, storage bin and five point harness. And here's the kicker: the price for all that is $119 (at Costco). We've also seen a similar model online at sites like IndoorsAndOutdoors.com for $130. The only downside to this model? The seat doesn't recline and the weight (at 30 lbs.) is a bit heavy. Like all products sold at warehouse clubs like Costco and Sam's, selection and availability is sketchy—you'll usually see just one color and if you don't buy it soon, it will be gone in a matter of days. But if you see one of these at Costco, we'd snap it up! ***Rating: B***

***Bertini*** (www.BertiniStrollers.com) This offshoot of Simo's U.S. importer has one claim to fame: their Chinese-made prams feature air-filled wheels that turn (most prams have fixed wheels). The problem? The price. The M5 at $310 has never won a wide audience, despite a raft of nice features (two position recline seat and height adjustable handle). The weight (27 lbs) might be a factor. **Rating: B**

**BOB** (www.bobtrailers.com). You gotta like the rugged look and features of the Bob "Sport Utility" strollers. BOB's big selling point is their "multi-position coil spring shock absorbers" which gives a very smooth ride. You can choose from 16" polymer wheels (the Sport Utility) or 16" aluminum alloy wheels. Weight capacity is 70 lbs. The fold is pin-free and takes about three seconds (among the easiest on the market). The downsides? The 70-lbs. weight limit is a bit skimpy, considering competitors' models now go up to 100 lbs. BOB's seats only partially recline (but, on the plus side, the seat is foam padded). Prices range from $280 to $325 for the Deluxe. A double stroller (the Duallie) is $400. New for 2004, BOB has switched to lighter weight materials, which means most models have shed two to three pounds in total weight. Also new: extended canopies, which addresses one previous drawback to this model. This year BOB also debuts an "Ironman" stroller with bright yellow fabric and smooth tires ($335). Quality is excellent. Bottom line: this is a great stroller for off-road and trail use. Hikers will love it. Serious runners, however, might be better off going for another model with 20" wheels. **Rating: A**

**Carter's. See Kolcraft.**

**Century** (www.centuryproducts.com). This company invented the travel system (infant seat that snaps into a carriage stroller), but parent Rubbermaid has recently decided to put this brand on ice in order to push the Graco name. You'll still see Century strollers on eBay and in second-hand stores; quality is only average. Most were made in Mexico. **Rating: B-**

**Chicco** (www.chiccousa.com). This stroller maker's claim to fame are two Chinese-made strollers, the Caddy ($50, 11lbs) and the London ($70, 15 lbs). The quality is good; look for Chicco to debut a new travel system in late 2004 or 2005. **Rating: B+**

**Combi** (www.combi-intl.com) Japanese stroller maker Combi built its business with the hot-selling Savvy, a super lightweight yet full featured stroller which offers a compact fold. Combi makes an excellent side by side, the Twin Savvy. Quality is good to excellent, despite a few recent hiccups with the Twin Savvy (we'll go into more details later). **Rating: A**

**CoPilot. See Bell.**

**Cosco.** (www.djgusa.com). The Kmart of stroller brands, Cosco churns out numerous low-cost strollers, both of the single and double variety. Made in China, you'll see Cosco stores in most major chains like Wal-Mart. In a savvy move, Cosco cloaks its identity by selling strollers under the Eddie Bauer and Safety 1st brands. Basically, these are the same strollers with upgraded fabric. What does Cosco have to hide? It's abysmal safety record, for one thing. Cosco has had several high profile recalls recently. On the plus side, Cosco at least is trying to innovate with their strollers—in the past few years, the company has rolled out more all-terrain and jogger models with the Eddie Bauer and Safety 1st names. In 2004, Cosco plans import several of parent Dorel's European brands. Already on sale: a $250 jogger from Quinny, a Dutch brand owned by Cosco (despite the Euro name, Quinny is made in China). **Rating: C-**

**Dreamer Design/Boogie Deluxe** (www.dreamerdesign.net). Formerly called Fitness First, this company focuses on good quality joggers (16" and 20" tri-wheel models) at decent prices. Most models feature aluminum alloy frames (there is one steel model), retractable canopies and a reclining seat. There is also one double model (the Ditto). Among the better models—the Suspension ($300) which features shock absorbers and an easy one-step fold. Prices range from $200 to $300, which is about $100 less than competitor's models. Weight capacity: 75 pounds. While we think Dreamer Design is good quality, we would rate their joggers as a notch or two below other high-end joggers. Dreamer's best feature: their large canopy with great coverage, which for some parents is a top priority. New this year is the Dreamer HT model ($279), which features an upgraded mesh sunshade. Also new: Dreamer's now have a bigger footplate and wide seats **Rating: A-**

**Eddie Bauer. See Cosco.**

**Emmaljunga** (www.emmaljunga.com). This Swedish brand of strollers withdrew from the US market in 2001. You'll still see their prams and carriages in second-hand stores though.

**Evenflo** (www.evenflo.com) Ohio-based Evenflo has played second fiddle to Graco and Cosco in the stroller market over the last few years. Evenflo clung to selling its bloated travel systems while the market moved to lightweight strollers (like the Combi Savvy) or all-terrain/joggers. Evenflo belatedly added a few lightweight models recently (the FeatherLight, InSight) but the company is still an also-ran in this category. Evenflo also makes strollers under the Osh Kosh brand name (same stroller, just different fabric) Quality is a notch above Cosco (Evenflo strollers are made in China), but not much better than Graco. Most Evenflo strollers run $50 to $100. ***Rating: C+***

***Fisher Price See J. Mason.***

***Graco*** (www.gracobaby.com). This company still dominates the chain store stroller aisle, despite its recent stumbles. Parent Rubbermaid has shaken up Graco's management and design team in the past year to reverse a sales slump. Talk with any parents about Graco's quality and you can see why sales are hurting—these strollers (manufactured in Mexico) are just poorly made. Yes, they look pretty in the store but they often break in a few short months. So even though Graco has stayed on top of market trends with lightweight models (MetroLite) and all-terrain styles like the tri-wheel Leisure Sport, the company's strollers are regarded as disposable by most parents. Defenders of Graco point out their lightweight strollers are so cheap, who cares if they break after a few months? ***Rating: C***

***Gozo*** (www.getgozo.com). This brand's claim to fame is their tandem (front/back) jogger, the only one on the market like it. The frame of these strollers can be configured with one or two seats. Gozo strollers also have five-point harnesses, quick release 16" wheels and sun canopies. Prices: $335 to $350 for a single version; the second seat is $135. Quality is good. ***Rating: A-***

***Inglesina*** (www.inglesina.com). Ingelsina strollers have always been an afterthought in the U.S. market, but they reversed that image a couple of years ago with the hot-selling Zippy. Despite a stiff price ($250), the Zippy's unique one-hand fold and low 17 lb. weight have made it a winner. The biggest news this year from Ingelsina will be a new side-by-side stroller, the Double Swift (22 lbs, $200). Quality is above average; all strollers are made in China. ***Rating: A***

***InStep*** InStep is Baby Trend's competition in the chain store aisles for low-end joggers. For example, InStep's 5K ($90) is a steel framed stroller sold exclusively at Target. You get stroller-like features (a parent tray with cup holder and covered tray), storage basket and quick release wheels. The only bummer? The weight limit is a skimpy 50 lbs. And the quality (all made in Asia) is merely average; these are no Baby Joggers. While InStep does several more models that are better suited to running (the $200 aluminum Pro, for example), this company's joggers are probably best suited to occasional use for neighborhood walks rather than serious runs or hikes. The biggest news this year at InStep is their debut of a travel system—InStep plans to debut their own infant car seat and pair it with a jogging stroller under the Schwinn brand name (which is an InStep license). Also new: the M3 model ($180) with a built-in weather shield and bigger seat plus one hand fold. **Rating: B-**

**J Mason** J. Mason makes Graco look like Mercedes—Mason's low-end strollers (made in China) are typically sold at bargain basement discounts. A typical offering is a $25 to $35 umbrella stroller with Sesame Street fabric. In the past year, J. Mason signed a deal to make strollers under the Fisher Price brand. Their first offerings include an aluminum stroller with one-hand fold for $70 and a $100 tandem version. J Mason's recent efforts to remake the brand with fancier looks (they even trotted out a French derivative of their brand name) largely have bombed. **Rating: C**

**Jeep See Kolcraft.**

**Kelty** (www.kelty.com). Yep, Kelty is better known for their backpack carriers but the company jumped into the jogger category three years ago. Kelty offers both single (the Joyrider $300) and double models (Deuce Coupe, $400). The Joyrider is available in 12″, 16″ or 20″ wheels; the Deuce Coupe just 16″ or 20″. Among Kelty's best features: lots of storage pockets (what else would you expect from a backpack company?), a unique umbrella-style fold, quick release wheels and big storage basket. Kudos for Kelty's hood design— "awesome" is how one parent described it; the canopy is big and adjusts to a low position to block low-angle sun. So what's not to like? Kelty's jogger handle is actually two handles (like an umbrella stroller), making one-handed steering a bit tricky. And the handle height is quite high—shorter parents (5′6″ or under) may find this height uncomfortable. Unfortunately, the seat doesn't recline for napping toddlers. Taller and wider children may also be uncomfortable in the somewhat tight Kelty seat. So it's a mixed review for Kelty: excellent quality, innovative features but a few major drawbacks that might be a deal killer for some parents. **Rating: B+**

**KidCo** (www.kidcoinc.com). KidCo used to be the distributor for Maclaren in the U.S. until they recently parted ways. KidCo responded by introducing their own line of Maclaren knock-offs (made in China). Example: the LS2000, an aluminum stroller with five position recline that weighs 16 lbs for $154. KidCo has excellent customer service (each model comes with a two year warranty), although some parents gripe the seats in their twin strollers are too narrow. **Rating: B+**

**Kolcraft** (www.kolcraft.com). Kolcraft has turned the corner in recent years, with the help of their Jeep brand. Their best-selling Jeep Liberty Urban Terrain—a three wheel stroller with turnable front wheel—is a good example. It has smart looks plus a raft of great features (parent tray, child snack tray, big basket, etc). And at $100, it is a good value. Of course, Kolcraft makes a wide variety of other Jeep strollers, but the Urban Terrain is probably the best of the bunch. **Rating: B+**

**Kool Stop** (www.koolstop.com). Kool Stop's joggers are loaded with all the features you'd expect from a high-end jogger: five-point safety harness, reclining seat, retractable hood, etc. Another unique feature: Kool Stop's rear wheels are angled by five degrees for improved tracking. The flagship "Senior" model comes in both steel and aluminum versions, ranging from $300 to $375. Most models have 20" rear wheels, making this a good choice for the beach or jogging. Weight capacities are 75 to 100 lbs. We liked the pin-free fold and quick release wheels. Another plus: the Kool Stop's models have a ratcheting, height adjustable handle and the size of their seats accommodate toddlers better. Both single and double models are available. New this year are bigger canopies on Kool Stops, as well as an easier fold. **Rating: A**

**Maclaren** (www.maclarenbaby.com). This British stroller brand's claim to fame is its pricey yet well made umbrella strollers. These super-lightweight models (both in single and double versions) are what moms in NYC and Boston swear by for their durability, despite prices that range from $100 to $300 for singles, $300 to $450 for doubles. So, what's not to like? In recent years, Maclaren shifted its production from England to China and some Maclaren fanatics say quality has suffered. Maclaren says they made the move to lower

## A good source for jogging strollers

Crested Butte, Colorado-based JoggingStroller.com specializes in just that—jogging strollers. While not a discount site, the prices are good and the selection of brands is excellent. JoggingStroller.com carries Dreamer Design, Kelty, Gozo, BOB, Baby Jogger, Bugaboo, Mountain Buggy and Yakima. Also cool: the site carries just about every accessory available for each brand. Their message boards let you post questions and get feedback from the site's owners about brands, features and more.

production prices, but retail prices for these strollers haven't budged. On the plus side, these strollers still retain their cache. Adding to that are several licensed versions of Macs now available, including a Kate Spade stroller. ***Rating: A-***

**Martinelli See Peg Perego**.

**Mountain Buggy** (www.mountainbuggyusa.com). New Zealand's Mountain Buggy's claim to fame is their Urban Single. This tri-wheel stroller's most talked about feature is its front wheel, which can swivel or be fixed. This gives the Mountain Buggy greater maneuverability, unlike other tri-wheel strollers with fixed wheels. The super lightweight aluminum frame (17-19 lbs. depending on the model) features 12" air-filled wheels with polymer rims (great for use near the beach), full reclining seat, height adjustable handle, one step fold and large two-position sun canopy. A slew of accessories includes a bug shield, full sun cover and more. Weight capacity is an amazing 100 lbs. If you don't need the swivel front wheel, Mountain Buggy also offers a model with a fixed front wheel (the Terrain Single). Mountain Buggy also sells two double models (the Urban Double with swivel front wheels and the Terrain Double with fixed wheels). So, what's the downside? First, price: these things are expensive. The Urban Single is $339, the Terrain Single $289. The Urban Double is $500; the Terrain Double $419. And Mountain Buggy is so new to North America that these strollers are hard to see in person. Nonetheless, if you have a dealer near by, they are worth a look-see. New this year: a mini version of the Terrain dubbed the Breeze with 10" wheels. This stroller runs $289 and weighs 14 lbs. ***Rating: A***

**Osh Kosh See Evenflo.**

**Peg Perego** (www.perego.com). The hottest stroller brand going, Italian-made Perego has won legions of fans for three reasons: quality, features and fashion. Quality is excellent, among the best in the business. Perego made a big bet on lightweight strollers (the Pliko family) a few years ago and that was prescient. Finally, the fashion— Perego makes the best-looking fabrics and styling in the business. Of course, all this quality ain't free. Perego strollers run $180 to $300 for singles, $300 to $400 for doubles. Perego is one of the few brands left that hasn't moved production to China; all strollers are still made in Italy. ***Rating: A***

**Phil & Ted's Most Excellent Buggy** (www.babybuggy.co.nz). Yes, this company wins the award for the best-named stroller company. And leave it to those scrappy New Zealanders to come up with great all-terrain strollers. These tri-wheel strollers are similar to joggers, but have smaller wheels and one major bonus—the front wheel can swivel or be fixed. The "Kiwi Explorer" (their main model) is $350. The only problem? These strollers have very limited distribution in the U.S. so it may be hard to see one in person. Quality and design, however, are excellent. ***Rating: A-***

**Regalo** (www.regalobaby.com) This brand tried to do better quality mass-market strollers, but all but disappeared in recent years. You occasionally see Regalo strollers pop up in discount stores, but they are hard to find. Most are $100 to $200; Regalo markets a knock-off of Graco's LiteRider and several jogging strollers. Quality was only fair. ***Rating: C+***

**Safety 1st** *(See Cosco).* Cosco has experimented selling jogging strollers under their Safety 1<sup>st</sup> brand, but scaled that back as of this writing. We did like their Two Ways jogger (now discontinued), which you still might see for sale online. Cosco/Safety 1<sup>st</sup> has been hobbled by poor quality and recall issues in the past year. But at least they are trying to do something innovative; other mass market brands often seem stuck in neutral. ***Rating: B+***

**Simo** (www.simostrollers.com) Norway's Simo tried and largely failed to bring Euro-styled prams to the U.S. The reason? High prices for one. Americans just didn't want a heavy, $400 pram, even if it had steerable front wheels. As a result, Simo is being "deemphasized" by their U.S. importer (see Bertini). ***Rating: B+***

***Swan See Baby Trend.***

**Teutonia** (www.britaxusa.com) Made by Britax's (the car seat maker) German subsidary, Teutonia debuted on the market in 2002. These pricey strollers ($400 to $500) attempt to bridge the gap between the indoor and outdoor models. Teutonia strollers have carriage-like frames with plush padding and full canopies, but then add air-filled tires for outdoor ruggedness. Despite a good reputation in Europe for quality, Teutonia stumbled early in the U.S. with the ill-fated Toni, a lightweight stroller beset with quality woes. Some of this might have been due to a production change—Teutonia recently moved their production from Germany to Eastern Europe. All this gives us pause in recommending the brand until they sort things out. ***Rating: C+***

**Yakima** (www.yakima.com). The newest player in the jogger market is Yakima, maker of bike racks, trailers and snowshoes. Yakima's "Beetle" ($325) features 16" wheels, alloy rims, aluminum frame, adjustable height and more. We liked Yakima's innovative features—a sippy cup holder inside the stroller, an angled frame so taller parents won't kick the frame when running and more. The only disadvantage? The skimpy canopy. Yes, it adjusts to block low angle sun, but the short length of the canopy is going to frustrate some parents. We'd also like to see a 20" wheel option. Yakima doesn't make a double stroller and don't look for any fancy accessories like a bug shield (there aren't any). Nonetheless, this is an intriguing new entry that is worth a look. Quality is excellent. **Rating: A-**

**Zooper** (www.zooperstrollers.com). Zooper occupies that niche between traditional strollers and joggers—that all-terrain user who wants a more rugged stroller for walks, but still needs all the comforts of a mall strollers. A good example: the Zooper Buddy ($250), a tri-wheel stroller that has earned kudos from parents. You get a plush, reclining seat, removable canopy, adjustable footrest, a large storage basket and front swivel wheel (which is new in 2004). And (get ready for this) the seat is reversible, so you can have your child ride facing you. The 12" air filled tires are great, as are the included accessories (wind/rain shield, full boot, etc). There's even an infant car seat attachment accessory. If you want a more traditional stroller (with four wheels), there is the Walk Air ($250) or Zooper's latest addition, the Kroozer ($300). New this year, Zooper has another model with a front swivel wheel (Jazz, 18 lbs, $169) which can hold an infant seat. Also new: Zooper's first twin stroller, the Tango (23 lbs, $169), a side by side model. The downsides? These strollers are not light, clocking in at 30 to 34 lbs. (depending on the model). That's about five to ten pounds heavier than other all-terrain strollers are. And the weight limits are rather skimpy, at 40-45 lbs. That makes these strollers great for younger toddlers (2-3 year olds), but we fear four or five year olds will quickly outgrow them. **Rating: A**

## Best Bets: Toddler Strollers

Well, here it is—our picks for the best strollers for toddlers, ages two to five. We divide our picks into roughly four areas: single and double strollers and inside and outside models. We define inside strollers as those best suited for the mall or for travel (airplanes, etc). We further break down the outdoor category into all-terrain/sport strollers and joggers. We'll explain more what we mean by those categories later in this section.

Readers of our *Baby Bargains* book may note that, in some cases, we will recommend different brands here than we did in that book. The reason is simple: strollers that work well for infants (birth to 2) may be different than what works for toddlers (age 2 to 5). In some cases, quality manufacturers make models for both age brackets (Combi, Peg Perego, Maclaren, for example).

So, let's break it down:

## Single Strollers

### MALL STROLLER (HIGH END)

This category covers strollers that are for the "mall crawlers": parents and toddlers that need a good stroller for the mall as well as neighborhood walks on good sidewalks. Like most folks today, we realize parents who live in their car need a lightweight stroller that can be set up and collapsed quickly, without taking up too much room in the trunk.

For those parents who live in urban areas, mall strollers are most helpful on public transportation when you'll have to navigate a set of subway or train platform stairs with baby in one hand, stroller in the other.

**BEST BET: PEG PEREGO ARIA LB**
**Stroller type:** Lightweight stroller.
**Weight:** 12.5 lbs.
**Price:** $179-199.
**Pros:** One hand steering, new extra large basket. Can use with Perego infant seat. Nice fabrics.
**Cons:** 40 lb weight limit means some bigger toddlers might out grow it too soon. Canopy is kind of skimpy. Lacks one-hand fold.
**Comments:** Perego's lightweight Aria is a winner—at just 14 lbs, it still packs an impressive number of features (child snack tray, cup holder, large storage basket).
**Bottom Line:** The best toddler stroller for the mall or neighborhood strolls.

**RUNNER-UP:** *Combi's Savvy Soho* ($100) is a pound lighter and $80 cheaper than the Aria but still has decent size storage basket. It works with Combi's new infant seat, so it has as much flexibility as the Aria. The only thing missing is a child snack tray or parent cup holder.

Another good runner-up: *Maclaren's Volo,* a bare-bones

mesh seat stroller that weighs a mere 8.2 lbs. Price: $100. Unfortunately, the canopy, rain cover and seat liner are an extra $50. If you want something from Maclaren with more features, consider the *Triumph*, which runs $150. It weighs 11 lbs. and has a full hood and a seat with a two-position recline.

## AIRLINE/TRAVEL STROLLER (LOW END)

Quick quiz: if you invest nearly $200 on a quality lightweight stroller like the Peg Perego Aria, should you take it with you on an airplane? Answer: not if you want to see your stroller again in one piece.

Airlines now force parents to "gate check" most strollers and the results are not pretty. It's a sad fact of modern travel: airlines are famous for mangling strollers; the more expensive ones seem especially marked for brutal treatment.

So, what should you do? We suggest buying a low cost, lightweight stroller that you use for airline travel or other road trips. If it gets destroyed by an airline baggage handler, at least there is less pain, cost-wise.

### BEST BET: GRACO BREEZE LITERIDER
**Stroller type:** Lightweight
**Weight:** 19 lbs.
**Price:** $48.76 at Wal-Mart
**Pros:** Low price. One hand fold. Two-position reclining seat. Nice canopy. Big storage basket.
**Cons:** It's made by Graco—don't expect it to last.
**Comments:** Not fancy and nothing to look at, but the Graco Breeze LiteRider will fill the bill as a good airplane/travel stroller.

**RUNNER-UP:** *Safety 1st's Acella LX* is similar in price to the Graco model (both are about $50), but the Acella weighs a bit more (24 pounds). On the plus side, you do get a few more items, including larger 8″ wheels and a special "one-hand fold and stand" capability. Bonus: the stroller includes an adapter bar to hold a Graco SnugRide infant seat.

## OUTDOOR: ALL-TERRAIN/SPORT STROLLERS

These strollers are sort of like the SUV of child transport—they feature rugged, air-filled wheels to handle rough roads/sidewalks, hikes or just about any off road adventure. Yet they offer surprising comfort features for baby including full canopies, comfy seats and accessories like bug shields, rain covers and more.

Our best bet in this category would be perfect for the beach, but also work well on trails and other gravel paths.

### BEST BET: MOUNTAIN BUGGY URBAN
**Stroller type:** All-terrain
**Weight:** 19 lbs.
**Price:** $339.

**Pros:** Front wheel can swivel or be fixed; enabling smooth steering. Lightest weight all-terrain on the market. 12" polymer wheels good for the beach. Fully reclining seat, height adjustable handle, one-step fold and two-position sun canopy. Lots of accessories. 100 lbs. weight capacity.

**Cons:** Expensive. Hard to find; Mountain Buggy is new to the U.S. and has few dealers so far, so it may be hard to see in person. Only comes in 12" wheel version.

**Comments:** Leave it to those Kiwis to come up with the perfect all-terrain stroller. Mountain Buggy's Urban Single has set our web site message boards abuzz with their well-designed stroller. Parents just love this thing. One bummer: New Zealand's Mountain Buggy is so new to the U.S./Canada that these strollers are hard to see in person.

**RUNNER-UP:** The *Zooper Buddy* ($250) is a tri-wheel stroller that combines all-terrain wheels (air-filled 12" tires) and the comforts of a mall stroller. The best feature: a reversible seat that lets you look at your toddler or have them facing forward. Also cool: a slew of included accessories like a rain/wind shield and full boot. New this year: the Buddy has a swivel front wheel like the Mountain Buggy.

## JOGGING STROLLERS: LOW END

Okay, you're no marathon runner, but you like the concept of joggers for neighborhood walks and occasional hikes on gravel trails. A low-price jogging stroller may just do the trick—since you don't need fancy wheels or a lightweight frame. One caveat: all of these models are made with steel frames; hence they would not be appropriate for the beach or salty air (rust would be a big problem).

### BEST BET: BABY TREND EXPEDITION
**Stroller type:** Low-end jogger
**Weight:** 29 lbs.
**Price:** $109 on BabiesRUs.com. Spotted for $99 in chain stores.
**Pros:** Low price. 5 point harness. Roomy seat. 16" wheels.

**Cons:** Heavy weight. Not recommended for running. Canopy doesn't block low angle sun. Difficult fold; bulky even when folded (may not fit into small car trunks). 50 lb. weight limit.

**Comments:** Yes, we do have a long list of "cons" for this stroller, but for a hundred bucks this is a good jogger for the mom that just wants to take occasional walks in the neighborhood. Don't kid yourself—this is not a stroller for runners. Baby Trend's mixed reputation for quality and durability means you shouldn't expect this stroller to last forever. But since most parents who use joggers aren't serious runners, this should fit the bill. FYI: Baby Trend also makes an "LX" version of this stroller that is $40 more; it has a few more plush features. Also, Baby Trend makes joggers under the name Reebok for Babies R Us; these sell for $170 to $200. See below for more on the Reebok strollers.

**RUNNER-UP:** *InStep's 5K* jogger ($90, exclusively at Target) features 16" wheels, steel frame, front and rear breaks, storage pouch and a reclining seat. It is very similar to the Baby Trend Expedition. If you want more features, look at Instep's new M3 model. This $179 stroller features a bigger seat, built-in weather shield, huge bubble canopy and one-hand fold. FYI: InStep also sells their strollers under the Schwinn brand name.

## JOGGING STROLLERS: HIGH END

Boy, it is hard to pick one best bet high-end jogging stroller . . . so we'll wimp out and pick two: the Baby Jogger III and the Dreamer Design Deluxe 20.

These high-end strollers are best for serious runners or for parents who plan to do more than just an occasional neighborhood run. Lightweight aluminum frames are a must, as are optional 20" (and even 24") wheels. Because runners require a stroller that doesn't wobble or steer to one side, these joggers must be of the highest quality. And of course, we also look for comfort for your child, including canopy size and extras like cup holders. Here goes:

### BEST BETS (TIE)
### BABY JOGGER III
**Stroller type:** High-end jogger
**Weight:** 16.5 lbs. for the 16" wheels, 20 lbs. for the 20"
**Pros:** bigger seat, only jogger on market with 24" wheel option, shock absorbers, and reclining seat.
**Price:** $340 to $400.

**Cons:** Expensive. Other brands fold easier, have better canopies.

**Comments:** Yes, it is pricey, but this is the only jogger on the market with big 24″ wheels (24″ on the back, 20″ in front). The bigger seat and foot plate make this stroller a better bet for toddlers than Baby Jogger's other models. For runners, this is a great choice.

### DREAMER DESIGN DELUXE 20
**Stroller type:** High-end jogger.
**Weight:** 26.5 pounds.
**Price:** $260 on JoggingStroller.com.
**Pros:** Incredible bubble canopy that blocks low angle sun. Same great features as high-end joggers, yet costs 25% less.
**Cons:** Weighs 25% more than similar models; slightly lower quality than other brands.

**Comments:** This is probably the best value for a quality jogger—at $260, it is $100 less than the comparable Baby Jogger III with 20″ wheels. Yet you get basically the same comforts and features. The killer feature: that bubble canopy has more coverage than just about any other stroller on the market. Weight capacity (at 75 lbs.) is a bit less than others, but it still should work for most children through age 5 and beyond. At 26.5 pounds, it is a bit heavier (3-6 pounds) than other brands' similar models. Overall, however, this is an excellent stroller and a good buy for the dollar. FYI: Dreamer is debuting a new model this year called the Dreamer HT—it is very similar to the Deluxe, but adds a cool recessed mesh sunshade, bigger foot plate and wider seat. It will also weigh a bit less than the Deluxe (25 pounds), but still hold up to a 75 pound child. It will sell for $280.

**RUNNER-UPS.** There are quite a few other choices that would also make good picks. The **Kool Stop "Senior"** ($370 for aluminum, 20″ wheels) is an excellent jogger with pin-free fold and height adjustable handle.

Taller parents might love the **Kelty Joyrider** ($340 for 20″ wheels), with its unique racing style handles. This stroller's numerous pockets and storage are a plus, but the seat might be a bit tight for larger toddlers.

If you've got rough roads, the **BOB Sport Utility Stroller** might be the best choice with its beefier suspension and quick fold that's among the easiest on the market. Unfortunately, there is only a 16″ wheel version (no 20″).

A dark horse choice might be the **Yakima Beetle** jogger ($325), a relative newcomer to the jogger market. The Beetle jogger has an impressive list of features, including an angled design so taller parents won't kick the back of the stroller when running. Yet, there is no 20″ wheel version and the skimpy canopy will frustrate users.

So, you want a jogger loaded with high end features, but don't want to spend more than $200? Impossible, you say? Well, there is good news—and a great bargain we found at Babies R Us. Their new **Reebok** strollers (made by Baby Trend) are loaded with goodies at a great price. The Extreme model is quite a deal—the frame is anodized polished aluminum, so the stroller is light weight yet still has a smooth glide. Check out the suspension system and plush padding for this model; we also liked the multi-position reclining seat, no rear axle (great for runners with longer strides), ratcheting sun canopy, boot and full rain cover. All that for $200. If you don't need suspension, boot and rain cover, then the more basic Velocity model might be a better bet at $170.

## Double Strollers

### TANDEM OR FRONT/BACK: MALL STROLLER

Can we talk frankly here? It's hard to recommend a good tandem (front/back) stroller. Most parents we've interviewed on this subject say they quickly come to hate their tandem strollers, no matter what the brand. Why? Even though tandems sound like the perfect solution to transporting an infant and toddler, most models become impossible to push in short order. It's simple physics—most of these models clock in at 30 lbs. empty. Add a 25 pound toddler and a 10 pound newborn (plus diaper bag, purse, etc) and suddenly you as are trying to push nearly 70 pounds of family. Given the elongated nature of tandems, this can be difficult at best. Most are as maneuverable as a tractor trailer.

Another factor: the brand choices here are lousy. Most tandems are made by Graco and Baby Trend. Neither company is known for its quality or durability. Yes, these tandems are affordable ($150 to $200), but they are no bargain if you are cursing a broken stroller after just three months. Other choices (like Cosco) have had serious safety concerns and recalls. Yes, Peg Perego makes two great tandem models (the Tender Twin and Duette)—but they cost $300 to $500, too expensive in our opinion. In case money is no object, we'll discuss these models later in this chapter.

So, what's a parent to do? Consider a side-by-side stroller, where the brand choices are better and most models are easier to push. Parents who use a tandem abandon it after a short while for a side-by-side stroller. Or, if you insist, grit your teeth and buy a tandem—just don't say we didn't warn you.

### BEST BET: GRACO DUOGLIDER

**Type:** Tandem, mall stroller
**Weight:** 37 lbs.
**Price:** $150 for the stroller, $230 for travel system
**Pros:** Price. Stadium seating, both seats have retractable canopies, rear seat fully reclines for an infant. Can attach a Graco infant car seat. Big storage basket.
**Cons:** Heavy; can be difficult to push when fully loaded. So large when folded it may not fit into small trunks. Graco is not the world's most durable stroller brand.
**Comments:** In a choice of lesser evils, at least this stroller is cheap! And the ability to attach a Graco Snug Ride infant seat is a big plus.

**RUNNER-UP:** *Baby Trend Sit N Stand* ($150, 31 pounds) isn't really a tandem but a push cart—the younger child sits in front while an older toddler can stand in back. A jump seat in back also provides a seating area. Cool feature: an infant car seat can snap in front. (See picture earlier in this chapter).

*Evenflo's* new *"Take Me Too!"* strollers are worth a look—we like the "My Step" side entry feature that lets toddlers in the back seat get out of the stroller by themselves. Like the Graco tandem, Evenflo has stadium seating, a huge basket, front child tray, compact fold and more. This stroller comes in two versions, a basic "Express" version for $90 and a more plush "Premier" model for $150. The basic Express version lacks cup holders for parents and extra storage pockets. In general, the parent reviews of the Evenflo tandem have been quite positive.

If money is no object, then we'd suggest the *Peg Perego Duette*—at $550 retail, it is a serious investment, but the quality of this tandem is much better than anything Graco or Baby Trend offers. You get two plush seats that can be configured to face each other or both forward. It also works with the Perego infant seat and features a larger storage basket. One caveat: this thing is darn heavy, weighing in at 45 lbs. And if you want it to fold really flat, you have to remove the front seat—a major pain.

A quick mention: the One Step Ahead catalog sells a "deluxe lightweight tandem" stroller for $120. It's made by J Mason (although the catalog doesn't mention that) and features a lightweight 23 lb aluminum frame and decent size storage basket. Parents who've bought it say it is a good buy for the money, although the quality is only average.

## SIDE BY SIDE: MALL STROLLER

### BEST BET: COMBI TWIN SAVVY

**Stroller type:** Side by side mall stroller
**Weight:** 18 lbs.
**Price:** $350.

**Pros:** Among the lightest weight side by sides on the market; "acoustic canopy" (headphones), two storage baskets, six wheel suspension. Five point harness. Extra large canopies with extended visors to block low angle sun.

**Cons:** Expensive. Two-hand fold. Previous Twin Savvy had quality problems.

**Comments:** In recommending the Twin Savvy last year, we were disappointed to hear from parents who complained about the stroller's "delicate" one-hand fold (translation: it broke). Combi went back to the drawing board and came back with an improved model this year (albeit with a two-hand fold now). Also fixed: the handle on this stroller, which cracked in a previous model. So, with its shaky history, why buy it? That's because this 2.0 version is still among the best-designed (and lightest) side by sides on the market.

**RUNNER-UP:** *Maclaren's Rally Twin* ($300) is a durable, compact and easy to maneuver side-by-side. The fully reclining seats are a major plus. One downside: at 25 pounds, it is much heavier than the Combi Twin Savvy.

*Peg Perego's Aria Twin* ($300) is a lightweight (14-lb.) stroller with five-point restraint and that fashionable Italian look. Best feature: one large storage basket under both seats. The only caveat to this model: the canopies don't offer the same amount of coverage as on the Combi Twin Savvy. Parents also complain the seats aren't as padded as they should be for this price.

Need a cheap side by side to take traveling? Don't want the airplane baggage handlers to man-handle your expensive double stroller? In that case, we'd suggest the *Kolcraft* side-by-side reclining umbrella stroller. At $60, it's a steal—you get individually reclining seats, a sun canopy and more. It weighs just 20 lbs. Okay, you don't get a basket and the stroller is almost 32" wide, which means it won't fit through most doorways. And Kolcraft's quality is not impressive (don't expect this stroller to last for years—one parent told us hers fell apart after just four months). But if you need an inexpensive side by side for airplane travel or other trips, this is a good option.

## SIDE BY SIDE: OUTDOOR ALL-TERRAIN/SPORT

### BEST BET: MOUNTAIN BUGGY URBAN DOUBLE

**Stroller type:** all-terrain double stroller.
**Weight:** 32 lbs.
**Price:** $560.
**Pros:** Only all-terrain with swivel front wheels. Just 29" inches wide. Light weight (32 pounds). Height adjustable handle.
**Cons:** Price.
**Comments:** This double version of the Mountain Buggy Urban has all the same great features and advantages of that stroller (see the review in single strollers for more details). In short, this is the best all terrain double out there. A perfect choice for the beach.

**RUNNER-UP:** The new *Zooper "Tango"* weighs just 23 pounds but has an impressive set of features, including newborn-friendly seats that fully recline, rain cover, boot and more. For $270, it is a great value.

## SIDE BY SIDE: JOGGING STROLLERS (HIGH END)

### BEST BET: InStep Ultra ALUMINUM JOGGER

**Stroller type:** double jogger
**Weight:** 23 lbs.
**Price:** $230.
**Pros:** Did we mention it is just $230? Folds easily, lightweight. 16" rear wheels.
**Cons:** Front wheel does not swivel.
**Comments:** This stroller accommodates two children up to 100 pounds; it is a great jogger and super lightweight. We were impressed with how easily it folds.

**RUNNERS-UP:** Like single jogging strollers, you can go high or low end with doubles. Again, we'd emphasize that low-end double joggers are great for occasional walks or hikes, not for serious runners or off-road use. On the low end, we'd suggest the *Baby Trend Expedition Double* ($170). Basically, this is very similar to the single version of the Expedition jogger—again, not good for the serious runner.

On the upper end, The *Dreamer Design Ditto* ($390) is a 40

lb. aluminum frame double with the same great bubble canopy you see on the single Dreamer Design strollers. There are separate canopies for each seat, which is a nice feature you don't see on other brands. It only comes in a 16" wheel version and has individually reclining seats.

Also on the pricier side, we like the **Kelty Deuce Coup**, which comes in both 16" wheel ($400) and 20" wheel ($420) versions. The only caveats to these well-designed double joggers: the weight (45-47 pounds) is a bit high and the seats don't recline.

For joggers who like to hit rougher roads, consider the **BOB Duallie**, which features their excellent suspension system. At $460, it's pricey but you do get two independently reclining seats and polymer wheels (great for the beach).

## Bike Seats and Trailers

What is the better investment, a bike seat or trailer? While we will address the safety aspect of this decision on the next page, let's look at the practical aspects of each product.

The bike seat is a better bet for younger toddlers (age two to three). Since your child is much closer to you than in a trailer, you can more easily talk to her (and hence, soothe a fussy two-year old).

The better bet for older toddlers (age three and up) is probably a trailer. Why? Bike seats have a capacity of 40 pounds—and that means a toddler will grow out of it much quicker than a trailer. Note: trailers typically have minimum age guidelines. Most brands do not recommend riding with a child until he is 18 months old.

What about bike trailer/jogger combos? Some bike trailers have stroller kits (for another $50 to $100) that convert a trailer into a jogging stroller. Great, right? Kill two birds with one stone? Well, yes and no. The converted trailers make decent strollers for that occasional neighborhood walk, but serious runners or hikers won't find this a good solution. That's because converted trailers are quite wide and bulky. And converting a trailer into a stroller can take ten minutes, even after you've mastered it.

 ## Safe & Sound

What are safer for toddlers, bike trailers or infant bike seats? Research says more injuries occur with bike seats (mostly head injuries) compared to trailers. But most bike seat injuries could be eliminated if parents followed these simple guidelines:

**1** **HAVE YOUR CHILD ALWAYS WEAR A HELMET.** We'll discuss helmets later in Chapter 8, Seasonal/Outdoor.

**2** **DON'T EXCEED THE WEIGHT LIMITS OF THE SEAT.** It's sometimes easy to forget to watch for this.

**3** **ALWAYS USE THE SAFETY HARNESS FOR THE SEAT.** While this seems like a no-brainer, quite a few injuries happen when toddlers aren't buckled in properly.

**4** **PRACTICE BALANCING WITH THE SEAT EMPTY.** It takes a bit of practice to get used to balancing a bike with a child seat on the back—before you set off on a trip with your child, take a few practice spins to get used to the seat.

We realize it doesn't sound like rocket science, but that's reality—hence, it is not like bike seats are inherently more dangerous than trailers. It's just that miss-use or not wearing a helmet can make the injury rate look worse than that for trailers.

With bike seats, should you go for a front or rear seat? Rear seats are more common here in the U.S. and Canada; meanwhile, in Europe and Asia you'll see front seats (where baby sits in front of the parent on the handlebars). Frankly, we think rear seats are safer—it is easier to balance a baby on the back wheel than the front. And safety advocates are concerned parents might be distracted by their child in a front seat, taking their eyes off the road.

And then don't forget the "stuff" factor—a trailer not only holds a toddler, but also toys, groceries and all the other stuff that seems to grow exponentially as your child ages. Bike seats don't have any extra storage capacity.

For that reason, we lean toward trailers as a better solution than bike seats. Bike seats make any bike more tippy—and putting in a child while trying to balance the bike is tricky. On the other hand, fans of bike seats say trailers are not easy to maneuver in and out of tight spaces. That's important if you plan to bike in more urban areas.

## Best bets: Bike Seats, Trailers, Tag-Alongs

## BIKE TRAILER

### BestBet: Burley d'Lite
**Price:** $400.
**Weight:** 20 lbs.
**Dimensions:** 32" wide, interior width 27", inside height 25".
**Capacity:** 100 pounds.
**Pros:** The Mercedes of bike trailers—features side windows, two-kid capac-ity, storage pockets, reflective material, lifetime warranty. Converts to stroller.

**Cons:** Expensive. If buying used, remember that older models do not fold!

**Comments:** Yes, this amazing trailer is the gold standard for bike trailers—just about every detail is well designed and thought out. You get five-point harnesses, quick release wheels and a fold that takes just seconds. If you can't afford one of these new, look for deals on Burley trailers on eBay and at yard sales. You can typically pick up one for 50% off from such sources. (Note the picture above is the d'Lite with the stroller conversion kit, which is additional).

***Runners-up:*** The *Yakima Tot Rod* and *Caddy Yak* trailers are also excellent choices if you can't find a Burley in your budget. The Tot Rod runs $375; the Caddy Yak $425. The differences are small: the Tot Rod has clear windows, while the Caddy Yak is tinted. The Tot Rod has pins you have to remove to take off the wheels; the Caddy Yak have push buttons (no pins). The fabric on the more expensive Caddy Yak is a bit thicker than the Tot Rod. Discount alert: we've seen the Tot Rod on sale as little as $240 on www.AgeeBike.com.

A reader from Canada emailed his recommendation for the ***Chariot Cheetah*** (sold on Brauns.com). This trailer (single version: $325 US or $430 Canada) can go hiking, skiing or be used as a bicycle trailer. "We have one and are very pleased," the reader wrote. "The only downside: the seats do not recline and one is advised to use it as a bicycle trailer when babies are old enough to sit upright unsupported and the head is big enough to wear a safe-ty helmet."

What about the cheap-o trailers you see at discount stores for $200? Frankly, we haven't found one with the quality or safety fea-tures we can recommend.

## BIKE SEATS

**BEST BET:**
**RHODE GEAR/CO-PILOT LIMO CHILD BIKE SEAT**
**Web:** www.rhodegear.com
**Price:** $90 to $110.
**Weight capacity:** 40 lbs.
**Comments:** This is our pick as the best bet for child seats—it has a safety bar, three-point restraint and a reclining seat. The footwells also adjust for comfort. A quick release mechanism lets you easily remove the seat from the rack that attaches to the bike. Note: Rhode Gear/Co-Pilot are owned by Bell Sports, which makes jogging strollers (reviewed earlier in this chapter).

## TRAILER BIKE

**BEST BET: ADAMS TRAIL A BIKE**
**Web:** www.norco.com
**Price:** $150 at REI.
**Ages:** Three to six (up to 85 lbs.).
**Comments:** Yes, literally a third wheel for your toddler to pedal along with you! This Trail-A-Bike attaches to the seat post of an adult bike with a universal hitch. You control the braking and steering, so your toddler can enjoy the ride. Adams offers three models—the starter ($150), the folder ($180, which folds up) and the shifter ($195, which has a five-speed grip shift shifting system and folds up).

## *Family Travel Tips*

When it is time to hit the road with your toddler, how do you make sure your vacation goes smoothly? Here are our top five tips:

**1 GO AT AN OFF-PEAK TIME.** As parents of a toddler, you have the luxury of traveling when other parents (that is, those of school age kids) are not. So, carefully think about when you plan to go—there is no reason to leave the Wednesday before Thanksgiving (when the immediate world is trying to get to Grandma's house) when the Monday or Sunday would be much less stressful.

The LEAST busy days for airline travel are usually Tuesday and Wednesdays (and sometimes Saturdays). Morning flights are less likely to be delayed than evening flights. If you can, fly direct instead of changing planes. The downside of non-stop flights: they usually are more expensive than a connection.

**2** **GATE CHECK YOUR STROLLER.** That means taking it through security and then checking it at the gate—that way, when you arrive at your destination, the stroller will be waiting for you in the jetway. Few airlines let parents bring a stroller on board these days, but it is always worth trying.

**3** **SYNC THE NAP AND THE FLIGHT.** If your child always takes a nap at 2pm, then try to fly during the time. Yes, getting on a plane is very exciting and some children may not want to nap—but it is worth a try.

**4** **BRING A CONVERTIBLE CAR SEAT.** The Graco Comfort Sport is our top pick for airline travel—it is affordable yet narrow enough to fit into most airline seats. Yes, that means paying for an extra seat . . . but it is worth it in terms of safety. Ask if the airline you are traveling on has any child discounts (yes, they are few and far between, but ask anyway). You may get a discount on that second seat. What about hoping that middle seat is empty? Don't bet on it—airlines are skilled at filling every last seat these days.

**5** **BRING LOTS OF LIQUIDS.** The air inside a jet is akin to the Sahara—and kids can get dehydrated much quicker than adults. A bottle of water is a must.

Now that you are all packed, where should you go on vacation? One of the top destinations for families is the water park, that unique American institution that is fun for all. As a public service, we visited the best waterparks in America in order to find the ones that are most kid-friendly.

## The Best Water Parks in America

We're on a mission.

A couple of years ago, we saw a Travel Channel special on the Top 10 Water Parks in the US. That was it—we were hooked. We vowed to visit all the Top 10 parks. What can we say? Everyone needs a goal in life.

So far, we've hit about half the list. Along the way, we realized some parks are simply more fun than others for families. In this special report, we'll share our experiences.

Water parks are on a roll. Across the country, attendance is up and families are making entire vacations out of visiting some parks. The parks themselves are adding bigger attractions, aimed at families.

Why are water parks so popular? Let's look at the reasons:

◆ *First and foremost, water parks are family-friendly—* most cater to ALL members of the family, with attractions suitable for toddlers through teenagers. Many of the new rides are "family raft rides" which let the entire brood enjoy an attraction.

◆ *Water parks are affordable.* Yes, tickets can run $20 to $25 at some parks, but kids are always less. And most parks run numerous coupon specials and other deals, so few ever pay full price to get in. Best of all, most parks let you bring in your own food. That right there is a big money-saver, as your own picnic will be much less expensive than the food at most parks. Parking? It's free at most parks.

So now that you have a few good reasons to visit a water park, which ones should you check out? Here's our take on the three best water parks in America.

## SCHLITTERBAHN

*Web:* www.schlitterbahn.com

What the heck is a Schlitterbahn? We're not sure what it means in German, but in Texan, it translates roughly to "Big Fun."

Schlitterbahn, located in New Braunfels, Texas, is the country's second biggest water park, weighing in at a whopping 65 acres. Opened in 1979, Schlitterbahn has pioneered some of the most amazing water rides and attractions.

(Actually, there are two Schlitterbahns now—the original in Central Texas is the one we are talking about here; there is also one on South Padre Island).

The water park is also a resort—it boasts 200 motel rooms, play areas and more.

So, what's unique about Schlitterbahn? Built on the banks of the Comal River, Schlitterbahn uses the river to feed some of its attractions and pools. Yuck, you say? Keep this in mind: the Comal is a spring-fed river that is 72 degrees year around. Also, the Comal is the shortest river in the U.S.—it starts in New Braunfels (fed by springs) and rolls three miles until it joins the Guadalupe. Hence, it is clear, clean and cool.

Because the park wraps around the Comal River, it is in the cen-

water parks

ter of town—not off the interstate. Not a big deal, as signs direct you, but it does take 10 minutes or so to drive through town to get to the park.

The best advantage to Schlitterbahn—the shade. Since it is built on the riverbank, much of the park is protected from the scorching Texas sun. Rides snake in and out of the trees and the pavement never gets that hot. We should note that the newer part of Schlitterbahn (Surfenburg & Blastenhoff) has less shade.

**WHERE IT IS.** New Braunfels, Texas. Where's that? Well, it is halfway between Austin and San Antonio. (If you are flying in, the San Antonio airport is closer, about a 30 minute drive).

**HOW BIG?** 65 acres. 40 attractions, broken into two major areas.

**LAY OF THE LAND.** Schlitterbahn is a bit intimidating for most first-timers. The park is divided into two areas: the older part (Das Lagune, Slidenplatz, Kinderlund and Wave Fest) and the new part (Surfenburg & Blastenhoff). The park runs a free, frequent shuttle service between the two areas but it is darn difficult to see it all in one day (see our tips section below). Download the map off their web site to get a better idea of how the park sprawls.

**THEME.** If Bavaria had a water park, it would look like this. You have castles, kiddie areas like KindeLund—you get it. To see photos of the park, go here:
http://www.schlitterbahn.com/media-center-photos-nb.asp

**CLAIM TO FAME.** Travel Channel voted this the top water park in America. Has the only water roller coaster in the nation.

*Blastenhoff, with the Master Blaster in the background.*

*Scenes from Schlitterbahn: The Raging River (above) includes a dip in the Comal River; the Cliffhanger tube ride is aptly named!*

**DEALS.** Most restaurants along IH 35 have discounts coupons off Schlitterbahn admission prices; you can also save if you stay at the park (there is a 20% discount). We found the discounted second day tickets to also be a great deal if you plan two days there.

### OUR TIPS:

◆ *Stay at the resort.* Rooms run $100 to $200—we stayed at a one bedroom unit with kitchenette for $175. No, no one will confuse these rooms with the Four Seasons. (And yes, the hotels out by the Interstate are half the price), but you do get some perks. First, there is a 20% discount on park admission. Second, the resort rooms are ON the property—meaning, you walk out your room and a few steps away, are the rides. You also get preferred parking, next to your room. And the resort has additional pools that are open after the park closes.

◆ **Pack you own food.** Schlitterbahn may be known for many things, but great food isn't one of them. It's basically a step above school cafeteria fare (and a small step at that). Most savvy park goers pack their own food and drinks.

◆ While buses move folks from one part of the park to the other (it takes about 10 minutes), we think it is better to try to **do Schlitterbahn in two days.** Shuttling from one part to the other takes a bit of time and effort.

◆ **Try to visit mid-week.** As you'd bet, the weekends are most crazy. Mid-week, you'll find the lines shorter at most attractions. As for the seasons, July through mid-August is the busiest time. So, go earlier or later in the season to find fewer crowds. (We were there in early June and had a blast).

◆ **Splash cash**—waterproof wristbands that you can use for money—is a great way to tote around cash. Meanwhile, there are lockers around the park for $6 a day (with a $2 refundable deposit).

◆ *Claim a picnic table early.*

◆ **Doors open about 15 minutes before the official "opening" time,** giving folks time to claim tables before the attractions open.

*Got a tube? The Lagoon pool in the original part of Schlitterbahn.*

**TOP RIDES.** The Master Blaster is the country's only water roller coaster, propelling two-person rafts with jets to up and down hills. (Get in line for this when the park first opens—lines for the Master Blaster can top one hour later in the day). In the old part of the park, the Raging River is the country' longest tube ride, running an amazing two miles!

Our kids loved the chute that blasts you into the lazy river at Surfenburg; and did we mention the heated swimming pools?

**MOST UNIQUE FEATURE.** Yes, Schlitterbahn is one of the few water parks with HEATED pools with swim up bars. Not just one, but

*What goes up must go . . . down! The Mater Blaster at Schlitterbahn.*

several that are located throughout the park. The water is heated to about 95 degrees. Okay, why do you need this in Texas, where summer temps routinely top triple digits? Yes, it sounds crazy but they are quite soothing.

The use of the Comal River is also an amazing feature, as one ride (the Tunnel Tube Chute) actually ends in the river.

**OTHER ATTRACTIONS IN THE AREA:** If you want to make this a weeklong vacation, consider spending some time in nearby San Antonio (which is about 30 minutes down the road). The Alamo, Fiesta Texas amusement park, Sea World and numerous other attractions make San Antonio a worthwhile place to check out.

**BOTTOM LINE:** It really takes two days at least to see it; little known (outside Texas) gem in the hill country.

# NOAH'S ARK

Web: www.noahsarkwaterpark.com

Okay, we'll spare you the biblical metaphors, but this water park is HUGE. In fact, Noah's Ark in the Wisconsin Dells is the country's largest water park by a mile—make that a couple miles. Noah's Ark boasts an amazing 60 attractions, all smack dab in the middle of the Dells, a long-time vacation haunt of Midwesterners for over 50 years.

Unlike Schlitterbahn's location in New Braunfels, TX (where there is not much to do besides the park), Noah's Ark is just the beginning of the family fun in the Dells. The area boasts magic shows, mini golf, and more. And did we mention the INDOOR water parks? Several major "water" resorts have opened around the Dells, each boasting huge indoor water parks. Just in case you don't get enough water at Noah's Ark.

But let's talk about the water park first. Here are the details:

**WHERE IT IS.** The Wisconsin Dells is about 60 miles north of Madison, WI. Or 125 miles west of Milwaukee, WI.

**HOW BIG?** 70 acres with over 60 attractions. Big draws include two wave pools and a myriad of slides, rides and thrills.

*Look at the upper right hand corner of this picture. That's someone questioning their sanity at this moment in time! Don't do the Stingray at Noah's Ark after lunch.*

*Doesn't look that intimidating, but check out the hair on this rider of Kowabunga. Part of the family fun at Noah's Ark!*

**water parks**

**LAY OF THE LAND.** Although large, the park is rather compact—attractions are crammed into every nook and cranny. Basically, the park is built on a sloping hillside. On the west side of the park is the Big Kahuna wave pool. On the north edge is the other major wave pool (creatively titled the "Wave").

As you first drive in to the main entrance, you pass by one of their signature rides—the Flash Flood. As it sounds, this mini roller coaster goes up one big hill and then down into a big pool—soaking everyone on board and those lucky (unlucky?) enough to be standing on a nearby bridge.

There really is no "main gate" but several entrances. When you buy a ticket, you get a wristband that lets you ride the rides.

**THEME.** Not sure there really is much of a theme here. You'd think everything would be biblical, but expect for the occasional animal pair, there isn't much more to the Noah theme.

**CLAIM TO FAME.** The country's biggest water park also has several non-wet activities, including a new attraction called Noah's Adventure and a mini-golf course and bumper boats.

**DEALS.** If you stay at the next-door Flamingo Motel, you get a free ticket for each night you stay (that promo was good last we looked). Also: second-day tickets are available at half price. You can also save 10% by ordering tickets online.

**OUR TIPS:**

◆ *WATER SHOES!* They are a must here! Noah's Ark is mostly black asphalt—and that gets hot to walk on in a hurry. We found the pavement to be quite rough on bare feet. Water shoes are a necessity.

◆ *Bring something waterproof to keep money in.* "Neck safes" are sold in the gift shop; unfortunately, Noah's Ark doesn't sell "splash cash" like other parks so you'll need to keep your greenbacks handy.

◆ *As you'd guess, the most popular rides (see below) and slides have long lines that form shortly after opening.* Do these rides first and then hit the lazy river or wave pools in the afternoon.

◆ *The park tends to empty around 4pm each day, as day-trippers head home.* But Noah's Ark is open until 8pm in the peak summer season—as a result, you can hit those popular attractions late in the day without big lines.

◆ *Parking can be a bit tight, as it is dispersed throughout the park instead of one main lot.* Arrive early. Also: the traffic on the main road outside the park can be nightmareish in the summer. Bring some patience.

◆ *As with most water parks, stake your claim early*—pick out a chair or picnic table and place your towels there when the park opens.

◆ *A few rides do have height limitations (see the web site for details).* For example, the Point of No Return requires all riders to be 48″ tall. Check out which ones have restrictions so not as to disappoint the smaller ones in your party.

◆ *July and August are the busiest months; June has the least crowds because some area schools don't let out until late in the month.* The best days to visit are Sunday, Wednesday and Thursday.

**FAVORITE RIDES.** We think Noah's Ark is perhaps the most fun for families with little ones (say the under four set). Many rides are family-friendly—including the Dark Voyage, a family tube ride in the dark (okay, that might be a bit much for toddlers). The list of family raft rides here is amazing.

The kids will love the floor show . . . that's right, one of the wave pools (the Wave) has live shows with "choreographed entertainment." Well, it isn't Vegas, but hey, the kids will love it.

We thought the Paradise Lagoon was fun for school age kids—

this neat area has two "cable drops," three cannonball chutes that drop kids into 11 feet of water (yep, that's our son at right), a jumping rock and more. This is a perfect example of what's missing at other water parks . . . a fun section kids can play in for an hour or more, without long lines. Altogether, there are five little kid areas and the aforementioned non-wet activities (including a mini roller coaster and bumper boats).

**MOST UNIQUE FEATURE.** We though the Thunder Rapids ride was quite interesting. It uses "hard tubes" (not the squishy inner-tubes) and sends riders careening down chutes on two different slides. The Stingray is best enjoyed by the brave—a double slide that sends you down a steep chute and back up the other side (like a skateboard half pipe).

Also unique: the Swirl River off the Wave pool—this area becomes the equivalent of a human washing machine when the waves hit this curved area. Mucho fun. As mentioned before, the live entertainment at the wave pool is quite unique as well.

**DOWNSIDES.** Well, no place is perfect. In their review of the best water parks, the *Wall Street Journal* knocked Noah's Ark for having cold water (68 degrees the day they visited). We didn't notice this, so it might have been a seasonal issue.

Another negative: there is little or no shade in the park. Snag a lounge chair in what little shade there is, because that is a rare commodity here.

And for all the hype, we found the Flash Flood log ride to be a bit of a let down. It's something you do once and then move on.

**ATTRACTIONS.** You'll either love or hate the Dells. This famous tourist area is a great throw-back to the old days. You'll find magic shows here, lake tours on the Ducks and as we mentioned earlier, the most amazing indoor water parks. We stayed at the Kalahari (www.kalahariresort.com)—which actually has both an indoor AND outdoor water park. Yes, if the weather turns nasty, you can always take the party inside (the room rate covers admission to both parks).

Detractors will probably not like the tacky tourist trap atmosphere of the Dells—and let's be honest, there are some silly things here. But you got to love a place that has a breakfast spot called (and we're not making this up) "Paul Bunyan's Famous Cook Shanty." Yes, that is a real restaurant that offers "fun, family dining 'lumberjack style' . . ." The price for a meal? It's 63 cents times the age of your child. Can you imagine this place anywhere else in America?

**BOTTOM LINE.** Noah's Ark is fun, but add to the experience by staying at an indoor water park resort and do a few more days seeing the sights in the Dells.

## BLIZZARD BEACH

Blizzard Beach is exactly what you'd expect from a water park run by Disney—efficient and fun with a clever theme.

And it's the theme here that is the most amazing part of Blizzard Beach. Basically, as the story goes, one winter it was so cold, they opened a ski resort in Florida. Unfortunately, thanks to Global Warming, the whole thing has started melting. Yes, there is a chair lift here and other parts of the "resort" that are in various stages of a melt-down. You get the idea.

**WHERE IT IS.** Orlando. Nuff said.

**HOW BIG?** 22 attractions make this a fun park that can be seen in one day.

**LAY OF THE LAND.** A 120 foot snow-capped mountain (Mt. Gushmore) is the centerpiece here. A ski lift takes you to the top or you can take the stairs. Circling the park is the Cross Country Creek, a long lazy river that dips through several "ice caves."

*A ski resort . . . with palm trees? Welcome to Blizzard Beach.*

**THEME.** Think we've covered that, right?

**CLAIM TO FAME.** While most of the rides here are available at other parks, it's the unique theme that gives Blizzard Beach its claim to fame. That and the kid's areas are phenomenal—Tike's Peak is a special area with a kid-sized version of

Mt. Gushmore and more. Teamboat Springs is one of the longest family raft rides anywhere (running 1100+ feet in length).

**water parks**

**DEALS.** This is Disney, so no deals right? Actually, if you buy a Park Hopper Plus ticket, admission to Blizzard Beach is part of the package. Disney's season pass (Annual Water Park Hopper Ticket) is quite a deal if you live near Florida—$106 for adults or $85.73 kids. It will pay for itself in three visits and is good at any of the three Disney-owned water parks.

### OUR TIPS:

◆ As with all Disney experiences, *you need a plan* that rivals the invasion of Normandy to maximize your fun here. For example, when the gates open, send ONE person to get a locker while the rest of the brood finds a place to put the towels. Snag a chair near one of the many entrances to the lazy river. Try to get a shady spot, but remember the sun moves through the sky—think about where it will be shady LATE in the day. The "pavilions" (brown squares on the map) are covered areas that are coveted—get there early!

◆ *Do the slides early and then the wave pool and lazy river later.* Yes, the lines for the slides will get very long as the day wears on, so don't delay.

◆ *The ski lift is a clever way to get to the top of Mt. Gushmore*—but the line will usually outweigh the advantage. Take the steps instead.

◆ *Coolers are allowed,* but no alcoholic beverages or glass containers.

◆ *Thanks to the warm Florida weather, Blizzard Beach is usually open year around.* The exception: Disney "rehabs" the park in January and February (and hence, it is closed).

◆ *Water shoes are a must.* That Florida sun can toast up the concrete in a hurry.

◆ *Worried about going to the water park in winter? Don't—Disney heats the water!*

**FAVORITE RIDES.** Wow, where do you start? The Storm Stormers (three flumes that are 350 long) are a hoot, swishing through a switchback course. The Teamboat Springs family raft ride can hold six passengers and is amazing.

As we mentioned, the kid's areas (Tike's Peak—see right—and Blizzard Beach Ski Patrol Training Camp) are fantastic. The latter is more of a school-age area, with rope swing, culvert slides and ice-flow walk.

**MOST UNIQUE FEATURE.** That ski lift has to be it, although the whole place is pure Disney—they take typical water park fare and turn it up to 11. Yes, Disney has two other water parks (Typhoon Lagoon and River Country), but let's be honest—it's all about the rides. And Blizzard Beach has the best.

**DOWNSIDES.** Did we mention the crowds? Like everything at Disney, the crowds can be overwhelming. Again, the key is to arrive early and do the fun stuff before it builds. Blizzard Beach is so popular it is sometimes closed when it reaches capacity.

And there is a reason why locals call this "Blister Beach"—there is very little shade. If it is a super-hot Florida day, you might consider one of the other parks (which have more shade). If you arrive early, try to snag a spot in a "pavilion" which has shade.

Most of the best rides in Blizzard Beach require scaling Mt. Gushmore (a gazillion stairs) or waiting to take the chair lift.

**ATTRACTIONS.** Did we mention this is in the middle of Disneyworld? You get the picture.

**BOTTOM LINE.** The most creatively themed water park in America.

**CONCLUSION.** Well, that's our take on the top water parks for families. Let us know what you think. Or let us know about a favorite park you've found. Email us at authors@windsorpeak.com.

## Bottom line

What's the best stroller for toddlers? When we are asked that question by parents, we always reply "Well, what do you plan to do with it?" For the mall, we liked the Peg Perego Aria LB, although the Savvy Soho is a good second bet. Folks on the East Coast swear by their Maclarens—the Triumph is a good choice in that line.

What if you want to do some airplane travel? Given what airlines do to strollers, you need something affordable yet decent enough to last at least for the length of the trip. For that, we recommend the Graco Breeze LiteRider. At $49, it will do the trick.

Planning to take a hike? All-terrain/sport strollers are all the rage, whether you plan to hit the trails or the beach. Our top pick here is the Mountain Buggy Urban, with the Zooper Buddy as a runner-up. These excellent strollers are pricey but very well made.

For joggers, parents are blessed with many choices, both at the high and low end of the market. If you just plan to walk around the neighborhood, the Baby Trend Expedition is a good deal at $100. If you want to really run with the jogger, go for a better quality brand like the Baby Jogger III or Dreamer Design Deluxe 20 or HT.

Double strollers can mean double trouble—many parents complain about the slim pickings here. For a tandem, we suggest the Graco DuoGlider, a good buy at $150. If you can splurge, the Peg Perego Duette at $500 is much better made and will last.

For side by side strollers, we pick the Combi Twin Savvy as the best bet, although the Maclaren Rally Twin and Peg Perego Aria Twin are great as well. The best all-terrain double is the Mountain Buggy Urban Double, while the best double jogger is the Baby Jogger Twinner II.

If you plan to go by bike, we liked the Burley trailers and Rhode Gear bike seats best. And don't forget about the Adams Trail a Bike—a cool product for the older toddler that's ready to tag along on bike trips.

# CHAPTER 8

## Seasonal & Outdoor
### Summer stuff, Halloween & more

### Inside this chapter

Gone are the days when you could just plop Junior down in the middle of the living room and he'd be happy chewing your keys. No, now he's learned to walk and talk and you're just trying to keep up. You have officially entered the active zone: Toddlerhood.

Let's be honest, kids want to get out and get moving. That means they want trikes, wagons, scooters and more. And what about ballet lessons, gymnastics, swimming lessons, soccer? Don't forget backyard pools, swing sets and sandboxes. But with all this comes some serious risk and responsibility. You'll have to consider everything from sunscreen to helmets and pads to pool alarms. This chapter's goal is to discuss the best choices for seasonal and outdoor items. We divided it by seasons, so we can focus on what's needed in the summer versus the winter. So let's get rolling.

## Spring and Summer

We can always tell when spring has sprung across the country, even if we are still snow bound here in Boulder. That's because our email starts to light up with those perennial spring and summer questions—"What's the best sunscreen?" "What's the best portable tent/cabana for the beach?" "What about backyard kiddie pools?" We'll answer those questions shortly, but first let's look at the best sources to find spring/summer items for your toddler.

## *Sources: Best places to find summer gear*

**1** **WAREHOUSE CLUBS.** The variety of products you'll find at warehouse clubs will amaze you. Along with the typical sunscreen and swim diapers, we've purchased goggles, wet suits (kids sizes!) and outdoor toys. We've even found great buys on rain coats and light jackets. Check frequently throughout the season since they get new products in all the time.

**2** **DISCOUNTERS.** Stores like Target, Wal-Mart, Kmart and others carry a wide variety of outdoor toys including swing sets, kiddie pools, sandboxes and sand, trikes, bikes and wagons. You'll also find safety equipment like helmets, pads and more. Of course, their huge selection of sunscreen and swim diapers are a plus as well. And if you want to encourage a budding sports star, these stores often carry beginner soccer, hockey and basketball sets sized just for little folks as well as sleds and skates. The only caution: safety may be sacrificed a bit for price. Be sure the equipment you buy is well made with no sharp edges. And check to see if gear meets government standards and the age of your child. Don't buy a bike helmet, for example, that is made for a school age child. Be sure to get a toddler helmet instead. Without much sales help, it's easy to buy the wrong item.

**3** **HARDWARE AND BUILDER STORES.** You'll find some impressive wooden swing sets at home stores like Home Depot. The disadvantage: they may need serious tools to put them together. They are also often very expensive compared to metal and plastic versions.

**4** **THE INTERNET.** The Internet is a great resource for terrific buys on warm weather gear, bikes, trikes, helmets, skates, pads, pool alarms and much more. You'll also find lots of product and safety information on sites like those run by the Consumer Product Safety Commissions (www.cpsc.gov) and *Consumer Reports* (www.consumerreports.org). Some sites are free while others charge a small fee.

Be careful with shipping charges—many over-sized items like swing sets are for sale online at bargain prices. At least it seems like a bargain until you factor in shipping. Be sure to get all the costs before placing an order.

**5** **SPORTING GOODS AND DANCE SUPPLY STORES.** While these specialty stores may be a bit expensive, they are great resources for advice on fit and quality. And they carry specialized shoes and equipment that you might need for lessons or activities.

**6** **GARAGE SALES/CLASSIFIEDS.** (And bargain newspapers like the Greensheets, Penny Savers). These are a great resource for swing sets, used equipment, yard toys, bikes, and more. And if your child thinks he wants to be a future Sammy Sosa, you won't have to invest a lot of dollars in case that dream is replaced by a new one.

**7** **RESALE SHOPS.** We love second-hand stores for gently used sporting equipment. Example: we found Nike soccer shoes for our youngest son for just $10 (retail: $30 and up). Kids grow out of this stuff so quickly, it only makes sense to buy second hand. And just in case your child's love affair with hockey dims, you avoid the big investment in gear at retail.

## Parents in Cyberspace: What's on the Web?

◆ *Have a budding ballerina?* Check out DanceSupply.com, All4Dance.com, and DiscountDance.com for bargain prices on dance supplies. For deals on soccer supplies, we liked SoccerSupplies.com and Absolute-Soccer-Equipment.com.

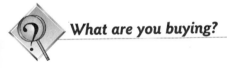

## What are you buying?

Maybe we should rename this section: "What are you NOT buying?" It's common to see over-excited parents run out to buy real baseball bats, balls and gloves when spring training begins. Or, in the case of some ballerinas-in-training we know, parents spare no expense to supply them with flouncy tutus when a simple leotard will do. But in reality, your best bet is to stick with specific items that are made just for your three, four and five year olds.

So instead of the high end wood play set with 20 foot tower, start with something simple: your little one may be better off with a Little Tikes plastic Swing Along Climber (right) with a small slide and safety swing ($109

at ToysRUS.com).

Regardless of what items you buy, safety and ability are important considerations with outdoor items. For example, you might want to buy a sand box with a top to keep neighborhood animals from using it as a litter box. Or if your little one wants to take up in line skating, check out an in line skate set from a manufacturer like Chicco or Fisher Price instead of a high priced pair from a sporting goods store.

And no matter the activity, sun and bug protection is paramount. Children are at greater risk of skin damage that can lead to serious and deadly complications in the future. Also, with the proliferation of mosquito-carried diseases, a good and safe bug repellent is important.

Ultimately, kids are at the age where they want to experiment with all kinds of activities from swimming to gymnastics to riding bikes in the neighborhood. Gear for these activities doesn't have to be an expensive investment in high quality professional-level equipment. Our bargain advice: shop at second-hand shops that resell "gently used" kids sporting equipment. That way if this week's soccer fascination gives way to next week's baseball obsession, you aren't out a wad of cash on fancy gear.

## Safe & Sound

**HELMETS AND PADS.** In April 2002, while writing the first edition of this book, a story appeared in our local paper about an eight year old skate boarder who was run over by a pickup truck. Bryce Peterson of Louisville, Colorado was wearing a helmet that day and it literally saved his life. The truck backed over his head but thanks to that helmet, Bryce was back in school just a couple weeks later. No brain damage, alive and well. Amazing, eh? And a potent reminder that children should wear helmets whenever they use equipment like trikes, bikes, bike trailers, bike seats, scooters, skates and skateboards.

The Consumer Product Safety Commission estimates that 800 bicyclists are killed each year and over a half million are treated in hospitals for bike injuries. While only 50% of bicyclists wear a helmet, the CPSC believes helmets will reduce the risk of head injury by as much as 85%. So what kind of helmet should you get? The good news is new federal safety regulations (in effect for helmets made after 1999) will help parents find and buy the correct helmet for their child. Once you buy the correct helmet, you'll need to make sure you use it correctly. Check out "What's New About

Bicycle Helmets" on the CPSC's web site (http://www.cpsc.gov/cpscpub/pubs/bike.html) for tips on using a helmet correctly.

If your child wants to try out a scooter, skateboard or skates, you'll need to find appropriate padding as well as a helmet. Padding for knees and elbows as well as wrist braces and gloves won't guarantee your child won't get hurt but may help them avoid serious injuries. Be sure to look for padding that is comfortable and fits well. It should be specifically designed for small children and should not interfere with their movement and ability to see or hear.

Don't forget to provide a soft landing surface around back yard play areas as well. See our next Safe & Sound tip for more info.

**2** **PLAYGROUND SAFETY:** According to a 1999 report from the Consumer Product Safety Commission there were 205,850 injuries on playground equipment, both public and private. Of the 147 deaths reported that year, 90% of them occurred on home playground equipment. One of the goals of the CPSC has been to increase public awareness of how to evaluate backyard playgrounds and create safer spaces for kids to play. The box on page 211 has a safety checklist produced by the CPSC to insure safe playgrounds.

**3** **FUN IN THE SUN:** parents know that it is important to protect their child from over exposure to the sun. Children are particularly vulnerable to sunburn which may lead to premature aging and even skin cancers. The importance of sunscreen, hats and protective clothing is a given. But a one-time slather of sunscreen is not enough to protect a child for the day—remember to reapply sunscreen frequently. And one of the best ways to avoid sunburn is to stay indoors during high UV index days and during times of the day when the sun is most intense (usually from 10 am to 3 pm).

Bugs are another concern for children playing out-of-doors. With increases in diseases like West Nile virus and Lyme Disease, finding and using a safe, effective bug repellent is imperative. One note about repellents: it is not recommended to use bug repellents on children under age 2. Also, children under six should only use it sparingly. Regardless of the type of repellent you use, be sure to wash it off with soap and water when your kids come inside. And don't apply repellent to broken skin or touch your child's eyes or mouth when applying it.

**4** **DRAWSTRING WARNING:** One of the most serious risks to a child when playing on playground equipment is the risk of strangulation. With that in mind, clothing manufacturers voluntarily began manufacturing children's clothing without drawstrings in the late 1990's. The CPSC stresses that parents avoid clothing with drawstrings and don't allow children to play on playground equipment with ropes, belts, or strings.

## Sun protection:
### UV clothing, sunscreen, sunglasses

Okay, you know it's important to put sunscreen on your child. But which sunscreens are best? Which SPF should you buy?

Suffice it to say that it is worth your time to protect your child from the sun. UVA and UVB rays can and do contribute to cancer in later life, which can be fatal. And kids receive most of their exposure to damaging sun before they turn 18—when you can make sure they protect themselves.

So what is UVA and UVB? UVB rays are the ones that cause your skin to burn and may be the main cause of serious cancers. UVA rays are absorbed deeper into the skin causing wrinkles and premature aging as well as immune suppression. The best sunscreens are "broad spectrum" formulas that help protect against both types of sunrays (Parsol 1789 is an ingredient to look for in broad-spectrum formula sunscreens).

And what about SPF? SPF is code for how long the sunscreen (or other cosmetic, clothing, etc.) will protect you from getting toasted. Think of it this way: if it takes you 20 minutes to begin to get a sunburn without sunscreen and you use a sunscreen with SPF 15 it will take you 20 x 15 or 300 minutes to get a burn with the sunscreen. SPF ratings higher than 30 have not been shown to be significantly more effective.

Next question: how do we know when the sun is going to be particularly dangerous on a give day? Good news: the National Oceanic and Atmospheric Administration now offers a UV Index forecast of the "probable intensity of skin damaging ultraviolet radiation reaching the surface" at mid-day in 58 cities in the US (check the Climate Prediction Center's web site at www.ncep.noaa.gov for a city near you). You can find UV forecasts on weather web sites like Weather.com and Weatherundground.com as well (a sample UV forecast map from the latter is reprinted on page 212).

So now that you know the UV forecast for your area, what action should you take? The chart on page 212 indicates the time to burn (given a certain UV index) as well as recommendation actions.

## *Home Playground Safety Checklist*

◆ *Install and maintain a shock-absorbing surface* around the play equipment. Use at least 9 inches of wood chips, mulch or shredded rubber for play equipment up to seven feet high. If sand or pea gravel is used, install at least a nine-inch layer for play equipment up to five feet high. Or, use surfacing mats made of safety-tested rubber or rubber-like materials.

◆ *Install protective surfacing at least six feet in all directions from play equipment.* For swings, be sure surfacing extends, in back and front, twice the height of the suspending bar.

◆ *Never attach*—or allow children to attach—ropes jump ropes, clotheslines, or pet leashes to play equipment; children can strangle on these.

◆ *Check for hardware*, like open "S" hooks or protruding bolt ends, which can be hazardous.

◆ *Check for spaces that could trap children*, such as openings in guardrails or between ladder rungs; these spaces should measure less than 3.5 inches or more than 9 inches.

◆ *Make sure platforms and ramps have guardrails to prevent falls.*

◆ *Check for sharp points or edges on equipment.*

◆ *Remove tripping hazards* like exposed concrete footings, tree stumps and rocks.

◆ *Regularly check play equipment and surfacing* to make sure both are in good condition.

◆ *Carefully supervise children* on play equipment to make sure they are safe.

*Source: Consumer Product Safety Commission*

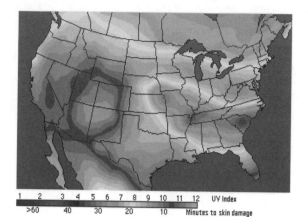

| 1 | 2 | 3 | 4 | 5 | 6 | 7 | 8 | 9 | 10 | 11 | 12 | UV Index |
|---|---|---|---|---|---|---|---|---|---|---|---|---|
| >60 | | 40 | | 30 | | 20 | | | 10 | | | Minutes to skin damage |

| UV INDEX LEVEL | MINIMAL | LOW | MODERATE | HIGH | VERY HIGH |
|---|---|---|---|---|---|
| | 0-2 | 3-4 | 5-6 | 7-10 | 11-15 |
| RECOMMENDED ACTION | | | | | 🏠 |
| | | | | ☂ | ☂ |
| | | | 👒 | 👒 | 👒 |
| | 🧴 | 🧴 | 🧴 | 🧴 | 🧴 |
| | 🕶 | 🕶 | 🕶 | 🕶 | 🕶 |
| MINUTES TO BURN | 60 | 45 | 30 | 15 | 10 |

🕶 Sunglasses Suggested   🧴 Sunscreen Suggested   👒 Hats Suggested   ☂ Shade Suggested   🏠 Staying Indoors Between 10 AM to 3 PM

*Source: Melanoma.com*

You'll notice that sunscreen is recommended no matter what the UV level. So, what's the best sunscreen? We'll address that next, plus discuss new UV kid clothing and sunglasses.

## Sunscreens

We'll recommend our top picks for sunscreens in just a second; first consider some general tips on using sunscreen, no matter what brand you use.

◆ The sun is strongest in the middle of the day from 10 am to 3 pm. This is the time to avoid extreme sun exposure.

◆ Apply sunscreen 15 to 30 minutes prior to going out in the sun. Sunscreen doesn't become effective immediately, so applying it before going out is important.

◆ Reapply after swimming and toweling off.

◆ Be generous when you apply sunscreen and don't forget areas like ears and behind the knees.

◆ Use at least an SPF of 15 (SPF 30 for fair skin). Studies have *not* shown an increase in protection with products that claim an SPF over 30.

◆ Reapply every two hours or after getting wet. Despite what the package might say, most sunscreens don't last all day.

## Best Bets: Sunscreen

Our top pick for sunscreen is **Durascreen**, a brand recommended to us by a dermatologist. Available in 15 SPF and 30 SPF formulas, we've found this sunscreen to be the best we've ever used (and Mom has incredibly fair skin!). Although it is expensive (about $8 to $10 per bottle) we have found it online at sites like www.ameri-carx.com and www.RxbyTel.com for less. It also can be ordered at a discount from wholesale clubs like Sam's and Costco (check with the pharmacy). One note of caution: Durascreen lotion stings when it gets in the eyes, especially during swimming. To avoid this problem, use the lotion on your toddler's body but then use Durascreen Sun Stick for their face, nose and near the eyes.

What if you don't want to spend the big bucks on Durascreen, what should you use? Most sunscreens are effective in meeting their SPF claim. However, don't assume that baby or kid formulations are going to be better. Children can use "adult" sunscreen without a problem. Remember that the benefits of any product rated over SPF 30 are questionable. And as with many combo products, it's more effective to apply a separate bug repellent than to use a combination of sunscreen and repellent. Why? Because sunscreen should be reapplied often (especially after swimming), while bug repellent should only be applied once a day and then washed off when you return indoors.

## *UV clothing*

Sun protective clothing is a bit different from the usual clothes we wear day to day. The Federal Trade Commission states that the fabrics used in these clothes are typically of a tighter weave and are usually darker in color. They may have a label on the garment listing its Ultraviolet Protection Factor (UPF) which is similar to an SPF in sunscreen. UPF describes the level of protection from UV rays or how much UV radiation is absorbed by the fabric—the higher the UPF the better the UV protection.

The FTC considers a UPF from 15 to 24 as "good"; 25 to 39 is "very good" and 40 to 50 is "excellent." And according to a study by University of Nebraska textiles professor Patricia Crews, the UPF protection does not wash out during laundering. One clothing product available now, Solumbra (www.sunprecautions.com) is the first clothing allowed by the FDA to claim an SPF of 30. Note: you'll see both UPF claims and SPF claims regarding UV protective clothing. Keep in mind you want at least SPF 15 and/or UPF 25.

Here are a few web sites to check out that sell UV protective clothing for toddlers: SunGrubbies.com, SunSolutionsClothing.com, and SunProtectiveClothing.com.

What if you don't want to spend the money on UV clothing? You have a couple options. You can put regular clothing on your

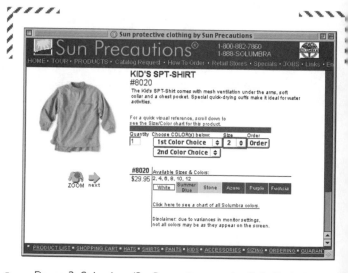

*Figure 2. Solumbra (SunPrecautions.com) sells kid's clothing and swimwear specially made to provide UV protection.*

child—the tighter the weave, the better. But this will only add another 5 to 9 SPF protection. Or you can try a new laundry treatment called "Sun Guard" from RIT, the folks best known for clothing dyes. They claim that clothes washed in this laundry additive "help block more than 96% of the sun's harmful ultraviolet rays from reaching the skin." They also claim it will not change the "feeling or comfort" or the "whiteness" of clothing. By the way, the Skin Cancer Foundation (www.skincancer.org) now recommends Sun Guard as part of your arsenal for skin protection. A six-pack runs about $20 but you can also find it as a single, a 12-pack ($40) and even a 5 lb. option ($150). You'll find RIT Sun Guard on a couple web sites: www.dermadoctor.com and www.seriouslyshady.com. Many national grocery chains also carry Sun Guard, or check out their web site at www.ritdye.com.

Finally, don't forget to add a hat to your child's summer wardrobe. And a baseball cap won't necessarily cut it. Look for the "French Foreign Legion" design (they really did use this stuff when fighting in the desert for a reason). The back and side flaps protect the neck and ears, two areas prone to serious sunburn. One of the most ubiquitous brands available is the Flap Hat from Flap Happy (www.flaphappy.com). They offer sizes up to three years and dozens of great colors and patterns. They also make wide-brimmed "Floppy" hats and "Prairie Flap Bonnets."

*Figure 3. RIT'S "Sun Guard" is a laundry treatment that adds UV protection to your toddler's clothes.*

## Sunglasses

Yes, sunglasses are important for toddlers, and not just because they make our kids look so cute. While most parents understand the importance of sunscreen for their kids, few toddlers wear sunglasses consistently. With the future risks of cataracts and other eye problems, this is important too. But they never stay on, you say? The kids lose them or break them? Yes, we agree that they can be a challenge, but so is any good habit.

So, what to look for? It is imperative that children's sunglasses block 100% of both UVA and UVB radiation. Lenses should also be large and close fitting. Teeny-tiny lenses may look cool, but they allow radiation to contact skin and eyes along the periphery. Finally, sunglasses don't have to cost a lot. Target and other discounters have affordable options.

One of the best brands of sunglasses we've discovered comes from Australia where they take their sun protection seriously. We loved *Baby Banz* (www.babybanz.com) designs with  their comfortable neoprene adjustable head band and polycarbonate lenses. They block 100% of UVA and UVB and meet stringent Australian guidelines. Price: $15. At the time of this writing they had sizes available from 0 to 3 years with 3 to 6 year sizes soon to be available. Another source: *SunGrubbies* (web: www.SunGrubbies. com). Their sunglasses are $9 for three to six year olds with 100% UVA and UVB protection.

## Beach Cabanas/Tents

Time to hit the beach? Yes, your little one is old enough to know not to eat sand. But how to keep them from broiling in the sun? The answer: a beach cabana or tent.

Several manufacturers make terrific pop up tents that have a UV coating to block dangerous rays. Thanks to great design and high-tech fabrics, most of these cabanas are lightweight, easy to carry and set up. Some of our favorites include the Kel-Gar (www.kelgar. com) line of Sun Stop'r tents. They  claim their tents block 98% of UVA and UVB radiation with an SPF of 50+. From the baby sized *Sun Dome* to the family size *Kwik*

*Cabana III*, the options all include the UV coating and easy set up. Prices range from $50 to $100 for the toddler and family options. We found Kel-Gar tents at sites like One Step Ahead (www.onestepahead.com), SunClothingEtc.com and Babies R Us.

Play Hut, makers of those pop up mazes and ball pits also has a small pop up tent with UV protection. My First PlayHut has a zip close door, mesh ventilation and even stake loops to secure the tent to the ground. Best of all it is a mere $35 (we found it at www.kidenergy.com). The only drawback—it's small so it's best for just one or two kids.

What about a large canopy for the entire family? Probably our favorite option was the Sun Screen POP Tent from Excalibur Electronics (www.excaliburelectronics.com). Just check out their web site and they have a video of how long it takes to set up this little wonder (try under 5 seconds!). Priced at $80 to $90 it offers UV protection, seats up to three people and weighs less than 5 pounds. Excaliber has added two more POP tents to its lineup: the Screen Room and the Sun Cabana. The Screen Room ($89) is designed with more see through mesh so you can keep your eye on the kids. The Cabana actually adds more privacy with opaque sides and enclosed, zippered front ($99).

Here's a new option for the beach: *Graco's Pack 'n Play Sport* (pictured). This new hexagonal play area weighs just 10 pounds and sets up with a one-step unfolding feature (see below). It features a removable canopy that blocks UV, water resistant floor, and a lockable play "hatch" that enables toddlers to crawl in and out. It will be available by the time you read this for $150.

We saw a demo of this new unit and were impressed—we liked all the features and portability (it even comes with a carry bag). But the $150 price may make it a tough sell when simple pop-up tents are under $50.

## *In the Swim*

Looking for some cool pools or pool toys to entertain the kids with this summer? What about life vests for that boat trip you've been planning for months. And how do you handle Junior at the beach or pool when he's still in diapers? Here are some solutions.

### SWIM DIAPERS

Most swimming pools and swim lessons don't allow children to wear standard diapers in the pool, as you might guess. The alternatives are either disposable swim diapers or cloth versions.

Disposable swim diapers from Huggies, called Little Swimmers, are a great option for parents who prefer disposable. We used them often when traveling or at the beach. The large size was $15 for a pack of 15 and fit kids 32 pounds and up. That's not cheap

---

## *Swimming Lesson FAQ*

In the old days (BC, before children), I taught swimming lessons to children to pay my way through college. I was fortunate to be trained by legendary swim teacher Lynnie Middledorf, who taught generations of kids how to swim here in Colorado. As a result, I'm often tapped for tips and info by friends and neighbors who want to know the best way to teach their child how to swim. So here is my advice:

### DENISE'S SWIMMING LESSON Q&A

*1. When should my child start swimming lessons?* Babies can get in the water with mom as early as 6 weeks. However, they aren't going to be doing the backstroke for a few years after that. My advice: get them comfortable with pools on your own or through mom-and-tot swimming groups, but formal lessons probably won't work well until they are three years old and out of diapers.

*2. Should my child wear water wings or sit in a floatie?* No kid can learn to swim wearing floaties or water wings. In fact, these devices can create a false sense of security for kids and parents. I can't tell you how many accidents happen each year when parents think their kids are safe in their water wings. These plastic inflatables can and do pop.

but for occasional use, they're great.

When we had our kids in regular mom-tot swimming lessons, we purchased a cloth swim diaper since the disposables were so expensive. Cloth works great as long as you choose a tight fitting size. The goal here is no leaks. And they are very affordable; we've seen them for as little as $5. *Flap Happy* (www.flaphappy.com) makes a variety of cute swim diaper designs in bright colors for kids up to 3 1/2 years. You'll also find versions available from the following web sites: DiaperBaby, EcoBaby.com, and BabyBag.com. Almost all cloth diaper suppliers also offer reusable swim diapers.

## FLOTATION DEVICES

As we discuss in the following box on swim lessons, we aren't big fans of using floatation devices to teach children to swim. Sure they can be lots of fun, but don't fool yourself. Only swim lessons

*3. Will my kid be safer in the water if we take him to swimming lessons?* Actually, your child will probably need even more supervision. Swim lessons should teach your child to be comfortable in the water, but they won't "drown proof" him. In fact, any swim school that promises to drown proof a baby should be avoided.

*4. What kind of program should I look for?* Find a program that is kid centered. Yes, that's easier said than done, of course. One clue: look for swim schools that operate year round, not just as a part-time summer business. Find a heated pool so your child will be comfortable and enjoy himself.

*5. What kind of instructors should be teaching my child?* Ask about the level of experience of the instructors and the number of years the instructors have been teaching. Find out about their training: Red Cross, YMCA, CPR, etc. Look for instructors that have at least a couple of years of experience teaching children.

*6. Should I visit a lesson before I sign up?* Absolutely. Look at this with the same critical eye as when you shop for a preschool. Are the teachers in the water with kids or standing on the side yelling at them? What's the teacher/student ratio? How do they handle a shy child who won't get in? Or another child who dominates the class and misbehaves? Most importantly, are the kids having fun? And do they get some free playtime at the end?

from a caring, well-trained swim teacher and encouragement from supportive parents will teach kids to be good swimmers and safe in the water.

So we recommend parents invest in fun water toys like diving rings, rafts, balls and squirt guns, but don't rely on float rings and water wings to protect your child from an accident. A couple great web sites for just such toys are PoolToy.com and Pools.com.

We've also found some great toys and gear at Target, Wal-Mart and Kmart. Remember you don't have spend a fortune on pool toys. A simple $5 raft from Target can provide hours of fun. A great web site for deals on pool rafts and toys is CoolSportsEquip.com. And don't forget to shop at end of the season sales. You'll find yard sprinklers, goggles, swim fins and more.

What about life vests for kids (also known as personal flotation devices or PFDs)? Yes, you need to purchase a life vest for your child if you have plans to go boating. And it is paramount that you find a life vest that fits your child well. While specific requirements for PFDs vary from state to state, the Coast Guard recommends that you buy a PFD that applies to your child's age, the type of boat and the specific type of boating you'll be doing.

Smaller children should have a PFD with a crotch strap and all kids PFDs should fit snugly and not ride up over the child's face. Remember a PFD will not prevent a child from drowning, rather it will only keep her afloat. Parental supervision is most important.

A great alternative to the bulky and uncomfortable life vest that most of us are familiar with is the "Aqua Force" from MyPoolPal. This is the only Coast Guard approved swimsuit PFD. Basically, the folks at My Pool Pal (www.mypoolpal.com) designed a swimsuit with foam inserts. This allows your child to wear one garment and meet the PFD requirements for kids. The suits don't ride up over their faces, don't need an uncomfortable crotch strap and are single pieces without extra straps, etc. Now, at $70, these guys are a bit expensive, but for serious boaters this is a great option. MyPoolPal makes both boy and girl versions of the Aqua Force (the girl's version is pictured).

Finally, what about those training suits with the inserts that can be removed or deflated? Their biggest disadvantage is that they keep your child in a vertical position making it tough to learn to swim horizontally. Once again we don't recommend these to teach swimming to small children.

## *Backyard play equipment*

Tired of schlepping the kids to the park or the pool? Looking for a bit of fun time at home instead? Let's talk about kiddie pools and sprinklers, swing sets and sandboxes. Consider the two schools of thought about toddler backyard equipment: buying big, semi-permanent equipment or buying less expensive transitional options.

School #1: those parents who want to buy backyard equipment only once. They'd prefer to put in those deluxe wooden swing set/climbing towers with twisting slide when their kids hit the toddler years. They figure the set will just hang out for years and years as their kids grow and will still be loads of fun for a ten-year-old.

School #2: folks who figure they'd rather have some small, plastic slides and climbers with cheap pools and plastic sandboxes so their kids won't be intimidated. They also won't worry as much about accidents when the climbing tower is only four feet off the ground as opposed to eight feet.

So, how do we come down on this? Well, as usual, it depends. We can see both arguments (how's that for commitment?) but with our kids we put off the big swing set until our oldest was about four years old. Some of our neighbors waited until their kids were in kindergarten. You have to measure how well your heart can take the thought of your three-year-old hanging from the top of a swing set! Remember that if you build it (or install it), they will climb it. And that leads to some safety tips.

## *Safe and Sound*

As we noted earlier, it is imperative that you pad the area around a play set with plenty of sand, bark chips or chopped up rubber (up to nine inches deep). Grass just doesn't cut it. Also don't forget to keep ropes and string away from play sets. Here are several other tips:

◆ *Don't allow children to play in a kiddie pool without supervision.* This means either bring the cordless phone outside with you or plan on not answering it or the front door. It takes only a few minutes for a child to drown.

◆ *Always empty out pools after your children are done playing with them.* We recommend turning them over so if it rains, there will be no water collecting in the pool. Remember, toddlers can drown in less than an inch of water.

◆ *Cover the sandbox after every use.* Your neighborhood cats (and other animals) will see it as a great supersized litter box. If it makes it easier to remember, buy a sand box that has it's own cover or just use a tarp.

◆ *Check for sharp edges and exposed hardware.* Any item that can snag clothes or skin and hair is a big red flag. Also look for smooth wood (if you choose this type of structure). Splinters can be a huge problem.

◆ *Follow the directions when building any structure.* If you've got any pieces left over, that could be a problem. If you're building an item (like a tree house) from scratch, make certain that you use screws whenever possible rather than nails which can pull out of wood more easily.

◆ *Follow the safety advice in the directions.* They aren't just trying to save their butts from a lawsuit; they really don't want your child to get injured. And neither do you. If you buy a used play set, see if you can contact the company to get a copy of the directions for your set.

## Best Bets: Play Sets

**PLASTIC:** Check out products made by *Little Tikes* (www.littletikes. com) and *Step 2* (www. step2.com). They offer a wide variety of plastic play sets from those for the very young to com-

plicated climbing towers and slides for older kids. Usually simple to put together with smooth parts and little exposed hardware, they are also the least expensive option out there. A simple Easy Store Slide Junior from Little Tikes is as little as $25 while a Playhouse Climber and Swing Extension can be as much as $530. Pictured here is the 8-in-1 Adjustable Playground System.

**METAL:** *Hedstrom* (www.hedscape.com) is the big name in metal playsets. They offer the traditional sets you remember as a kid, plus a large number of

add on products. They have been through a series of recalls, so if you're buying a second hand set, you'll need to check with the CPSC on recalls (www.cpsc.gov). Available at Toys R Us, they start at about $180.

**WOOD:** These are available from a huge variety of sources including building supply stores, toys stores, even specialty stores. *Rainbow Play* (www. rainbowplay. com), a manufacturer of red-

wood play sets, sells their products through a network of 250 retailers across the US. Prices start at (are you sitting down?) $2500. Hedstrom, mentioned above, also manufactures wooden sets.

Want to build one yourself? Check out Home and Garden TV's web site (www.hgtv.com) for plans and instructions. EHow.com (www.ehow.com) is another do-it-yourself web site with plans.

## *Arsenic and old playground equipment?*

Here's a scary topic that was recently reported in the press: arsenic used as a preservative to treat wood. And that wood has found its way into many a play set. What's up with that?

In February of 2002, the Environmental Protection Agency announced that they would be ordering pressure treated wood with arsenic in it off the market at the end of 2003. Like us you're probably saying, "Why did they wait?" Well, the feds say they had to give the industry time to come through with an alternative.

How do you spot arsenic treated wood? Look for pressure treated wood with caution labels—and DON'T buy it. Instead, consider using cedar or redwood (more expensive but naturally pest resistant woods). Another option: look for a new version of pressure treated wood called ACQ (check out this site, www.treatedwood.com/ news/, for a news release on ACQ). Be careful about purchasing second hand wooden play sets too. And don't forget plastic and metal swing sets are still out there at typically cheaper prices.

## Wading Pools

Nothing is more fun to a toddler than a backyard pool sized especially for them. But you don't have to spend a fortune to get something that's fun. Here are the key things to look for:

◆ **Price:** The majority of most kiddie pools are incredibly reasonably priced. If you spend more than $60 on a pool, we'll have to vote you off the island. The plainest of basic pools should be $15 or less.

◆ **Size:** Look for a pool that will fit more than one or two kids. Having a backyard pool is a great way to entertain kids during summer play dates and maybe Dad or Mom will want to get in on a particularly hot day.

◆ **Features:** Kids love bells and whistles. And bright colors. For example, we found the *Pool Sports Center Play ground* inflatable pool on Amazon.com (see picture) that had two

pools divided by a volleyball net, a basketball net and a t-ball accessory. Even better, one half of the pool was covered cabana-style. And the price? Only $25, half off the $50 retail. Hard to beat all those features for so little money. Another cool option to check out: SummerToy.com's playground pools ($25 to $50). Even if you go for a basic plastic pool, be sure to choose a colorful one.

◆ **Durability:** Most pools are so cheap, they are considered disposable—and few last beyond one season. However, if you have a particularly rambunctious group, molded plastic seems to be the way to go. And remember some inflatable pools come with a pump, while others require you to buy a separate pump.

## Fall/Winter

Whew! Spring and summer seasonal stuff is quite overwhelming. Fall and winter, on the other hand is more simplified. There are basically two major events here: Halloween (our favorite holiday) and winter. First, let's look at the best web sites for Halloween costumes and crafts. Then, we'll finish with winter gear.

## HALLOWEEN

Here are three great web sites for costumes, advice and crafts:

### *About.com*
*Web Site:* www.about.com; search for Halloween.
*What It Is:* A huge web site that has all kinds of info on everything you could need or want.
*What's Cool:* It's a great place for ideas on Halloween costumes. Under the Arts and Crafts sub-topic we found all kinds of suggestions on making your own costume. There are over 800 entries including a cardboard box fire engine, a bumblebee and even a glow-in-the-dark skeleton. You can also submit your own ideas. So if you're looking for inspiration, About.com is a terrific resource.
*Needs Work:* Start with a search for Halloween costumes. Otherwise, you'll spend your whole day browsing around trying to find the right stuff.

### *Family Fun*
*Web Site:* www.familyfun.com
*What It Is:* This Disney-owned web site is an extension of their great Family Fun magazine.
*What's Cool:* The holiday crafts include décor, party ideas and, of course, costumes. The costumes range from simple ideas using around-the-house items to complex creations. We loved the "Pick of the Litter" costume where your child is dressed like a mommy dog carrying a box of puppies. Too cute! They even have a costume contest every year and you can check out last year's winners for ideas.
*Needs Work:* Some ideas require sewing which is not always an option.

### *Halloween Street*
*Web Site:* www.halloweenstreet.com; pictured on the next page.
*What It Is:* An extensive resource for children's costumes and accessories.
*What's Cool:* They have quite a large selection of kids costumes affordably priced ($10 to $35 in most cases). We found costumes ranging from Winnie the Pooh and Big Bird to Angel Barbie and Power Rangers. Accessories are also available.
*Needs Work:* There aren't pictures for every costume option, leaving you to guess what the "Twinkle Fairy" really looks like. They also mix in baby costumes with toddler options, which forces you to look through everything if you're trying to get some ideas.

seasonal

Other web sites to consider: One Step Ahead (www.onestepa-head.com), Lillian Vernon (www.lillianvernon.com), Baby Style (www.babystyle.com).

## Safe & Sound

Remember the cute little costume you bought for your babies first Halloween? They looked so adorable for pictures, but when your doorbell started ringing, your little monkey was ready for bed. Fast forward to today: your little one is finally ready for the main Halloween event: trick or treating. Certainly by the time they're four or five (some earlier), toddlers will want to trek around the neighborhood in the dark (even if it's only your block) and collect some yummy goodies.

And here's when things get complicated. You're walking around in the dark on uneven sidewalks to collect candy from, in some cases, complete strangers. It may be cold, it may be raining or snowing and there are other ghosts and goblins out as well. How do you keep kids safe during this exciting but chaotic holiday? Here are a few tips:

**1 MAKE IT FLAME RETARDANT.** When buying a costume, check that it is flame retardant. And if you'll be making your munchkin's costume check that the material you chose is flame retardant as well (polyester is a good choice).

**2** **DRESS FOR THE WEATHER.** Even though your little ballerina may balk at wearing sweats and a jacket over her beautiful tutu, remind her she'll be able to collect more candy if she's warm and toasty.

**3** **REFLECT ON IT.** Either buy a costume that has reflective fabric on it (front and back) or head to the fabric store for reflective strips to sew on your child's costume. Pick bright colors as well.

**4** **NO MASKS.** Sure your guy wants to look as much like Spider Man as he can, but nix the mask. Instead use kid friendly face paint to achieve the look. Then you can be sure his eyesight isn't obscured by a sliding mask.

**5** **AVOID HIGH HEELED SHOES.** There are plenty of beautiful princess shoes out there that don't require your little one to stand on her tip toes. Weather conditions may be wet or snowy and you don't need to exacerbate the risk with high heels.

**6** **DON'T BE A DRAG.** Avoid costumes that drag on the ground—these are a tripping hazard when traveling in groups. Test this out before the big day to be sure.

**7** **LIGHT ME UP.** Buy small flashlights or glow sticks to light up them and their surroundings. Older kids can wear them around their necks in some cases.

**8** **NO SNACKING.** Don't let kids snack as they walk. It makes them inattentive and parents won't have a chance to look over the candy in advance. Especially with highly allergic kids, go through the candy first before they eat it.

**9** **ALTERNATIVES.** If you don't feel comfortable trick or treating in your neighborhood or don't want to take your kids out in iffy weather, consider alternatives like local malls. Check parenting newspapers for options.

**10** **ALWAYS GO WITH YOUR CHILDREN OR SEND THEM OUT WITH OTHER RESPONSIBLE ADULTS.** If they trick or treat with another family or group, write down emergency info on the inside of your child's clothes, or put an emergency contact paper in their pocket. That way, if they get separated, someone can help them get home.

◆ **Shopper Tip:** *Buy Halloween costumes with a bit of room if you live in a cold climate.* You may find it necessary to add leggings or even sweat pants to your child's costume when they go out to trick or treat. The extra room is key to comfort.

◆ **Waste of Money:** *Buying costumes for next year.* Yes, you think you're being smart when you see those Barney costumes on sale at the end of Halloween. You'll just buy the next size up because you just know Junior will still love the Big Purple One. But really, kids' tastes change as fast as. . . well, yours. So don't bother. Now if you want to buy a few packs of make up or colored hair spray or neutral wigs, etc., it might be worth it. But never assume you can predict your child's future Halloween costume preference.

## WINTER GEAR

Here's our top pick for a great winter gear web site:

### Cool Sports Equipment
*Web site:* www.coolsportsequip.com
*What It Is:* A great sporting goods site with plenty of kids' options.
*What's Cool:* If you're looking for off-season bargains on good quality sporting goods, you'll find them here. We saw ski helmets on sale in the spring for 40% off. And in season items are widely varied as well. Look for kids' skis, helmets, sleds, clothing and more. Brands include Molehill, Head and Giro. Best of all, they promise to "do their best" to beat any other web site's prices.
*Needs work:* You sure have to go through a lot of windows to get to the items you're interested in.

◆ For winter sports gear, also check out Sports4Kids.com, REI.com, Sno-Ski.net, SierraTradingPost.com, Campmor.com

 Safe & Sound

1 **REMOVE ANY HOOD DRAWSTRINGS.** Although clothing manufacturers have voluntarily removed drawstrings from most children's clothing, you may find some drawstrings on used clothing, particularly coats and jackets. Remove them immediately, as they are a strangulation hazard.

2 **BUY AND WEAR HELMETS AND OTHER PROTECTIVE GEAR.** Even adults are recognizing that they should wear ski hel-

mets, but it's even more important for kids. As with bike helmets, your child can avoid serious brain injury with a properly fitted ski helmet. And don't forget to insist on pads when playing hockey or ice-skating. Especially at first, kids are going to crash a bit; padding will cushion the blow.

**3** **INVEST IN SKI LESSONS.** Most ski resorts have "learn to ski" packages for youngsters—they teach the basic turns and safety advice (like getting on and off a ski lift safely). If your child has a disability of any sort (physical, mental, learning) that you can document, many resorts offer terrific lesson options including private, one-on-one instruction for a reduced rate. Don't be afraid to ask.

## Smart Shopper Tip

◆ *Look for mitten clips to help you keep track of the little buggers!* You can also buy some mittens on a string that you thread through the coat. This may save your sanity a bit. One tip: teach your child to stuff hats/gloves into coat sleeves to prevent them from getting lost.

◆ *When buying rain gear, make sure it's lined.* Sure, it's cheaper, but a rain coat without a lining can chill you to the bone. Same thing goes for rain boots. Those hard plastic and rubber books need a bit of lining or some thick socks to keep tootsies toastie.

◆ *Label everything.* Whether your child attends preschool, daycare or just heads over to a friends' house for a play date, label every piece of outdoor clothing they've got. Replacing this gear is expensive, so you'll want to keep your track of it.

## Wastes of Money

◆ *Jackets that go on over your child's head.* We found this one of the most difficult feats to accomplish when dressing kids to go outside. Not to mention that you just spent all morning combing their hair only to mess it up when they put on their coat. Instead buy coats that button, snap, velcro or zip up the front.

◆ *Expensive mittens/gloves.* We can't begin to count the number of singles and pairs of mittens we've lost. And we've certainly heard our own parents complain that we were even more irresponsible when we were kids. So don't buy those Patagonia ski gloves that cost $60 when an affordable fleece pair will do in most cases. See our money saving tips below for specific places to buy affordable gloves. The exception: if you're buying ski gear for a budding Pikabo Street, get the warmest gloves you can find. Check out some of the web sites we mentioned earlier for deals.

◆ *Hats.* Now wait a minute before you protest. We have kids who hate to wear hats and they lose them all the time anyway. So we compromise. We buy coats with hoods. Or we buy ear muffs/head bands that are cheaper than hats in most cases. Now, if you're lucky and your toddler will do whatever you ask, ignore us and buy a couple hats.

◆ *Umbrellas.* We know, kids love to play with umbrellas. But they can get expensive if damaged. Your best bet is a rain coat with hood or a rain hat. Hand them one of your old beat up umbrellas for playtime.

## Money Saving Secrets

**1 eBay.** We've found incredible bargains on designer name clothing online at eBay. Upper end clothing stores often use this site to get rid of last season's items. For example, we found a girls' Austrian boiled wool jacket by Geisswein on eBay for a mere $100. Sounds expensive, but this jacket originally sold for $300. Not a bad savings.

**2 Garage Sales.** Jackets for $5 (or maybe $1), mittens for 50¢ and skates for $10—we've seen these bargains and more at yard sales.

**3 Shop early or late.** When it comes to winter gear it pays to be early—or late. We've noticed many outdoor stores have winter gear/ski sales in August. And again in early spring with their season clearances—we found a $100 winter coat for just $20 at a department store winter clearance.

**4 Target.** This discounter is our favorite source for affordable winter gear (gloves, hats, boots). We saw one fleece hat and mitten set for $12. Later it was marked down to only $6. Fleece tops regularly priced at $10 were marked down to $5.

**5** **WAREHOUSE CLUBS.** We've found kid's ski pants at Costco for just $15. Heavy duty ski jackets were only $30 and fleece lined rain coats $15.

### Bottom Line

Hit warehouse clubs like Sam's and discounters like Target for the best deals on seasonal gear (swim goggles, outdoor toys, swim suits, hats and gloves etc). We also found the web to be a great source for specialty items like pool toys.

The best sunscreen for toddlers is Durascreen. We also were impressed with the new sun protective clothing from Solumbra and kid-size sunglasses from Baby Banz. The best beach cabanas are made by Kel-Gar and Play Hut. And we thought Excalibur's Sun Screen POP Tent was a winner.

When summer turns to fall and little children think about Halloween, surf to HalloweenStreet.com, FamilyFun.com and About.com's Halloween section for the best selection of Halloween costumes and tips for do-it-yourselfers.

For fall/winter gear, we liked the deals on CoolSportsEquip. com. Don't waste your money on jackets that go over your toddler's head—they aren't worth the fight.

# CHAPTER 9

## Toddler Proofing
### *Affordable safety advice*

### Inside this chapter

**"W**ant to see something really scary?" *Yes, that catch phrase from the old Twilight Zone TV show could easily apply to the world of child safety. Sample scary fact: 146,250 kids were injured by toys alone in 2002, according to the Consumer Product Safety Commission.*

Not a day goes by without some horrific story about dangerous products crossing the newswires or flashing across TV. It's enough to make you seriously consider securing your child in a plastic bubble inside an empty, non-toxic round room. Or at least wrap them in bubble pack before you let them out the front door.

Before you panic, it's smart to realize that an ounce of prevention can head off most of the accidents that injure kids. That's the bottom line of this chapter: toddler proofing your house, safety around your pool and at the public playground, first aid kits and requirements, fire safety and more.

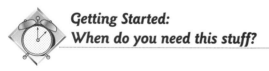

### Getting Started:
### When do you need this stuff?

You probably already have your house baby proofed with toilet locks, cabinet locks, outlet plugs and more. But now that your little one is even more mobile and even more curious, you'll find that some of those items you didn't cover earlier will become an issue. For example, we never thought our 18-month-old would be able to open the fridge so those appliance straps seemed a bit useless. But then at three, he was retrieving the ingredients to fix his own omelet. Whoa!

But there is good news: older kids can participate in learning to be safe. Fire safety is a topic you can begin to broach with books, videos and even a fire safety plan. Toddlers also want to start playing with older kid toys like Legos and Barbies. But parents are still going to have to watch out for age appropriate toys and accessories.

## Toddler Proofing: Affordable Ideas, Advice

How is safety-proofing for a toddler different than a baby?

Well, you may find that it is time to take down some of safety devices and add a few more. For example, you'll have to provide access to toilets for a toddler who is potty training. But, on the other hand, now that your toddler has become an accomplished climber, you might want to consider adding window guards, especially in warmer weather. Here are a few other suggestions:

◆ **Outlets.** It's still a great idea to keep most of them covered up, but those cheap plugs may need to be replaced. Parents (and our experience) tell us that their toddlers have figured out how to dislodge plugs. In this case, consider the type of plate cover that slides to the side. Kidco (www.kidco.com) makes one called the Standard Outlet Cover for about $5. Although they are more expensive they are also more effective at thwarting little fingers.

◆ **Appliance straps and locks.** As we mentioned, our little guys did eventually manage to pull open the fridge door, not to mention the front-loading washing machine. If you don't want her munching indiscriminately, we'd recommend appliance straps. And don't forget to the dishwasher and oven locks. Another recommendation: if your stove is not anchored to the floor, now is the time to do it. Most appliance and hardware stores have a piece of hardware that will secure your stove so it doesn't tip over if Junior is hanging on the oven door.

◆ **Furniture anchors.** Securing furniture to the wall especially in your child's room is very important. Chests of drawers and bookshelves are tempting targets for budding mountain climbers but can crush a child if they tip over. Anchors for such items are an important investment. Mommy's Helper offers a tip resistant furniture safety bracket for about $5 (www.mommyshelperinc.com). Another major tip hazard: TV's. Secure a TV in a cabinet that is anchored to the wall; or

## The Best First Aid Kits

One of the best things we've ever invested in was a pre-packed first aid kit from *First Aid Only* (www. firstaidonly.com). Inside you'll find a huge assortment of band aids, hand sanitizer, first aid guide, scissors, ace bandages, antiseptic spray and more all in a handy carrying case. We can't tell you how many times this has come in handy for our kids. The kit with

144 pieces sells for $27 although we've found it at warehouse clubs for much less. The company also makes a specific kit for vehicles for $18. It has fewer items, but will do the job. Hint: Keep one in each car, as most first aid needs seem to happen at parks or away from home.

By the way, one reader wrote recently to complain about the poor quality of some types of band aids available. She recommended staying away from no-name brands since they didn't really stick well. On the other hand, Band-Aid, Curad and Nexcare are among the best at sticking. No matter the brand, be sure to avoid putting any lotions on the cut (a bit of antibiotic ointment directly on the wound is okay) since lotion keeps the adhesive from sticking. But consider buying some of those cheap band aids for those days when you child wants to wear them as a fashion statement. Seems every toddler goes through a phase of covering his entire body with band aids.

If your child spends a lot of time in the water (for example, in the summer at the pool or beach) and bandages constantly fall off, consider a liquid bandage. Made by Band-Aid (there is a generic version as well), Liquid Bandages are 100% waterproof, flexible and easy to use on hard-to-cover areas. You merely apply the liquid seal to the cut and let it dry. Then your child can do whatever she likes without worry. As the wound heals, the liquid bandages wears off. Or it can be removed with baby oil.

make sure your TV can't tip over on your toddler.

◆ *Don't display tempting food, toys or gifts where a child can see them, but not reach them.* You may think that putting something up will keep your child from getting it. However, they may just be motivated to grab a step stool or a chair or even climb some shelves to get to the "prize." Be sure to hide items both high up and at the back of cabinets and shelves. And don't let them see you hide it!

◆ *Keep ladders and step stools put away and even locked up.*

◆ *Lock doors.* If you have a security system, set it to chime every time a door is opened. That way you can be advised if Elvis has left the building. If you don't have a security system, be sure to close doors to the outside or garages and basements. You may want to consider installing a keyed lock or a hook and eye high up on your doors to keep kids from wandering into basements or garages.

Another idea: there are devices that can be installed on both sliding doors and regular doors that cause the door to automatically close behind you. This is a great idea for doors that open onto pool areas.

◆ *Cabinets and drawers.* We'd continue to keep the locks on cabinets with dangerous appliances or sharp implements. And continue to lock up medicines and household cleaners and poisons. Four and five year olds can probably handle having cabinets with dishes and silver ware available. After all, it's time to get them to help set the table and other chores. So you can begin to loosen up a bit on many of your cabinets.

◆ *Keep the Poison Control number handy.* Betsy Jaffe, a reader of our *Baby Bargains* book, emailed this tip: there is now one universal toll free phone number for parents to contact in case of a poisoning: (800) 222-1222 (web: www..1-800-222-1222.info). This new national poison control center can answer questions about emergency treatment, medicine, household and outdoor poisons.

## Toy Safety

Since your life has become consumed by your child's desire to collect more toys than any other kid on the planet, it's important to consider toy safety. No matter how many toys your child has, you'll still be harassed to buy the newest Blues Clues character or get the latest Happy Meal toy from McDonalds. But how do you keep your child safe when she's playing with My Little Pony?

◆ *Read the label.* If you have a three-year-old, don't buy a Lego set with a label for 8+ years. Chances are the parts are a choking hazard plus it will be complicated to build. In the case of Legos, the

## *A helping of ELF STEW*

Don't call PETA to protest our inhumane treatment of elves—ELF STEW is our easy way to remember what to keep in mind when buying toys for kids. So here goes:

**E.** *Electrical Toys:* Make sure that battery compartments require a screw driver to open them. You don't want Junior playing with those batteries.

**L.** *Loud Noises.* Children's ears are particularly susceptible to damage from loud sounds. Check it out before you buy it. And if the item has a volume control, keep it down.

**F.** *Flying Objects:* Projectiles are big no-no's for little kids. Besides losing parts, your child can get hit in the eye or hit someone else's child.

**S.** *Sharp Edges and Points:* Run your fingers over the entire toy to check for sharp edges. Also pointed objects should be avoided. When skiing once, we asked a ski instructor why the littlest skiers never have poles. Answer: they will use them as weapons!

**T.** *Tiny Parts:* Anything can end up in a child's mouth, even when your little one is school age. Best to avoid the temptation altogether. And don't forget there may be other children in your house who are younger and even more vulnerable to snacking on toy parts.

**E.** *Emotional Hazards:* "There's nothing scarier that a clown!" is one of our favorite lines from *Sex in the City*. And let's be honest: clowns ARE darn scary. My parents made the rookie mistake of hanging a clown painting in my room—the source of many nightmares! So think about the scare factor when buying toys for your child—some monsters and characters may seem cute, but be careful.

**W.** *Wrong Toy for the Wrong Age:* There is an age limit on all toys for a reason—to keep small or dangerous parts away from small children. Don't assume the age limit is advisory or related to ability. Later on, some toys like Legos will have an age ability range, but with kids five and under, the limit is all about safety. Make sure relatives follow age guidelines as well.

*Thanks to Dr. Ari Brown for her ELF STEW acronym. Dr. Brown is a pediatrician in Austin, Texas and author of the book, Baby 411: Clear Answers & Smart Advice for your Baby's First Year (www.baby411.com).*

parts often break off and get lost.

◆ *Even if the toy is appropriate to your child's age, make sure your child's behavior doesn't render the toy dangerous.* For example, if your child still mouths toys at four years of age, stay away from toys with small parts that could be a choking hazard.

◆ *Look for toys that are well constructed.* Take them out of the box and really give them the once over before you buy. Tug on small parts like button eyes to be sure they are secure.

◆ *Avoid toys that have sharp edges or points.* If you buy electric toys with a heating element (like an Easy Bake Oven), make sure there is adequate adult supervision.

◆ *Immediately throw out the plastic packing that many toys are wrapped in.* It could be a suffocation hazard.

◆ *Keep toys intended for older children away from younger brothers and sisters.* This may be difficult, but take great care not to introduce inappropriate toys to younger siblings.

◆ *Finally, insist that family and friends abide by the same guidelines.* This is one of the hardest parts of parenting: policing the buying habits of your family. Just tell them up front to be aware of buying age-appropriate gifts. And be prepared to return items or hide them until your toddler can actually safely play with them.

## Pool Safety

In *Baby Bargains*, we discuss pool alarms and pool safety. In short, our recommendation is that you choose an underwater alarm since it can also be used with a pool cover. Other tips include alarming doors leading to the pool, installing self locking gates with latches out of reach of small children, as well a power safety cover when the pool is not in use, and locks on ladders or steps to above ground pools. If a child is missing, be sure to check the pool first—seconds count.

## Public Playground Safety

No doubt you've already visited your local playground and argued with your child about eating sand, throwing rocks and climbing up the slide the wrong way. But playground safety is a serious issue. Almost a quarter million injuries occurred on public playgrounds last year, according to the CPSC. The following checklist can help you evaluate your neighborhood playground. If you find anything lacking, contact your local parks and rec department and push to have any problems corrected as soon as possible.

◆ Make sure surfaces around playground equipment have *at least 12 inches* of wood chips, mulch, sand, or pea gravel. Also acceptable: mats made of safety-tested rubber or rubber-like materials.

◆ Check that *protective surfacing* extends at least 6 feet in all directions from play equipment. For swings, be sure surfacing extends, in back and front, twice the height of the suspending bar.

◆ Make sure play structures more than 30 inches high are *spaced* at least 9 feet apart.

◆ Check for *dangerous hardware*, like open "S" hooks or protruding bolt ends.

◆ Make sure *spaces* that could trap children, such as openings in guardrails or between ladder rungs, measure less than 3.5 inches or more than 9 inches.

◆ Check for *sharp points* or edges on equipment.

◆ Look out for *tripping hazards*, like exposed concrete footings, tree stumps, and rocks.

◆ Make sure elevated surfaces, like platforms and ramps, have *guardrails* to prevent falls.

◆ Check playgrounds regularly to see that equipment and surfacing are in *good condition*.

◆ Carefully *supervise* children on playgrounds to make sure they're safe.

When you visit your local playground, make sure your child's clothing doesn't have any strings attached. Also, if you see ropes or string that other children have left behind, trash it. Strangulation is a real hazard when string or rope is available.

Use age appropriate equipment as well. Toddler swings with waist belts or leg openings should be used by smaller children until they reach a level of development that allows them to use traditional swings. Don't let children climb too high on their own—a fall from a great height could be life threatening.

## Fire Safety

Here's a topic we all wish we didn't have to discuss. But as your toddler gets older, he or she is ready for this important lesson. You'll definitely need to start talking about matches, candles and fire with children as young as two years of age.

To help facilitate discussion, we'll recommend some great books. And now is the time to develop a fire plan and practice it. Some tips:

◆ *Check all battery powered smoke detectors routinely and change out the batteries.* It is recommended that you place smoke detectors on every floor of your home and in bedrooms. You'll also need to change out batteries—we do it in the spring and fall when the clocks change.

◆ *Develop a fire plan and practice it.* Go over with your children that they should get out of the house as quickly as possible and call 911 from a neighbor's house.

Be sure to go over the quickest routes to get outside. Emphasize leaving everything behind and getting help. Be sure to decide on a place for everyone to meet in case some family members aren't home when an emergency occurs (designate a neighbor's house).

◆ *Get some great books on the subject.* For very little kids, check out *Dinofours: It's Fire Drill Day* and *Barney and BJ: Go to the Fire Station.* Older kids will love *Arthur's Fire Drill* and *No Dragons for Tea: Fire Safety for Kids (and Dragons).* All these titles are available from Amazon.com. What about videos? We liked "Kids for Safety: Bicycle, Fire and Personal Safety" by Mazzrella Productions (www.mazz. com). Check your library for titles like *Sesame Street Visits the Firehouse* (1990).

◆ *Have a two story house?* Then consider a fire escape ladder. Check out www.babycatalog.com for affordable options. We've also seen escape ladders occasionally at warehouse clubs and discounters. If you see one, snap it up. Measure your house to be sure you buy the right length.

## *Bike Helmets: What to look for, how to buy*

Good news on the helmet front: since 1999, the Consumer Product Safety Commission (CPSC) has mandated standards for

## *When to visit the hospital.*

We hope this never happens to you, but chances are you'll find your way to your local emergency room at least once in the years your children are young. So how do you know when you can safely head for your pediatrician's office and when you need to call out the ambulance? Here are the times you need to get to a hospital:

safety

◆ If your child has trouble breathing, particularly if hands and feet are turning blue. It doesn't take long to suffocate so don't wait to call an ambulance.
◆ Profuse bleeding.
◆ Unconsciousness.
◆ Suspected broken bones (although you may have an option for using urgent care through your pediatrician). You may be able to drive your child to the hospital or doctor yourself in some cases.
◆ Continuous vomiting/loss of fluids.
◆ Severe abdominal pain.
◆ When your pediatrician/urgent care facility is closed.
◆ Fever over 105°.
◆ Suspected poisoning.
◆ Convulsions.
◆ Bloody bowel movements.

And remember, there is no wrong question. If you think you have an emergency, call the ambulance. Better safe than sorry.

By the way, our son has a life threatening peanut allergy for which we carry an Epi-pen. When we asked his doctor if we should call and wait for an ambulance or if we should drive him to the hospital ourselves, he said:

"If you can see the hospital out your front door, drive him over. But if you aren't that close call the ambulance." His belief is that Emergency Services personnel are well equipped to handle everything quickly and get your child to the hospital. Use them, that's what they're for.

bicycle helmets. So all helmets sold today must have a CPSC sticker on them. But . . . how do you know which helmets are best and easiest to use? Not to mention how do we know when a helmet is on right? Here's our primer for you on helmet safety:

There are two types of helmets: hard shell and soft shell. A soft shell is made of exposed, but extra thick polystyrene foam. They are usually covered with cloth or a coating. A hard shell, on the other hand has an outer shell of plastic. Hard shell helmets are most common. The shell helps hold the Styrofoam together in case of a crash but they are heavier than the soft shell option. Both types are approved by the CPSC. Helmets are available in toddler and youth sizes. Toddler is best for two three and some four year olds. Five year olds may be too big for a toddler size, so a youth helmet will work well.

When shopping for a helmet, fit is paramount. Your child will be able to wear his helmet for a few years before outgrowing it, so you want one that fits, is adjustable and is comfortable to wear. The helmet should fit squarely on top of the head and cover the upper forehead–DO NOT TIP IT BACK. Make sure the helmet doesn't slip. The chin strap should be snug but not too tight. Rule of thumb: if you can slide one finger between chin and strap, you're OK.

A great tip: Have your child walk into a wall with the helmet on. If the helmet hits the wall before your child's nose, you have it on right. See the pictures below for a guide.

Evaluate the fit occasionally. You can remove pads as your child grows to help maintain proper fit. For even more technical advice on fitting a helmet correctly (it can take 15 or 20 minutes the first time), check out the web site for the Bicycle Helmet Safety Institute (bhsi.org).

And which helmet makers offer toddler and youth helmets? Here are a few: Bell, Fisher Price, SportScope and PRO. Your best bet for affordable helmets are stores like Walmart and Target. Bike shops will carry some options, but may be rather expensive. Look for sales or ask for a discount if you buy both the bike and the helmet at the same store.

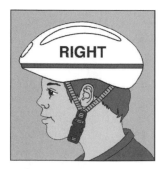

# CHAPTER 10

## *Happy Birthday!*
### *Birthday ideas on a budget*

### **Inside this chapter**

H*ow can you celebrate your toddler's birthdays with a fun party, but without breaking the bank? We'll discuss the ins and outs of affordable birthdays in this chapter, with tips from the pros—that is, parents who've been there and back.*

If you're like us, you celebrated your baby's first birthday with great fanfare but mostly with close family and a few adult friends. The idea of a gaggle of one-year-olds running around probably wasn't appealing to you and might have been too overwhelming for your child. But now, she's hitting two, three, four, or five and it's time to bring in the supporting cast: her friends.

So what do you do for a three-year-old? Do you hire a petting zoo? Head to the local children's museum? Or just hang out in the backyard? Our readers had definite opinions and tips on this and much more when it comes to planning memorable birthday parties for the toddler set. You'll see their ideas and suggestions scattered through this chapter.

## Getting Started

If your children are like ours, they are busily planning for their next birthday as soon as the last one's over. Our kids have already picked the flavor for their next birthday cake, discussed who should attend and so on.

Of course, you don't need to plan eight months out like our kids. But, if you're having the party at a site other than your home, you will want to start checking into it two to three months in advance. If the site is especially popular or hip like a hot children's

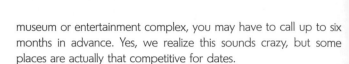
museum or entertainment complex, you may have to call up to six months in advance. Yes, we realize this sounds crazy, but some places are actually that competitive for dates.

If you're planning a home party but want to have outside entertainment, it wouldn't hurt to start calling entertainers two or three months in advance. If you won't need to hire entertainment, you can start planning your home event about a month out. This will give you time to pick the theme and get the invitations together.

## Sources

Beyond the obvious party stores there are other sources you might consider checking out like Target and Wal-Mart, especially for character themes like Bob the Builder or Hello Kitty. Don't forget to look for alternative sources like Home Depot for a construction party or a beauty supply store for a Make Over party. The web offers numerous options for parents looking for party supplies as well as advice and ideas.

### Parents in Cyberspace: What's on the Web?

### Birthday Express
**Web site:** www.birthdayexpress.com
**What it is:** This site specializes in every kind of character party supply and helps put together party packages. Parents we interviewed love this site, especially for ideas.
**What's cool:** If they don't have it, nobody does. Their selection is amazing. Short on time? Birthday Express has "one stop" packages that include everything you need for different themes. They also offer party planning advice and ideas, as well as a place to share ideas with other parents. And don't forget to check out the bargain bin. One parent also noted that you can buy a package for a certain number of kids, then buy additional items a la carte. So if you have a party of 9, you don't have to buy another 8 pack. This means you won't waste money on buying extras you don't need. Another plus: if you decide to purchase some of their craft activities or other products, check out their feedback section—it's got some great tips.
**Needs work:** Some items are a bit pricey. Many parents complain that they can find the same stuff locally for less.

birthdays

## Birthday Party Ideas

*Web site:* www.birthdaypartyideas.com

*What it is:* Here you'll find hundreds of party ideas submitted by other parents.

*What's cool:* If you can think of it, someone else has already done it and written in to describe how! Want to have a fishing party? A hoe down? A princess party? We found over 80 new ideas the day we visited, plus many more "old" ideas that had been on the site awhile. And more get added daily. Each month, they offer a prize to the best idea submitted, so we checked out some of the winners. The extent to which some parents went was amazing, but you could definitely cherry pick ideas. And another nice touch: many of

the parties came with an age moniker so you could stay away from party ideas for older kids and focus on toddlers.

***Needs work:*** This site can be slow to load. And sometimes the descriptions are difficult to read as there are no paragraph breaks (unless the parent adds them in!). Finally, expect to see lots of banner ads.

◆ ***Other web sites to check out***: Parents we interviewed suggested these sites for ideas and supplies:

> ***BoardmanWeb.com*** for party ideas
> ***PersonalizedPartyFavors.com*** for party favors
> ***FamilyFun.com*** part of Disney
> ***Factorycard.com*** party tips
> ***PBSkids.org*** fun and games
> ***FisherPrice.com*** birthday planner
> ***PartyPro.com*** party supplies and ideas
> ***NickJr.com*** more party ideas
> ***Wilton.com*** cake and cookie decorating ideas

Looking for sites with game and activity ideas? Surf here:
> ***dltk-kids.com***
> ***PreschoolEducation.com***
> ***PerpetualPreschool.com***
> ***BirthdayInaBox.com***
> ***BHG.com*** Better Homes and Gardens site—search for birthday party games
> ***AmazingMoms.com*** search for kids birthday parties
> ***PartyGameCentral.com***

# What Are You Buying?

What does the average birthday cost for a toddler? Parents spend on average $150. Although there are no rules about what to buy for birthday parties, it seems they most often include many if not all of the following items:

◆ ***Party supplies.*** Cups, plates, flatware, tablecloths and such that you need for any typical party. These can be basic solid color items or character designs ranging from Smiley Faces to Finding Nemo. Of course, you'll need enough table settings for each kid and/or adult at the party. Unfortunately, many preprinted designs only come in sets of eight, leaving you with extras more often than not. Here's where sticking with solid colors is a plus: you can use them again for anything while Blue's Clues plates don't seem as adaptable.

Party supply kits from a web site or catalog like BirthdayExpress. com can range from $25 to $35 for eight children depending on how much is included. Solid colored items would be much less expensive.

◆ **Decorations.** From the simplest crepe paper to the most elaborate piñata, decorations can be quite a slice of your budget. Very small toddlers will be happy with a few balloons and streamers, but older kids will begin to crave the elaborate centerpieces and wall décor marketed in those packages and displayed in party stores (full-size cardboard Darth Vader anyone?). Plenty of moms told us they thought a few well-chosen decorations were preferable to an explosion of Barbies on walls, tables and ceiling.

Look for piñatas to start at $10 and go up to about $20. The more elaborate designs will cost more. And don't forget to budget for the candy and prizes to fill it up. A centerpiece might cost upwards of $5 each. Crepe paper and balloons are the least expensive option and cost as little as $5 for enough to decorate a whole room. If you have a party store fill a dozen balloons, the price is about $10 for a plain color. Mylar balloons start at about $1 inflated for a plain heart shape. Elaborate shapes and printed messages start at $3.

◆ **Entertainment.** Universally, parents told us (and we agree) the only entertainment two and three year olds need are their friends and a room full of toys. Older kids may need a bit more structure and certainly will enjoy a craft or two and some great games. If you have a child with a particular interest like bugs or firemen, a visit to a firehouse or a party at a bug museum may be a great idea. Hiring a clown or magician may be overkill and might even scare younger kids so we recommend forgoing that type of entertainment.

Craft items to go with theme packages run the price gamut. You can buy kits from party supply sources like the ones we saw on line at BirthdayExpress.com. For a pirate theme they sell gold paper mache treasure chests. Kids can decorate the boxes with jewels that come with the kits. Cost: 2 boxes for $10. Craft stores sell unfinished boxes and birdhouses among other items that might be a more

birthdays

affordable option for craft activities.

As for hiring entertainment, the prices and options vary so dramatically from town to town that we can't give you an "average." We've rented those big party bouncers (see picture) for neighborhood block parties for about $150 to $200 depending  on how many hours you need it. Clowns and magicians probably range about the same.

◆ **Food.** No matter what type of celebration you organize, you'll want a cake. Interesting note: one study on birthday costs we saw pointed out that only one-third of all cakes are homemade. That means the rest are store or bakery bought. Once you pick a type of cake, you'll have to address other food items. If you plan a party between meal times, cake and ice cream will be enough. But if you plan for a lunch or dinner party, kid friendly foods are a must. Hot dogs and pizza were our readers most frequent suggestions, complimented with fruit and veggies.

Cake prices range from the cost of a box of cake mix to $15 for a warehouse club cake to $20 for a grocery store cake to $30 or more for a deluxe bakery cake.

◆ **Favors/Goodie Bags.** Do you have to have them? Nope. But will you be pressured to? Yep! But remember if you do favors they can be as simple as a decorated cookie or a craft item made at the party as part of the entertainment. Our personal request: please don't send home whistles and other noisemakers. We've been the victim of many of these types of favors and we usually want to strangle those parents by the end of the day!

The favor boxes and bags that compliment the birthday party kits from on line party suppliers are about $4 each. You can find inexpensive filler and bags from your local Wal-Mart or Target for a lot less. And you'll read later about some great ways to create your own favors for very little.

◆ **Location.** Not surprisingly, surveys show that 65% of all kid birthday parties are held at home. This was echoed by our readers who mostly felt this was the best option, especially with the youngest toddlers. Parents who want to have a party elsewhere could spend as much as $175 for a party at Gymboree or similar sites. Other options like the zoo or a museum are usually just the cost of admission. Some sites seem expensive, but may provide entertainment, the cake and all the decorations and supplies in that price. In cities like Los Angeles or New York City, a popular kid birthday party destination could top $200 or even $300.

## Safe & Sound

While you might not think of birthday parties as an area of safety concern, you'd be surprised at the potential problems that crop up. For example, at a party for some kids from our son's school the parents had a carrot cake with chopped walnuts. One of the boys had a nut allergy, but the parents of the birthday boy were unaware of this. The child did ask if the nuts were cashews, but when told they weren't, he went ahead and ate the cake. That child ended up in an ambulance to the hospital with a serious allergic reaction. This was a scary lesson for the rest of the families from school.

◆ *Ask each parent when they RSVP if their child has a food allergy.* Some allergies are life threatening like nut allergies while

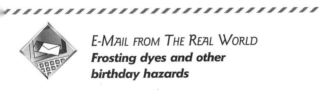

*E-MAIL FROM THE REAL WORLD*
**Frosting dyes and other birthday hazards**

*Because birthday parties feature special treats, your child may be exposed to new foods for the first time—and the result might be an allergic reaction. Check out the following story from reader Jennifer Peterson for just one such example.*

"One bit of information that I hope you will pass on to your readers is to give the child plain cake with dye-free icing. Our son broke out in awful hives after his first birthday party. We were racking out brain to figure out what caused it. When we took him to our pediatrician he asked if our son's cake came from Publix (our local grocery chain), which it had. He said that all of his little patients have the exact same reaction right after their first birthday because of the dyes used by the bakery there! Here we thought we were getting a great deal. It seems such an obvious thing, but at the time we were concentrating more on how much sugar he might ingest not ever giving thought to the potential danger in the dyes."

others may just make a child break out (like strawberries). Either way, best to know ahead of time. And remember to read the ingredients on any candy you give in favor bags or in piñatas. A smart move: avoid any candy with nuts or peanut butter.

## *5 Ways to Make Your Toddler's Birthdays Special*

Every parent wants to make his or her child's birthday special. But in this pre-fab, time-crunched world we all live in, how can you really do that? We polled readers of our book to get their best ideas and we were amazed. Here are their thoughts.

1 **SUNRISE SURPRISE.** Christie Williams of Anderson, SC starts the party at sunrise with a decorated bedroom as a surprise for the birthday child.

*"Birthdays are a big deal for me and I make them as special as possible. It is their day so the whole day is special, not just the party. Waking up to see what treats the birthday fairy has left for them is a fun way to start the day. Balloons are in the room so that as soon as they wake up—it's official—it's their birthday!"*

2 **CREATIVE MEMORY MAKING.** Several parents created lasting memories as gifts to make the party special. Recinda Sherman-Seitz of Portland, Oregon told us her idea:

*"Although my daughter only turned one, I started a 'tradition' that I hope to maintain for at least the next four years. I created an ABC book using digital pictures from her first year. For instance, "A is for Avocado, your first solid food!", etc. The book had a picture for each letter of her involved in whatever it was. The last few pages had general pictures of family and friends. Although she may not appreciate it now, she may enjoy it later in life. The friends and family who came to her party enjoyed it, too, because many of the pictures included them. And I felt I really made an effort and didn't feel guilty about not spending a lot of money on a gift."*

Jennifer Meeuwnberg echoed many other parents with her idea for preserving the moment:

◆ *Be careful with balloons.* Latex balloons can be a hazard if they are either un-inflated or if they break. Children can swallow balloons or pieces of them leading to death in some cases. So keep an eye out for any balloon breakage. And if you have great concern over the environmental cost of balloons, consider mylar instead of latex.

*"We bought a plate from a ceramic shop and put my son's handprint in the center of the plate using the glaze paint from the shop. We then had all of our guests sign their name in pencil around the plate. My mother in law then painted over the pencil with a special paint, took it to the shop and had the plate fired for us. We now have a wonderful memento to our son with all of the guests at his first birthday party! We plan to do one every year! It looks great on his wall!"*

**3 KEEP IT SECRET.** Parents definitely need to consult with their toddlers about the kind of party they want, especially the theme, the cake and the food. Not to mention whom to invite. But be sure to keep some details a secret. For example, plan a treasure hunt or invite a special guest your child isn't expecting. The photos will be more than memorable.

**4 DRESS FOR SUCCESS.** Kids love to dress up and many parents suggest using a birthday as an excuse to buy a new costume to coordinate with the theme or a fancy outfit to make a child feel special.

**5 LET KIDS GET IN ON THE ACT.** Instead of doing everything for your kids, let them get involved.

One parent told us she made cupcakes for her child's birthday and let the kids decorate them themselves. For a construction party, get wood, nails and tools for the kids to help put together a play structure. Now this seems a bit complicated, but our son went to just such a party for a four year old. The birthday boy's dad pre-drilled all the pieces and in about an hour the kids had put together a rudimentary house "by themselves."

Got some young ladies who'd love a "makeover?" Buy some supplies at a discount store and let them paint their nails or put up their hair.

If you've got a great idea for making a child's birthday special, feel free to email us at authors@windsorpeak.com. We'd love to print even more suggestions in future editions.

◆ **Beware small toys in gift bags**. Remember the age of all the children you're inviting. In mixed-age parties it is especially important not to give small toys to the under-three year old set that would be at risk of choking on them. Better bet: avoid toys altogether and go for a food gift or craft item.

◆ **Constantly supervise children.** While this may seem obvious, we know that parents sometimes get distracted with conversations or setting things up. Especially if you have a pool or hot tub on your property, you must keep a constant eye on the kids you invite. Don't hesitate to ask parents to stay and help you at the party. And consider limiting the number of kids so you can supervise more easily.

# Wastes of Money

### Waste of Money #1
*Hired entertainment for young children is often overkill*

" My neighbor invited my two year old to her daughter's party. When we arrived they had hired a petting zoo as entertainment. Most of the kids lost interest in it pretty quickly and spent most of the day playing with each other and the birthday girl's toys. But now we're wondering if we need to get some sort of entertainment for our child's party."

Small children are usually so excited to have a chance to play with someone else's toys in someone else's yard, that they won't miss expensive entertainment if you don't have it. Free play and cake and ice cream are probably the best options for kids so don't feel the need to spend loads of money on superfluous entertainment.

### Waste of Money #2
*Coordinated decor*

"When we went to the party store to buy supplies, my son became enamored with every single coordinating item he saw. In fact, he threw a fit in the aisle when we balked at buying the lighted construction helmet for everyone ($5 each!). Do we really need all this stuff to have a great party?"

Of course not. It can be tough getting through a party store with your little one (and you might want to consider leaving him at home when you do this). And it's even harder when you see the array of items party stores tie into different themes. For example, on BirthdayExpress.com, you'll find eleven theme items pitched along with the Rainbow Fish party supplies. These range from fish candles ($4 each) to squirt fish (8 for $5). A few tasteful theme items will evoke the idea without wasting all that money.

### Waste of Money #3
Favors

*"What's with all these gift bags full of trinkets I see given out at birthday parties as favors? At one party we attended the parents gave an entire knight outfit complete with sword and shield to every child. The parents said they spent $20 a child! That's outrageous!"*

We don't mean to get off on a rant here, but what is it with favors? At what point was it decided that at all kids birthday parties, every guest needs to be sent home with a "goodie bag" full of trinkets? Of course, some parents go off the deep end here, giving their kid's birthday party guests a lovely parting gift of Waterford crystal goblets.

Just kidding . . . but the knight example above is a true story. Readers tell us they are amazed at the booty their children come home with after a party.

Is it just us or have we all gone crazy? In the good old 1970's when we last attended a birthday party as a child, we were darn lucky to get some cake at a party. Favors? Never happened.

And ask yourself, do ten of your child's friends need some plastic tchotchke that will be thrown away or lost within a few minutes of arriving home? We think not. As a parent, spend your energy putting on a fun party (games, etc.) and skip the favors.

If you live in a town where you might be arrested by the Birthday Party Police for following this advice, then do a simple favor—a decorated sugar cookie as a parting gift.

 Money Saving Secrets

1 **GO PLAIN.** Character-emblazoned party supplies are cute but grossly overpriced. One of our readers' most popular tips: buy solid colors and a few theme decorations at a huge savings. For example, if you wanted to buy Clifford theme dinner plates you'd pay about 39¢ per plate while solid red dinner plates are only 16¢ each—a 60% savings. You can still do the Clifford theme, just chuck the Clifford plates and cups.

2 **LOCATION, LOCATION, LOCATION.** Where you have your party can be lead to significant savings. Obviously a home

party is the least expensive option and probably the best for parents of two and three year olds. If you're looking for someplace different to hold an older child's party, look for offbeat sites and civic options. For example, we've had parties at a local rec center in the past. Included in the affordable $85 (for eight kids) fee was the cake, decorations, a staff member to lead some games and swimming at the rec center's fantastic, kid-friendly pool. Couldn't beat that for a deal! Off beat sites might include a zoo, municipal airport or local nature center. In many cases, there are small or no fees. You may have to bring your own supplies but check to see if anything is included.

Another way to save: have a party at your child's day care. Do this during a regular school day and organize some party games, serve a cupcake snack and avoid the mess and hassle of a home party. Best of all, you won't get inundated with gifts—a problem if you have a house full of toys already.

**3** **FAVOR SAVERS.** We know that you're wondering about this tip since we ranted on about favors earlier, but even we have succumbed to the pressure and handed them out on occasion. So what to do to save a few bucks? Here are some suggestions from our readers:

◆ One reader gave out **Sippy cups** as favors for a crew of small kids. We've also seen plastic cups with cool designs and pop up straws. At least this is practical and a reminder of a fun party.

◆ *If you're "crafty" check out stores like Michaels or Hobby Lobby for ideas to make affordable favors.* One reader made her own soap from supplies at Michaels and inserted duck erasers inside the glycerin bars. This matched her Rubber Duck theme and were included with a washcloth and squirting duck from Wal-Mart. A small washtub to hold the trinkets completed the favor—all total, she spent only $3 each for these creative favors. The downside: it takes time to make things yourself.

◆ *Check out dollar stores.* More than one reader recommended the Dollar Store or Job Lot for unbelievable deals. For a dog-themed party a reader bought mini books of dog stories for only 50¢ and made bone shaped cookies to go with them.

**4** **BE CRAFTY.** Crafts are a fun activity for any party; you can save by having the guests take home their projects as favors. Use your imagination—most craft stores have supplies to make birdhouses, jewelry or other fun items. One example: decorated flow-

erpots. Michaels Arts & Craft Stores (www.michaels.com) have 4"
pots for $1 each and paints run $3.50 for eight colors. Skip pricey
catalogs like Pottery Barn if you follow this tip; that catalog had a
flowerpot painting kit with three pots and paint for $24. You'd save
nearly 70% by buying the supplies at craft stores.

**5** **TAKING THE CAKE.** The cheapest
option for the cake is to make it
yourself. But what if you aren't impressed with
box mix cakes and don't want to try a
"scratch" cake? Check out *The Cake Mix
Doctor*, a great book by Anne Byrn. This cook-
book offers easy and tasty ideas for additions to
the standard box cake. You can also find ideas and a newsletter
online at her web site, www.cakemixdoctor.com.

Another idea: consider taking a cake-decorating course. While
it costs money up front, once you learn this skill, it's yours for a lifetime of birthday cakes! Reader Kay Walter wrote to us saying: "I'm
taking a cake decorating class at a local craft store for $25, supplies
are $20. I'm the only one attending and am getting private lessons!"
You'll find classes at craft stores and local junior colleges or civic
education programs.

Finally, no matter whether you make a cake or buy one, we
have a suggestion. You and your adult friends may like almond
genoise cake with apricot filling and orange-infused buttercream
icing, but kids just want a plain cake. Their biggest dilemma will be
deciding between white and chocolate. Heck, they often only eat
the icing! And don't impose your "no sugar" rule on your kids on
their birthday. Remember they can stick to a healthy diet 364 days
of the year. Let your hair down on this one.

**6** **WAREHOUSE CLUBS.** Here you'll find the ultimate savings on
paper goods, favor ideas (books, candy, toys) and even
birthday cakes. Speaking of cakes, one reader told us she buys
sheet cakes at Costco for a mere $12 to $15.

## Do It By Mail

### ORIENTAL TRADING COMPANY

*To Order Call: (800) 875-8480*
*Web: www.OrientalTrading.com*
*Shopping Hours: 24 hours a day, seven days a week*

*Credit Cards Accepted: Amex, MC, Visa, Discover*

Possibly one of the kitschiest looking catalogs we've received in the mail, Oriental Trading Company nevertheless offers up some of the best prices on favors and party decor. For example, you can buy 12 rubber ducky squirts for $5. Looking for something more tactile? How about a dozen glitter silly putty eggs for $5. Beyond favors, Oriental Trading sells paper products like their Zoo Animal party assortment (includes plates, cups, napkins and invitations for eight) for a mere $5. Parents told us they think this catalog/web site is one of the cheapest sources out there for party supplies.

## Bottom Line

The least expensive route for a birthday party: have it at home and bake your own cake. But spice it up with home-made crafts, a few theme decorations and solid color paper products.

If you want to do a little less of the work or punch up the theme but still save money, parents look to web sites like BirthdayExpress. com or OrientalTrading.com for affordable kits, coordinating decor and favors.

The most expensive party options are destination events like taking ten kids to Gymboree. If you decide to go this route, we've found that it pays to look for sites with packages that include the cake, entertainment, etc.

The overwhelming advice experienced parents give about birthday parties for the toddler set is KEEP IT SIMPLE. Don't get sucked into the Olympic Competition for Most Money Spent on a Three-Year-Olds Birthday Party. It won't make it any more memorable or enjoyable. And it won't do much for your wallet either.

# CHAPTER 11

## Toys & Media
### Best bets, classic toys and more

### Inside this chapter

**3**.8 billion. Yes, that is the number of toys and games sold each year in this country.

Some days, it feels like we own about 3.4 billion of those toys. As the only grandchildren on both sides of our family, our two boys have been fortunate (in their opinion) to be on the receiving end of an avalanche of toys, both educational and just plain fun. So, as parents, we've been able to see what's worked . . . and what gets consigned to the yard sale box.

Our mission in this chapter is to show you how to pick the best toys for your child. Small task, no?

Of course, with the plethora of toys out there, it isn't our goal to review each and every best toy for toddlers. That frankly, would probably require another book the size of an unabridged dictionary. Instead, we'll boil it down to our best bets by age. And we'll discuss our picks for educational toys and classic options. We'll give you general buying guidelines and what to look for by age as well.

Since we can't review every best toy out there, we'll give you several cyber resources to finding toy reviews. Finally, we'll take a look at educational software. And that biggest purchase of all for every toddler: their first tricycle.

### Parents in Cyberspace: What's on the Web?

The U.S. toy industry is a $25 billion a year business—and that figure even excludes the $6 billion in video games Americans buy each year. That works out to $328 per year for every child in the U.S. and Canada. Not surprisingly, grandparents buy one out of every four toys sold in North America.

Given the scope of the toy biz, it's no surprise that quite a few authors and web sites have made a career out of reviewing toys. Here's our list of the best sites that review toys:

◆ **Oppenheim Toy Portfolio** (www.toyportfolio.com). The Oppenheims are the Ralph Naders of the toy industry: true consumer advocates who've been reviewing and rating toys since 1989. They publish a series of books, a quarterly newsletter and host a web site. Granted, the web site isn't going to win any design awards, but you can search their online database by keyword and see a sampling of their toy reviews online. Best bets: check out their list of toddler toys *to avoid*. We also recommend their book, *The Oppenheim Toy Portfolio Baby & Toddler Play Book* (2nd Edition, $6). The Oppenheims list several myths about baby toys that we'll discuss in the box on the next page.

◆ **Dr. Toy** (www.drtoy.com). Dr. Stevanne Auerbach (a.k.a. Dr. Toy) is the author of three books on toys and a syndicated columnist. Her web site has lists of the "100 Best Toys" and picks for classic toys, vacation toys, links, toy history and more. While Auerbach consults for the toy industry (and hence is not a true consumer advocate), we found her advice and recommendations to be sound and worth a look.

◆ **Parent's choice** (www.parents-choice.org) probably has the best-designed web site in this category. This non-profit consumer's guide to books, toys, videos, software and more has been around since 1978. Their "Parent's choice" awards (judged by moms, dads, teachers, librarians and, of course, kids) provide a great list of toys to consider. There's also an email newsletter and additional reviews on their site that cover kid's TV shows and magazines.

◆ **The National Parenting Center's** (www.tnpc.com) "Seal of Approval" program has been independently testing toys since 1989. Parents, children and educators do the testing; their web site lists the winners for the last ten years. The National Parenting Center tests books, videos, software, educational products, games, dolls, crafts and more.

◆ **Traveling Tikes** (www.travelingtikes.com). Well, this site doesn't review toys. But they do have great prices on trikes, bikes and other outdoor toys (we'll discuss our picks for best trikes at the end of this chapter). This site carries the quality Kettler line at good prices. And ground shipping is free. FYI: this site also carries jogging strollers, booster car seats and other to go gear at great prices as well. Traveling Tikes also has a small twins discount for parents of multiples.

 *Safe & Sound*

As we mentioned in the safety chapter, toy-related injuries send 146,250 children to hospital emergency rooms each year. Taking a few simple steps could prevent many of these injuries:

**1** **WATCH OUT FOR SMALL, REMOVABLE PARTS.** Remember the Under-3 Rule—children under three should not play with toys with small removable parts. These are a choking hazard. Use a toilet paper tube to test small parts: if it is small enough to fit

---

## Top 3 Toy Myths

In their book, *The Oppenheim Toy Portfolio Baby & Toddler Play Book* (2nd Edition, $6), consumer advocates Joanne and Stephanie Oppenheim discuss several myths about toddler toys. Here are some of their points:

◆ **Myth #1:** *"Smart toys" are better than classics.* Reality: yes, manufacturers have become more creative in making innovative toys using computer chips and technology—but toddlers can often have just as much fun with simple classic toys. The Oppenheims say "so-called smart toys are really only enriching to the bottom line of stores and manufacturers." We agree.

◆ **Myth #2:** *Classical music makes babies smarter.* Reality: No, Mozart will not raise your toddler's IQ. Yes, there was a 1993 study that showed that link among *college students*, but subsequent studies on babies show classical music does not make it more likely your toddler will get into Harvard. Of course, that doesn't mean your child shouldn't listen to classical music. In fact, toddlers should listen to a wide variety of music. Ours preferred the Barenaked Ladies and the Fountains of Wayne, but, hey, that's just our family.

◆ **Myth #3:** *You've got to start working on numbers and letters at an early age.* Reality: most babies and toddlers simply can't handle abstract number or letter concepts. Reading and singing to your child is more effective at expanding their vocabulary than any fancy hi-tech educational toy.

through the tube, it is small enough to be swallowed. Examples: marbles, balloons, small balls, etc.

**2** **WATCH OUT FOR TOYS WITH STRINGS OR CORDS LONGER THAN SEVEN INCHES.** These can be a strangulation hazard.

**3** **BE ON THE LOOK OUT FOR ANY TOY WITH SHARP EDGES OR POINTS.**

**4** **MAKE SURE ALL PAINTS, CRAYONS AND MARKERS ARE LABELED "NON-TOXIC."**

**5** **CHECK ALL HAND-ME-DOWN TOYS OR THOSE BOUGHT AT YARD SALES FOR HAZARDS**—missing parts, broken pieces, etc.

**6** **BE AWARE OF PACKAGING.** The best advice is to throw it all away (or recycle it). Plastic peanuts, bags and other packaging can be hazardous.

**7** **WEAR A HELMET.** Motorized toys are fun (even though foot power is just as fun), but be sure to wear protective gear like a helmet, pads, etc. Never use motorized toys without direct adult supervision at all times. (see Chapter 9 for safety for tips on buying a helmet).

**8** **YES, YOU MUST READ THE WARNING LABELS, INSTRUCTIONS AND AGE RECOMMENDATIONS.** Just because your two-year-old is "advanced" it does NOT mean he can play with a toy designed for five-year-olds. And be just as adamant with grandparents. They often purchase items without checking the age appropriateness.

**9** **STAY ON TOP OF RECALLS.** Sign up for our free newsletter (toddlerbargains.com) or check out a site like SafetyAlerts.com for the latest recalls. Look for past recalls on the CPSC's web site, www.cpsc.gov. Yes, we realize this can seem overwhelming (the number of recalls has jumped in recent years), but it is the only way to stay on top of which toys have been found to be dangerous.

## Smart Shopper Tips: Toy Guidelines by Age

Here are our shopping tips for picking the right toy for your toddler or preschooler:

**Children under age 3:** This age group still sticks everything in their mouths—everything that they haven't figured out how to destroy yet. And a toddler can get easily frustrated. So it's important to pick toys that can stand up to abuse: blocks, pounding toys, push and pull toys, etc. Our tips:

◆ *Test it out.* If you can't figure out how to pop the Jack in the Box, will your toddler? Make sure the toys do what they say *before* you leave the store to prevent toddler frustration.

◆ *Make it hard to destroy.* Wood Brio trains are a winner; electric trains are not for this age group. Look for machine washable toys and durable materials like hard plastic.

◆ *Skip the SAT prep toys.* Lots of toys aimed at this age group claim to teach toddlers their ABC's and numbers. We say don't sweat that yet—choose toys that stimulate your child's imagination (yes, that can be blocks with letters on them), but don't worry about whether he is learning advanced calculus.

**BEST BETS:** Blocks, pails, toy telephones, wooden trains, toy construction sets, tea party sets (but beware of small parts). We'll have more specific recommendations later in this chapter.

**Children age 3 to 5.** Okay, finally, not everything goes into the mouth. Now you can transition to more complex toys. Here are our shopping tips:

◆ *Do it yourself.* That's the mantra of most older toddlers and preschoolers. They want to take that ride-on toy for a spin or try to figure out how to put together a 10-piece puzzle.

◆ *Tests of strength.* Toddlers have boundless energy and their toys should harness some of that. Look for pushing and climbing toys. Getting messy with art toys is an important part of developing motor skills and creativity.

◆ *Social toys.* Costume boxes or toy props (light sabers, anyone?) make playing with friends fun. Toddlers age 3 to 5 now want to play with friends and their toys should reflect that.

**BEST BETS:** Books, tape players (with secure battery compartments), sand box toys, dress up clothes. Outdoor toys like slides, baseball tees, swings, etc. Cash registers, puzzles, and art toys are winners now. See later in this chapter for some specific recommendations.

## Money saving tips

**1** **HIDE IT.** So your toddler is bored with a toy? Hide it for a few weeks and then bring it back—presto! Now it is brand new and fun to play with again.

**2** **SWAP IT.** There's no more exciting a toy than your neighbor's. Organize a toy swap with your neighbors or play group to make this happen. Meet for a play date with three toys you want to swap. Make sure the toys are in a similar price range and the same condition. Of course, a toy swap can also be more informal with neighborhood kids.

**3** **RENT IT.** Books, CD's and videos are expensive—rent/borrow them first from your library to make sure your toddler enjoys them before buying.

**4** **eBAY IT.** The online bazaar is a toy wonderland. You can often pick up "gently used" toys for half or more off retail.

**5** **CLUB IT.** Warehouse clubs like Sam's and Costco are big into toys. You'll often find the hottest stuff at rock-bottom prices. As always, our advice: if you see it, buy it. It may not be around for much longer.

**6** **YARD SALE IT.** Garage and yard sales are great places to pick up toys at bargain prices. Be sure to check the toy for broken/missing parts or if it has been recalled (www.cpsc.gov).

**7** **COUPON IT.** If you want to buy toys online, use a web coupon to save. Check sits like DealOfTheDay.com for a list of current deals. When we last visited that site, we saw deals for $10 off a $50 sale at Amazon.com and free shipping deals at other sites. Just enter the coupon codes when you place an order to get the discount.

**8** **CLEARANCE SHOP IT.** Clearance sites like OverStock.com and SmartBargains.com have toys at 50% off retail. Check out their "Gifts, Gadgets & Toys" section for preschool toys and rack up the 50% or more savings on new-in-the-box toys.

### Best Bets: Classic toys

Many of today's popular toys date back many years. For example, did you know that Raggedy Ann and Tinker Toys date back to the early 1900's. Cool stuff.

Here are some of our favorite classic toys:

### CORN POPPER

**Age Range:** 1 year and up
**Made by:** Fisher Price (www.fisher-price.com)
**Price:** About $10 ($13 for a counting popper)
**What's Cool:** Can't beat the original Corn Popper for a terrific push toy. We had them when we were kids and we loved pushing them around again when our kids were toddlers. While this toy violates our unwritten rule of not buying noisy toys, it isn't nearly as loud as many electronic toys our kids have played with.

### MAX THE DOG PULL TOY

**Age Range:** 1 to 3 years
**Made by:** Ambi (ambitoys.com)
**Price:** About $20
**What's Cool:** When you pull this black and white dog around the house he barks, wags his tail and shakes his head. Not too noisy and with the world's best facial expression. Your early walker will love this guy as her companion. Other doggie pull toys: Fisher Price's Lil' Snoopy (about $8) and Playskool's Walk'n Sounds Digger the Dog (about $15).

### RAGGEDY ANN AND RAGGEDY ANDY

**Age Range:** 3 and up
**Made by:** Applause/Dakin (applause.com)
**Price:** $20
**What's Cool:** The star of over 25 childrens' books from the late 1910's, Raggedy Ann is a huge part of Americana. I vividly remember my Raggedy Ann playing with my brother's Raggedy Andy out in the playhouse in our back yard (and I'm not *that* old!). Nowadays they don't have the button eyes so they're very safe for your toddler and will bring back sweet memories to you and your child's grandparents.

### DUPLO/LEGO Blocks

**Age Range:** 2 to 6 years for DUPLO; 5 to 10 years for LEGO

**Made by:** LEGO Systems, Inc. (www.lego.com).

**Price:** A tub starts at about $15 and goes up from there.

**What's Cool:** Start your child's LEGO or DUPLO collection now and there's no knowing what cool things he or she can build. Our kids started with tall towers made from chunky DUPLOs and have now graduated to space ships and speeders with regular LEGOs. And you can keep adding new systems like the Animal Adventures bucket ($11) with animals and people you can build.

### CANDY LAND

**Age Range:** 3 to 6 years

**Made by**: Milton Bradley (www.miltonbradley.com)

**Price:** $10

**What's Cool:** Kids love candy. So why not incorporate it into their first board game? Invented in 1949 by a polio-inflicted child (Eleanor Abbott) to while away the hours in a hospital, Candy Land is a terrific way to interest your child in board games. What we like best is kids don't need to be able to read. The game uses colors and pictures to help kids race their gingerbread boy pieces around the track to the finish line. This is a great way to teach taking turns, color recognition and winning and losing graciously. Another great game: Chutes and Ladders ($9).

### RADIO FLYER WAGON

**Age Range:** 2 to 5 years (although our kids grandpa managed to get pulled for a ride not long ago!)

**Made by:** Radio Flyer (www.radioflyer.com)

**Price:** $35

**What's Cool:** What's not cool? The ultimate transport for kids was first introduced to the world in the 1920's (Italian immigrant Antonio Pasin made them of wood first, steel came around in the 30's). But they're still incredibly popular today. You can buy the original steel red wagon or check out several plastic and wood models. In the end, the many imaginative uses of this simple red wagon make it the most classic toy of all time.

TOYS & MEDIA

## Best Bets: Fun Toys

Note, these are our best bet picks for fun toys for children two to five. Be sure to note these age recommendations as some of these toys are for older toddlers or preschoolers.

### UNBELIEVABLY SOFT BABY

**AGE:** 2 and up
**MANUFACTURER:** Goldberger Doll Manufacturing (www.goldbergerdoll.com)
**COST:** $20
**WHAT IT IS:** A great first doll, the Unbelievably Soft Baby is as advertised: soft and cuddly. The cool part is she has an air pillow inside her body that can be inflated to exactly the right firmness or softness. And this doll has lovely soft skin to cuddle next to too.

### JUMBOJET

**AGE:** 2 to 6
**MANUFACTURER:** Hooray! (www.huggybuggy.com)
**COST:** $12
**WHAT IT IS:** This airplane-shaped toy has a soft, easy to grasp exterior with wheels so a budding pilot can ready it for take off. Hooray! also makes the Huggy Buggy car, dump truck and fire truck.

### SILLY SAM TALKING BROOM

**AGE:** 2 to 4
**MANUFACTURER:** Kidz Delight (www.kidzdelight.com)
**COST:** 2 to 4
**WHAT IT IS:** Okay, you dream of a future where your child helps you clean up all those messes he makes, don't you? Introduce him to Silly Sam, with his googly eyes, sweeping sounds and infectious giggle, and you may just spark an interest here. He even talks to your child as he sweeps!

### WOODEN TRAIN SETS

**Age:** 3 and up
**Manufacturer:** Brio, Learning Curve (Thomas the Tank Engine), TC Timber

**Cost:** Starter sets as low as $20

**What it is:** These wooden trains with magnetized couplers come in bright colors with their own grooved track. The Thomas series is especially popular since they have faces and stories that go with them. Add-ons are incredibly numerous including tables, additional train cars, many types of tracks and tunnels and bridges.

### FELTLAND DOLL HOUSES
**Age:** 3 and up
**Manufacturer:** Small World Toys (www.smallworldtoys.com)
**Cost:** Starter set is about $25
**What it is:** These modular dollhouse rooms are covered with bright colored felt. The starter set comes with two rooms plus felt door, outside lights, one window, a fireplace, picture, TV, fish tank, rug and two books. Furniture is also included along with two adult dolls. And you can add on many more rooms and accessories until a mansion is erected in your humble home!

### WIGGLY WORM TUNNEL
**Age:** 2 and up
**Manufacturer:** Playhut (www.playhut.com)
**Cost:** $25

**What it is:** With its goofy smile, antennae, feet and tail, this is one caterpillar you'll be happy to have around the house. Kids love running around and through tunnels and they make great, safe hiding places. This terrific tunnel toy collapses flat for easy storage.

### GERTIE BALLS
**Age:** 3 and up
**Manufacturer:** Small World Toys
**Cost:** Start at $5
**What it is:** These ultra soft, squishy balls are easy to catch and won't hurt your little ones when they inevitably get one in the face. They're lightweight and come in many sizes, colors and textures too. A great first ball for your budding athlete.

### COZY COUPE II
**Age:** 2 to 4
**Manufacturer:** Little Tikes
(www.littletikes.com)
**Cost:** $40

**What it is:** This classic riding toy is one of the favorites of our neighborhood. Even kids too big for it seem to want to go for a drive. Now it comes with a remote key clicker and four sounds for an updated and modern driving experience.

### COLOSSAL BARREL OF CRAFTS
**Age:** 4 to 8
**Manufacturer:** Chenille Kraft Co.
**Cost:** $30

**What it is:** Colossal is no understatement when it comes to this craft and activity jar. We love all the stuff it contains: pom-poms, craft sticks, beads and string, foam shapes, pipe cleaners, googly eyes, glitter, metallic spangles, cutters, and more. A great rainy day pick-me-up.

## Best Bets: Educational Toys

### TEACHING CASH REGISTER
**Age:** 3 to 5
**Manufacturer:** Learning Resources
(www.learningresources.com)
**Price:** $45

**What it is:** Here's a great way to introduce math concepts and even entrepreneurship with your child's very own cash register. Although ts on the expensive side (can you say "Grandma"), it comes with coins, bills and credit cards. There are also built in games to teach Coin Identification and Place Value among other things.

### FISHING FOR NUMBERS
**Age:** 3 and up
**Manufacturer:** International Playthings
(www.intplay.com)
**Price:** $20
**What it is:** This game lets kids practice

number skills while trying to catch brightly colored fish. Includes fishing poles with magnets, fish and worms.

### SING WITH ME MAGIC CUBE
**Age:** 2 to 7
**Manufacturer:** Munchkin (munchkininc.com, click on Embryonics)
**Price:** $40
**What it is:** An extension of Munchkin's Magic Cube series, the Sing With Me version of the interactive cube plays favorite songs including Itsy Bitsy Spider and Pop Goes the Weasel. Your child can add or subtract different musical sounds to the songs, teaching them to recognize sounds and how they work together.

### POWER TOUCH LEARNING SYSTEM
**Age:** 3 and up
**Manufacturer:** Fisher Price (www.fisher-price.com)
**Price:** $50
**What it is:** This interactive story book reads the story to your child but allows her to participate at the touch of a finger. There are interactive games and activities and the "book" is portable as well.

### CIRCLE OF FRIENDS MATCHING GAME
**Age:** 3 to 6
**Manufacturer:** Briarpatch (www.briarpatch.com)
**Price:** $15
**What it is:** Using old friends from the Little Golden Book series (Pokey Little Puppy, et al), this game helps kids develop matching and memory skills.

## Best Bets: Children's Software

While most children's software is available in both Mac and PC configurations, be sure to check before buying. Also check for minimum system requirements to make sure your computer can handle it. You'll find most of these titles on Amazon.com, FreeSoftwareNow.com or KidsClick.com.

## *Beyond Raffi: Music CDs for kids*

While there are an unbelievable number of great CD's and tapes out there for kids, here are a few of our favorites beyond Raffi. (You can find any of these CD's or tapes at Amazon.com).

◆ Joe Scruggs: One of our kids' favorites has always been this Austin, Texas children's artist. His CD's *Traffic Jams, Deep in the Jungle, Ants, Late Last Night, Even Trolls Have Moms* and *Deep in the Jungle* are warm, witty and fun. We still love to sing along to "This Little Piggy" and other favorites. Joe's web site is HelloJoe.com.

◆ *Inside-Out Sleep Game:* Sung by Pattie Teal, this is a terrific collection of bedtime songs to help kids settle in at night.

◆ *Classic Disney* (volumes 1-5): This excellent collection of Disney hit songs past and present is a terrific series. For example, you can sing along with "Spoon Full of Sugar" from Mary Poppins or "Can You Feel the Love Tonight" from Lion King. With 25 songs on each CD/tape, it is a good value.

◆ *Yummy, Yummy* (The Wiggles): You might have seen these hilarious Aussies in between shows on Disney Channel doing the "Shaky Shaky" and wondered what was up with these guys! But they really rock the toddler set with their catchy, easy-to-sing-along tunes.

◆ *Mary Sue & Cari:* Looking for songs that are silly and fun? Check out Mary Sue Rogers and Cari Minor's CDs *Music with Kids* and *Here We Go Again*. Songs about germs, bugs and ponys—what else is there to a little kid? CDs are $15 and can be ordered on line at www.cdbaby.com.

◆ *Songs About America-Celebrating American History* (Kimbo Educational, www.kimboed.com):Each song on this CD reflects a particular period in American History—a sort of jumping off point to talk about this great nation and it's past with your kids. There also a guide included with the history of the songs, games and activities.

### CANDYLAND ($10)

The classic board game is now available for your computer screen in both Windows and Mac versions. The goal is still to be the first to get to the Candy Castle, but now you'll meet animated characters along the way. Parents thought this game was good for teaching basic skills. And one even noted it was tough to get her child to stop playing it. (3 years and up)

### JUST GRANDMA AND ME ($15)

Living Books by Broderbund pioneered the interactive CD-ROM book with this Little Critter adaptation. When our kids were as young as 18 months, they clamored to plays this CD. Little Critter and his grandma find all kinds of fun things to do at the beach in this sweet story. The surprises abound with clickable shells, clouds, animals and more. The surprises are unbelievable fun and your child can read along with the narrator as well. Living Books also makes the Arthur series based on Marc Brown's books, Dr. Seuss, Reader Rabbit and more. (3 years and up)

### CLIFFORD THINKING ADVENTURE ($18)

This CD-ROM from Scholastic finds Emily Elizabeth trying to find the supplies to throw Clifford a special birthday party. Your child can explore Birdwell Island while practicing shape recognition, sorting and self-expression. There are more Clifford options beyond the Thinking Adventure if you have a big red dog fan in your house. . (4 to 6 years)

### ALPHABET ($20)

A visual panorama of color, Alphabet (by Tivola) morphs mere letters into interactive visual and auditory experiences. Inspired by artist Kveta Pacovska's book, this is fun and exciting for kids of all ages. You can use keyboard strokes, mouse dragging or even your computer's microphone to manipulate the letters. This computer game has won every possible award—we highly recommend it. (3 and up).

## Best Bets: Tricycles

### TOUGH TRIKE
**Age:** 2 to 5 (may work better for tall two year olds)
**Price:** $20
**Manufacturer:** Fisher Price; (www.fisher-price.com)

**What's Cool:** This all-plastic trike is a terrific low-end option. It comes in wonderful bright colors with stickers, a key in the handlebars and a secret compartment in the seat. Except for complaints that two year olds may be too short to use the pedals (no adjustable seat), kids seem to love this trike. There are a couple versions of this trike: the Barbie and the Kawasaki Ninja. Fisher Price also makes an Action Sounds Trike for $40 that comes with motorcycle sounds.

### RADIO FLYER TRIKES
**Age:** 2 1/2 to 5
**Price**: $45 to $75
**Manufacturer:** Radio Flyer (www.radioflyer.com)

**What's Cool:** Maybe you remember riding a metal trike when you were a kid. This Classic Red Trike is mostly-steel and comes with air filled tires, handlebar pad and handlebar grips. Best part: your child sits up higher on this trike than most and really feels like a big kid. Other Radio Flyer trikes come with push bars, another with storage and cup holders among other things.

## All By Myself videos

Looking for a video to help your child master those little tasks like dressing themselves? We'd recommend "All By Myself," a video series by Lady Bug Productions that does that just. Their first product focuses on how toddlers can dress themselves and more videos are planned. Check it out at www.allbymyself.com.

### KALYPSO TRIKE

**Age:** 2 and up

**Price:** $90

**Manufacturer:** Kettler International

**What's Cool:** This trike has to be one of the best-made toys we ever bought our kids. It is made of steel and high quality plastic in brilliant colors. The beauty of the Kalypso: it has a detachable push bar for parents. And for kids the seat has four positions, a rear wheel footplate, high back seat and slip resistant pedals. You'll find that Kettler has a trike for just about every one in every price range. We even saw a two-seater for those of you with twins! While it's not a cheap trike, if you have the money, this is a great investment.

## Bottom Line: Our Top Picks

Who's got the best advice on toys? If you are a parent looking for toy info or a grandparent who wants to make a splash with your next gift, first surf to Oppenheim Toy Portfolio (toyportfolio.com) and Dr. Toy's web sites (www.drtoy.com). You can check out reviews on which toys are best and which to avoid.

For toddlers under three, skip the educational toys that claim to teach kids their ABC's. Instead, focus on fun toys that stimulate their imagination, but can withstand abuse. The best classic toys for this age group include DUPLO/Lego blocks, Fisher Price's Corn Popper and Radio Flyer's wagon.

For older toddlers (age three to five), consider more "social toys" like costume boxes or toy props, etc. These older toddlers can now enjoy a simple game like CandyLand, wooden trains and Feltland Doll houses.

As for the best kid's software, we recommend the Living Books' "Just Grandma & Me" as a way to introduce toddlers to the computer. "Candyland," "Clifford Thinking Adventure" and Tivola's "Alphabet" are other excellent choices. For music, we suggest Joe Scruggs or Pattie Teal's "Inside-Out Sleep Game."

Who's got the best kid's tricycles? We pick Fisher Price's "Tough Trike" as a best buy, although the excellent Kettler Trikes (good sample model: the Kalypso Trike) are worth the splurge.

No matter what toys you pick for your child, be sure to follow the safety guidelines we list in this chapter—beware of small parts for the youngest toddlers and always read the age guidelines and instructions to insure safety.

# CHAPTER 12

## What Does it All Mean?

**H**ow much can you save from using this book? Let's tally up the savings from just a handful of our tips.

Yes, raising a toddler can easily run $10,000 or more a year. Even when you factor out fixed expenses like housing, transportation and child care, the "running costs" of a toddler work out to $2670 a year.

So, how much can you save from our advice? Let's look at some real figures based on the tips from this book:

◆ **Toddler Bed.** Skip buying this unneeded piece of furniture and you'll save $100 to $200. Instead, we advise going straight to a twin bed. Decorating with Wallies and other affordable decor tricks we discuss in Chapter 2 will save you about $300 over expensive wallpaper or paint treatments.

◆ **Clothes.** Yes, most parents spend about $400 per year on toddler clothes and shoes. But if you hit the discount stores (Old Navy, Target, Kohl's), outlets (Stride Rite) and other deals like eBay, we estimate you can slash that bill by $200 or more.

◆ **Potty training.** An affordable toilet insert runs $10, saving you $20 to $30 off the cost of regular toddler potties.

◆ **Food.** Yes, it costs $1260 per year to feed a toddler, but you can slash those bills by following our tips. One suggestion: skip the pre-packaged "toddler meals" and juices that can run 30% more than non-toddler foods (that are just as nutritious). We estimate this tip alone would save $400.

◆ Use a **web coupon** to buy your child's booster seat. This can save $20 to $30, depending on the deal (20% off or free shipping).

◆ **Jogging strollers** are hot today, but you can save $100 to $200 by buying a no-frills steel version from Baby Trend or InStep. If all you plan is to tool around the neighborhood (instead of jogging), that's all you need.

◆ ***And more.*** As always, saving money is often dozens of small tricks that can add up big over time. For birthday parties, consider eliminating character plates and cups (just go with the plain ones)—that can shave $20 or more off your costs. For summer sports gear, buy second hand or at yard sales and you'll save 50% or more. The same advice applies to toys—swap toys with friends, scour second hand stores and rent tapes/CD's/software from libraries. Over time, these tips will save you $100, $200 or more.

***Bottom line:*** follow all this advice and we think you can shave $1000 to $1200 a year off what it costs to raise a toddler. And a $1000 is nothing to sneeze at these days.

We'd like to thank all those parents, readers and other experts who helped contribute ideas to this book. As always, we encourage readers to surf our web page's message boards to get the latest scoop on how to save for babies and toddlers. If you find a great deal, post it! We view this book as a work in progress, so feel free to email us your tips, suggestions and advice at the address at the back of this book.

# APPENDIX D
## Web Site Directory

Wonder where these contact names appear in the book? Check the index for a page number. Remember that many of these contacts do not sell to the public directly; the web sites are so you can find a dealer/store near you. Refer to the chapter in which they are mentioned to see which companies offer a consumer catalog, sell to the public, etc. Note: we've omitted the "www." prefix before the web address for space reasons.

| Contact Name | Web Site |
| --- | --- |

### Chapter 2 Furniture/Decor

| | |
| --- | --- |
| Babies R Us | babiesrus.com |
| Pottery Barn Kids | potterybarnkids.com |
| Baby News | babynewsstores.com |
| USA Baby | usababy.com |
| Baby and Kids Express NINFRA) | ninfra.com |
| Rooms to Go Kids | RoomsToGoKids.com |
| Ethan Allen | EthanAllen.com |
| HGTV's web site | hgtv.com |
| Wallies | wallies.com |
| | Domestications.com |
| | JCPenney.com |
| Seaman's Kids | seamanskids.com |
| Lands End | landsend.com |
| Company Store | thecompanystore.com |
| | PoshTots.com |
| Ebay | ebay.com |
| Modellbahn Ott Hobies | prissprints.com |
| Sam's | samsclub.com |
| Costco | costco.com |
| BJ's Wholesale | bjswholesale.com |
| The Container Store | containerstore.com |
| American Home Showplace | carpetsofdalton.com |
| Kimberly Causey | smartdecorating.com |
| Gothic Cabinet Craft | gothiccabinetcraft.com |
| EG Furniture | egfurniture.com |
| Flexa | flexa.dk |

### Chapter 3 Clothing/Shoes

### Chapter 4 Potty Training

| Baby Bjorn | regallager.com |
| Dr. Merry's PottyPal | pottypal.com |
| Fisher Price | fisherprice.com |
| Graco | gracobaby.com |
| Safety 1st | safety1st.com |
| Totco Inc. | tot-co.com |
| DrugStore.com | drugstore.com |
| DermStore.com | dermstore.com |

### Chapter 5 Meal Time

| Stokke KinderZeat | stokkeusa.com |
| PecoWare | pecoware.com |
| California Innovations | californiainnovations.com |

### Chapter 6 Booster Seats

| Baby Trend | babytrend.com |
| Basic Comfort | basiccomfort.co |
| Britax | britaxusa.com |
| Century | centuryproducts.com |
| Cosco | djgusa.com |
| Evenflo | carseat.com |
| Jupiter | jupiterindustries.com |
| Safety Baby/Nania | team-tex.com |

### Chapter 7 On the Go Gear

| Aprica | apricausa.com |
| Baby Trend | babytrend.com |
| Baby Jogger | babyjogger.com |
| BOB | bobtrailers.com |
| Chicco | chiccousa.com |
| Combi | combi-intl.com |
| Dreamer Design/Boogie Deluxe | dreamerdesign.net |
| Emmaljunga | emmaljunga.com |
| Evenflo | evenflo.com |
| Gozo | getgozo.com |
| Inglesina | inglesina.com |
| Kelty | kelty.com |
| KidCo. | kidcoinc.com |
| Kool Stop | koolstop.com |
| Maclaren | maclarenbaby. |
| Mountain Buggy | mountainbuggyusa.com |
| Peg Perego | perego.com |
| Phil & Ted's Most Excellent Buggy | babybuggy.co.nz. |
| Regalo | regalobaby.com |
| Simo | simostrollers.com |

web directory

## Chapter 8 Seasonal/Outdoors

## Chapter 9 Safety

## Chapter 10 Birthday

Birthday Express      birthdayexpress.com
Birthday Party Ideas      birthdaypartyideas.com
     BoardmanWeb.com
     PersonalizedPartyFavors.com
     familyfun.com
     factorycard.com
     PBSkids.org fun
     FisherPrice.com
     PartyPro.com
     NickJr.com
     dltk-kids.com
     PreschoolEducation.com
     PerpetualPreschool.com
     Wilton.com
     Family.Go.com
     eBubbleMachines.com
     BirthdayInaBox.com
     cakemixdoctor.com
     OrientalTrading.com

## Chapter 11 Toys

Oppenheim Toy Portfolio      toyportfolio.com
Traveling Tikes      travelingtikes.com
Dr. Toy      drtoy.com
Parent's choice      parents-choice.org
National Parenting Center's      tnpc.com
OverStock.com
Yesterday Land      yesterdayland.com
Ambi      ambitoys.com
Applause/Dakin      applause.com
LEGO Systems Inc.      lego.com
Milton Bradley      miltonbradley.com
Radio Flyer      radioflyer.com
Small World Toys      smallworldtoys.com
Playhut      playhut.com
Little Tikes      littletikes.com
International Playthings      intplay.com
Poetry Pals      poetrypals.com
Munchkin      munchkininc.com
Kidzup Productions      kidzup.com
Joe Scruggs      Hellojoe.com
Lady Bug Productions      allbymyself.com

web directory

# INDEX

index

index

index

index

index

# Notes

# Notes

# Notes

# How to Reach the Authors

Have a question about

## Toddler Bargains?

Want to make a suggestion?

Discovered a great bargain
you'd like to share?

Contact the Authors, Denise & Alan Fields
in one of five flavorful ways:

### 1. By phone:
### (303) 442-8792

### 2. By mail:
### 436 Pine Street, Suite 600,
### Boulder, CO 80302

### 3. By fax:
### (303) 442-3744

### 4. By email:
### authors@ToddlerBargains.com

### 5. On our web page:
### www.ToddlerBargains.com

If this address isn't active, try one of our other URL's:
www.DeniseAndAlan.com or www.WindsorPeak.com.
Or call our office at 1-800-888-0385
if you're having problems accessing the page.

**What's on our web page?**
◆ *FREE updates on this book.*
◆ *NEW BARGAINS suggested by our readers.*
◆ *CHECK out parent reviews/ratings on our message boards*
◆ *CORRECTIONS and clarifications.*
◆ *Sign up for a FREE E-NEWSLETTER!*

# Our Other Books

## *Baby 411*

*Clear Answers & Smart Advice For Your Baby's First Year*
*$11.95 (1st Edition)*

*400+ pages of questions and answers for new parents with detailed advice from an award-winning pediatrician.*
*Co-authored by Dr. Ari Brown, M.D.*

- ◆ How to pick a pediatrician with detailed questions to ask and insider tips.
- ◆ The latest scoop on hot topics like cord blood banking, optional newborn screening, the vaccine/autism debate and more!
- ◆ The truth about "old wives tales" and Internet rumors—how to separate medical fact from fiction online!
- ◆ Detailed nutrition info with a step-by-step guide for successful breastfeeding, introducing solid food and the "new and improved" formulas.
- ◆ Sleep. The best way to get your baby to sleep through the night.
- ◆ The top web sites to find the most reliable medical info for your baby

*Go to Baby411.com for more details*

**Order online at www.WindsorPeak.com**
*or call toll-free to order!*
**1-800-888-0385**

# Our Other Books

By Denise & Alan Fields

## Baby Bargains

*Secrets to saving 20% to 50% on baby furniture, equipment, clothes, toys, maternity wear and much, more!*
*$16.95 (5th Edition)*

Hooray! A baby book that actually answers the big question about having a baby: How am I going to afford all this? With the average cost of a baby topping $6000 for just the first year alone, you need creative solutions and innovative ideas to navigate the consumer maze that confronts all parents-to-be. Baby Bargains is the answer! Inside, you'll discover:

◆ The best WEB SITES that offer the biggest discounts.
◆ NAME BRAND REVIEWS of bedding, monitors, high chairs, diapers and more!
◆ FIVE WASTES OF MONEY with baby clothes and the best outlet bargains.
◆ Seven tips to SAVING MONEY ON CRIBS, plus in-depth reviews of crib brands.
◆ THE TRUTH ABOUT STROLLERS—and which brands work best in the real world.
◆ The SEVEN MOST RIDICULOUS BABY PRODUCTS, plus gift do's and don'ts.
◆ Dozens of SAFETY TIPS to affordably baby proof your home.
◆ SMART SOLUTIONS for maternity wear, baby announcements and nursery furniture.

**Order online at www.WindsorPeak.com**
*or call toll-free to order!*
**1-800-888-0385**

# Our Other Books

## By Denise & Alan Fields

# *Your New House*

The alert consumer's guide
to buying and building
a quality home.
$15.95 (4th Edition)

- ◆ HOW TO USE THE INTER-
  NET to plan your new home,
  with web addresses for
  builders, product suppliers
  and more!
- ◆ BEST BARGAINS on
  everything from lighting to
  carpet--save 20% to 50%
  off!
- ◆ THE TRUTH ABOUT "PRODUCTION HOMES"
  and how three simple steps can save you from
  buying a lemon.
- ◆ HOW TO REALLY screen builders and find the
  one who's right for your house.
- ◆ SMART SOLUTIONS to finding the lowest rates
  for mortgages, plus helpful advice on how
  much new home you can really afford.
- ◆ RATINGS AND REVIEWS of windows, plumbing fixtures and more.
- ◆ SAVVY QUESTIONS to ask inspectors, lenders
  and architects, plus tips on how to negotiate
  the best deals.

**As seen on ABC's 20/20**
*"This is, by far, the best book available on how to
buy and build a new home!"*
—Robert Bruss, *Chicago Tribune*

**Order online at www.WindsorPeak.com**
**or call toll-free to order!**
**1-800-888-0385**

# Our Other Books

## *Bridal Bargains*

Secrets to throwing a
fantastic wedding on a
realistic budget
$14.95 (7th Edition)

- ◆ How to save up to 40% on a brand new, nationally advertised wedding dresses.
- ◆ The best web sites to save on everything from flowers to gowns, invitations to, well, you name it.
- ◆ Fourteen creative ways to cut the catering bill at your reception.
- ◆ How to order flowers at wholesale over the internet.
- ◆ Eleven questions you should ask any photographer—and seven money saving tips to lower that photo expense.
- ◆ How to do your invitations on a computer, saving 70%.
- ◆ A clever trick to save big bucks on your wedding cake.
- ◆ Plus many more money-saving tips on wedding videos, rings, entertainment and more!

**As seen on DATELINE NBC Oprah and People Magazine**

**Order online at www.WindsorPeak.com**
***or call toll-free to order!***
**1-800-888-0385**

*Additional information on all our books is available on our home page **WindsorPeak.com***
*Mastercard, VISA, American Express and Discover Accepted!*
*Shipping to any U.S. address is $3 ($4 for Canada)*

# Our free e-newsletter

*Sign up for our free e-newsletter! The latest bargains, safety recalls, product news and more.*

## Go to ToddlerBargains.com click on "e-newsletter"

**Privacy policy:** We hate spam too. Therefore, we will NOT sell or disclose your email address to any third party. We will just use it to send you our newsletter. You can unsubscribe at any time!

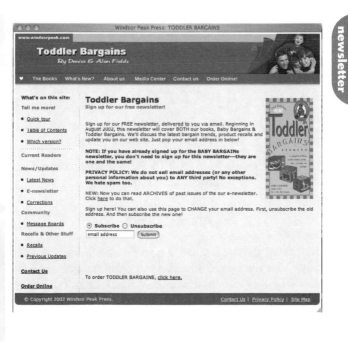

## *If this book doesn't save you at least*

# $250

*off your toddler expenses, we'll give you a complete refund on the cost of this book!*

## NO QUESTIONS ASKED!

Just send the book and your mailing address to

**Windsor Peak Press • 436 Pine Street, Suite Q Boulder, CO, 80302.**

If you have any questions, please call
**(303) 442-8792.**

Look at all those other baby books in the bookstore—no other author or publisher is willing to put their money where their mouth is! We are so confident that *Toddler Bargains* will save you money that we guarantee it in writing!